AF531238

EFFECTIVE SCHOOL CURRICULUM

EFFECTIVE SCHOOL CURRICULUM

By

Dr. Marlow Ediger
Professor Emeritus of Education
Truman State University
P.O. Box 417, 201 W 22nd St
North Newton KS 67117
United States of America

&

Dr. Digumarti Bhaskara Rao
M.Sc., M.A., M.A., M.Ed., Ph.D.
Reader & Research Director
R.V.R. College of Education
Guntur – 522006, A.P.
digumartibhaskararao@rediffmail.com

DISCOVERY PUBLISHING HOUSE PVT. LTD.
NEW DELHI-110 002

First Published-2010

Reprinted-2011

ISBN 978-81-8356-585-1

Published by:

DISCOVERY PUBLISHING HOUSE PVT. LTD.

4831/24, Ansari Road, Prahlad Street
Darya Ganj, New Delhi-110002 (India)
Phone: 23279245 • Fax: 91-11-23253475
E-mail: parul.wasan@gmail.com
info@discoverypublishinggroup.com
Website: www.discoverypublishinggroup.com

Printed at:

Sachin Printers, Delhi- 53

Preface

School curriculum is the head, heart and hand of the course work. As the curriculum is the total spectrum of the content, resources, methods and materials of teaching through which the purposes of the course and the education are achieved, it must be organised properly and effectively. The curriculum when constructed properly, the students get benefit out of it and become successful individuals in every waik of life.

The book on 'Effective School Curriculum' provides various means and modes to improve the syllabi of various school subjects. This book will be of use to school curriculum designers and school teachers along with school administrators.

DIGUMARTI BHASKARA RAO

Sri Sai Soudha
D-43, S.V.N. Colony
Guntur-522006
India

Contents

1

Philosophy of Education and Social Studies

Teachers of the social studies need to develop a philosophy of education in teaching pupils. Philosophical schools of thought provide guidance to the teacher in choosing objectives, learning activities, and appraisal procedures. Indepth study of each philosophical school of thought is a must. It varies much when selecting from one school of thought, as contrasted with another, in how teaching and learning will occur.

Too frequently, in higher education courses in the philosophy of education, professors may not be able to make practical application of each, nor will pupils see each philosophy of education be implemented in the classroom, Each teacher in the public schools should be knowledgeable about and be able to implement different schools of thought in philosophy,

REALISM AS A PHILOSOPHICAL SCHOOL OF THOUGHT

Realism stresses the world of science with its accuracy and preciseness. Reality can be known as it truly is, according to realists. Thus, one can receive a replica of what actually exists. Perhaps, the great educator E.L. Thorndike (1874–

1946), best stated the philosophy of realism in teaching and learning. He stated, "Whatever exists, exists in some amount, and if it exists in some amount, it can be measured." This statement exemplifies what is believed in chemistry whereby any molecule is comprised of atoms in exact amounts. Water, which all are familiar with, contains two atoms of hydrogen and one atom of oxygen. This can be stated as a chemical formula. Or another common molecule, sugar, contains six atoms of carbon, twelve atoms of hydrogen, and six atoms of oxygen.

Objectives, too, for pupils to achieve then need to be written with precision. As stated in the objective, all need to agree upon what a learner is to achieve as a result of teaching. "To develop the democratic citizen" is much too broad as a stated objective and leaves leeway for much interpretation. The following, as examples, are stated precisely and leave no room for reading between the lines in terms of what is to be taught:

* the pupil will list in writing three causes of World War II.
* the pupil will write a sixty word paragraph on casualties of World War-II (Ediger and Rao, 2002).

To achieve the two above listed objectives, as well as others, the social studies teacher must select learning activities which will assist pupils to be successful in goal attainment. The learning opportunities must relate directly to the objective(s) being emphasized in teaching students. A variety of concrete (objects, items, and excursions), semi-concrete (video tapes, transparencies and the overhead, pictures, illustrations, as well as power point presentations), and abstract (reading, writing, discussions, speaking, and listening experiences) in the social studies must be in the offing to provide for individual differences. Tests measuring the stated objectives emphasized in teaching then need to be written with precision, generally in multiple choice form. Immediately, as soon as possible, the learner should receive feedback on the adequacy of his/her responses. Hand scoring for teacher prepared tests and machine scoring for mandated tests should be available. Tests need to measure higher order thinking skills (hots), such as critical and creative thinking, as well as problem solving. To indicate precision in testing, from test results, a definite percentage of either correct or incorrect responses must be in the offing for each pupil, with no vagueness in the written test items, according to realists. If standardized tests are given, student results from testing may be recorded with numerical results such as in the following:

* percentiles in which a pupil's score will be between the zero and the 100th percentile. Out of every hundred students then having taken a standardized test, a student being on the sixtieth percentile, for example, will have forty above and sixty below in achievement results. Or, a pupil being on the fifth percentile will have five below and ninety five above, for every hundred students having taken the test. The spread of scores will be indicate as being one, two, or three standard deviations above and below the mean.
* stanines whereby a pupil's achievement will be indicated on a band of nine levels. Each band will cover a certain percentage of the total in the norm group. The teacher's student scores are then contrasted with those in the norm group
* grade equivalents such as grade one, two, three . . . twelve. In the manual of the standardized test, the grade level achievement for the norm group will be indicated. The test score for each pupil in one's class/ school can be matched with the appropriate matching score in the norm group. It will then state which the appropriate grade level is in achievement progress for that pupils' grade equivalent.

The reader is asked to read statistical information from a reputable university level statistics textbook to become knowledgeable about testing/measurement information.

Realism, as a philosophy of education, stresses the following salient concepts:

* specific objectives of instruction upon which there is "perfect" agreement as to their meaning in teaching and learning situations
* learning activities which assist pupils to achieve what is contained in the objective
* numerical results from testing to show pupil attainment
* objectivity and specificity are ideals to strive for in the social studies curriculum (See Guilfoyle, 2006).

Experimentalism, as a second philosophy of education, stresses that one cannot know the real world, as it truly is, but can only experience the natural/social world. Since one can only experience, but not know reality as it truly is, the involved person perceives societal changes as being ongoing. With change, problems arise which need identification and related solutions sought. Problems which need identification and solutions include the following:

* peaceful, agreed upon solutions pertaining to wars and rumours of wars
* statesmen who are willing and able to be ambassadors of peace and willing to negotiate disagreements
* spokes people who believe in human rights as a way of life for all
* fair elections for all nations and peoples in deciding upon who to vote for at the ballot box
* the rule of law and its honest interpretation for all people
* clean air and water being a right for all
* full employment for adults with adequate wages and salaries for decent living

* quality education for each student in order to reach maximum potential, regardless of educational path pursued
* the right to adequate, safe food, clothing, and shelter.

For each of the above, objectives may be written which are, in degrees more specific, be one a behaviourist with realism as a philosophy of education or experimentalism with gradually more open ended objectives for problem solving (Ediger, 2007).

ISSUES IN EDUCATION

There are a plethora of issues in education which need a philosophical approach in their solutions. Cognitive objectives are generally stressed to the minimizing of attitudinal goals. Both kinds of objectives are important and need some kind of rational balance. Intelligence quotient tests have been with us for some time, such as the Stamford Binet or the Wechsler Intelligence Scale for Children (WISC). Rather recently, there have been educators and psychologists who have emphasized emotional intelligence as being equally salient. People lose jobs and positions due to not getting along well with others. Quarrelsome, rude individuals are difficult to work with and this hinders productivity in any field of endeavour. Selected public schools have developed lessons and units of study dealing with the emotions. The state of Illinois has adopted standards for the social and emotional skills that K-12 students should be taught and include:

Goal 1. Develop self-awareness and self-management skills achieve school and life success:

(A) Identify and manage one's emotions and behaviours.

(B) Recognize personal qualities and external supports.

(C) Demonstrate skills related to achieving personal and academic goals.

Goal 2. Use social awareness and inter-personal skills to establish and maintain positive relationships.

(A) Recognize the feelings and perspectives of others.

(B) Recognize individual and group similarities and differences.

(C) Use communication and social skills to interact effectively with others.

(D) Demonstrate an ability to prevent, manage, and resolve inter-personal conflicts in constructive ways.

Goal 3. Demonstrate decision-making skills and responsible behaviours in personal, school, and community contexts:

(A) Consider ethical, safety, and societal factors in making-decisions.

(B) Apply decision-making skills to deal with academic and social situations.

(C) Contribute to the well being of one's school and community (Viadero, December 19 , 2007, 1 and 15).

Social skills and the academics interrelate since one assists the other if emphasized in a positive way. Thus, pupils take part in discussions and social skills stress respecting the thinking of others as well as learning to take turns in presenting ideas. In small groups, pupils need to harmonize their efforts with others as in developing a purposeful product within a project method of teaching. Being able to work together is a must! Treating others fairly and equitably aids in pupils achieving more optimally. Giving help to others as necessary makes for better sequence in learning. Being able to stress quality standards in peer interactions as well as in peer teaching maximizes learner performance. Giving support to others minimizes fear of failure in a given learning opportunity. Sometimes, a pupil will not participate for fear of experiencing failure. Providing help as needed provides the necessary impetus in moving forward in goal attainment. Recognizing the feelings of others and acting within that framework might well make for reciprocity. I'll will, rudeness, and feelings of superiority minimize opportunities in getting along well with others. Each pupil needs to develop feelings of having a good self-concept for learning. Positive attitudes assist in achieving well in attaining academic content (Ediger and Rao, 2001).

It was in the mid-nineties that the term Emotional Intelligence took the business world by a storm. It was Daniel Goleman who popularized it through his research on Emotional Intelligence (EI). It is said that IQ alone is no more the measure for success; it only accounts for 20%. Emotional and social intelligences, and luck account for the rest (Goleman, 1995). It was also found that whereas people with high IQ were real flops in real life, in their families and in the community, people with high EI have proved themselves successful in these areas...

One reason the EQ caught on so quickly is the belief—Goleman and others—that the EQ can be taught, whereas IQ (Intelligence Quotient) is genetically fixed and less malleable. Where IQ is a fixed capacity for processing cognitive information, EQ is an acquisitive skill for making great decisions, living with integrity and connecting with others. IQ and EQ are complimentary parts of a whole and healthy person. Great intellect does not diminish emotional capacity, and "emotionality" is not at odds with rational thought (Darsana, 2007).

Pupils in the classroom and school setting may have both motivational problems and attitudinal problems in acquiring subject matter. The two concepts might well interact. A low self-concept hinders in achieving academic objectives. Confidence in the self must be there to feel that it is possible to think critically and creatively, and to solve problems. Feelings of curiosity propel the individual to ask questions and to seek answers. Not being able to work well with others hinders in the ability to engage in co-operative learning whereby ideas need to circulate among its members. Feelings of hostility work in opposite ends of self-control. Individuals regret frequently what they have said in social situations due to a lack of self regulation of behaviour. It may take a long time to heal these wounds. Whereas in working well with others in co-operative learning, achievement of goals in ongoing lessons and units of study is possible. Social studies teachers need to provide a plethora of learning opportunities in which students may learn to work harmoniously.

Vygotsky (1978), a Russian psychologist, advocated that pupils work in small groups in discussing new ideas obtained. Within a discussion setting, pupil's ideas are circulated and appraised, resulting in clarity of thought and higher levels of cognition. The learner then has a chance to see his/her thinking evaluated, and revised if necessary. Vygotsky was a constructivist in educational philosophy. He believed that pupils should sequence their very own learnings with teacher supervision. It is the pupil that needs to do the learning, not the teacher in lectured centered approaches in teaching. With social constructivism, pupils are stimulated and encouraged to raise questions. They are guided to find their own answers in ongoing learning activities. Through social interaction, cultural tools (materials used in learning), and an activity centered curriculum, pupils ideas, thought, and sequence shape their development. The environment then shapes pupils thinking.

In contrast to Vygotsky, Jean Piaget, a Swiss psychologist, believed that pupils mature and go through different stages in life such as:

* psychomotor development from birth to age two years
* the pre-operational stage from two to seven years of age
* the stage of concrete operations from seven to eleven years of age
* the stage of abstract thought from age eleven and on.

As children mature, their intelligences and how they think changes. The process of biological maturation is involved here. Maturation of the individual then makes for different levels of cognition. The pupil possesses schemes which are organized actions and thoughts for each level of maturation. To receive new learnings, the pupil *accommodates* the new within the schemes, resulting in *assimilation* (*Hoy and Miskel*).

Social studies teachers may well study Piaget's thinking to notice what kinds of learning opportunities harmonize with the different levels of maturation. On the pre-operational level (ages two to seven, the latter includes the nursery school through the first grade), pupils tend to see one variable in objects which are shown and discussed. They are limited in making comparison and contrasts. On the pre-operational level, pupils need to experience concrete objects together with the abstract such as discussions, whereas on the stage of abstract thought, pupils may not need as many concrete materials along with reading, writing, listening, and speaking experiences.

Metacognition is another concept which has important implications for teaching the social studies. With metacognition, pupils think about thinking. Thus, in reading social studies subject matter, the pupil monitors if he/she is obtaining ideas being read rather than reading words only. Comprehension is the major goal when reading. Sometimes, a pupil when reading, reads words only without obtaining the related subject matter. Comprehension must go beyond securing facts, but include also analytic, creative, and evaluative reading. The student needs to monitor if he/she is fulfilling these ideals. The teacher needs to model aloud metacognition strategies in teaching and learning situations. Through criteria for metacognition use and actual modeling by the teacher, students may acquire key ideas pertaining to metacognition. Monitoring of metacognition application in each of the following assists pupils to understand and apply its use:

* rehearsing and analyzing how a previously taught problem was implemented

* reviewing critically why a lower test score, than desired, was obtained

* evaluating how to present a better oral book report than one given previously
* assessing a project completed in the social studies, emphasizing what might be improved therein.

There is much thinking about thinking which occurs when one makes plans for learning subject matter or skills in an ongoing unit of study. The planning component involves concentrating on how to pursue in these processes to ascertain what might work in moving forward. Purposes are inherent when finally deciding upon each step to pursue. Reasons then exist for achieving, growing, and developing. In viewing contents in a basal textbook, the student, for example, may preview the subject matter. This is done to obtain an overview of what will be read. Predictions are then made of the ensuing ideas to be gleaned. Facts, concepts, and generalizations might well result from these predictions. The predictions made will be tested when the student is engaged in the ongoing reading activity. Rereading is needed to determine if a prediction did not harmonize with the subject matter read. Based on the prediction, the student may evaluate if a new strategy needs to be used in making predictions (Balu, 2006).

In closing social studies teachers need to possess a thorough understanding of major philosophies of education. They need to be able to apply chosen strands.

Teachers in many cases diagnose learner progress and notice weaknesses. Pupils then are taught using appropriate methods to remedy deficiencies. A somewhat different approach is to identify strengths of pupils individually. Then, the teacher needs to assist learners to build on these strengths and interests. In his book *Frames of Mind*, Howard Gardner, psychologist at Harvard University, identified intelligences possessed by learners. Teachers might then identify and build learner achievement on each of these intelligences possessed:

* verbal intelligence as in reading and writing activities
* logical intelligence as in reasoning to secure information

* spacial whereby the pupil does well in artistic endeavours in using space properly
* musical/rhythmical as in writing lyrics and setting the words to music
* intrapersonal whereby the learner works by the self and achieves more optimally as compared to being involved in group work
* interpersonal in which the pupil achieves more optimally in small group endeavours as contrasted with working individually
* bodily/kinesthetic whereby pupils learn best through manual dexterity. There are a plethora of objects, items, and models to construct in ongoing lessons in the social studies.
* scientific intelligence emphasizing object thinking.

REFERENCES

Balu, A. (2006), *Effectiveness of Metacognitive Orientation Among Teacher Trainees on Developing Competencies in Teaching Social Studies*. Ph.D thesis from Alagappa University (India), evaluated by the writer.

Darsana, M. (2007), "Relationship Between Emotional Intelligence and Certain Achievement Facilitating Variables of Higher Secondary School Students", *Edutracks*, 7 (4), 25.

Ediger, Marlow (2007), "The Substitute Teacher in Reading Instruction", *The Sub-Journal*, 8(2), 67-72.

Ediger, Marlow, and D. Bhaskara Rao (2001), *Teaching Social Studies Successfully*. New Delhi, India: Discovery Publishing House, Chapter Four.

Ediger, Marlow, and D. Bhaskara Rao (2002), *Philosophy and Curriculum*. New Delhi, India: Discovery Publishing House, Chapter One.

Guilfoyle, Christy (2006), "NCLB: Is There Life After Testing?" *Educational Leadership*, 64 (3), 8-13.

Hoy, Wayne K., and Cecil G. Miskel (2005), *Educational Administration, Theory, Research, and Practice*. New York: Mc Graw-Hill, 66-67.

Viadero, Debra (December 19, 2007), "Social Skills Programs Found to Yield Gains in Academic Subjects", *Education Week*, 27 (16),1 and 15.

Vygotsky, Len (1978), *Mind in Society; the Development of Higher Psychological Processes*. Cambridge, Massachusetts: Harvard University Press.

2

Social Studies and Psychology of Learning

There is much the social studies teacher may do to enhance pupil learning. They need to study, analyze, and synthesize recent studies from the psychology of learning. There are different schools of thought, here, in assisting pupils to achieve more optimally. The reason for this is that learners differ from each other in terms of methods and approaches which are beneficial to achievement, development, and growth. Social studies teachers, also, must observe and learn from their own students to notice what assists in increased achievement, without harmful side affects entering in.

TEACHING AND LEARNING IN THE SOCIAL STUDIES

There are selected criteria which social studies teachers need to follow in teaching and learning situations. As a university supervisor of student teachers, the writer always made certain observations of productive classrooms. Students need to be involved in the ongoing lesson and unit of study. It is generally easy to observe which students are not paying attention in the ongoing learning activities. They are inattentive and their attention must be refocused on the learning opportunity in evidence. This may emphasize a change in the learning opportunity being offered. The following might be offered as a change of materials in teaching and learning situations, from what was to something more appealing:

* use of a video tape (audio and visual being used) instead of a discussion of abstract ideas
* use of library books instead of sole use of basal textbooks (library books may be more developmentally appropriate)
* use of transparencies and the overhead to clarify ideas
* use of committee endeavours to supplement individual endeavours
* use of dramatic experiences, based on the previous lesson, instead of extended seat work activities (See Balu, 2006).

Other materials of instruction which might be used include constructing a model pertaining to subject matter acquired; doing a mural; making drawings; designing a bulletin board in its entirety; keeping diary and journal entries of content acquired. Thus, if pupils are disconnected from the lesson, the social studies teacher may change the type of learning activity being stressed.

The method of instruction used may also be changed. The new method may include the following:

* problem solving instead of lecture
* inductive instead of deductive learning
* activity centered versus subject centered
* committee rather than individual endeavours
* peer mediated as compared to large group instruction
* rubric use in place of testing to notice achievement
* pupil choice of sequential tasks at a learning centers instead of assigned work (Ediger and Rao, 2001).

The above indicates approved methods to be used in teaching. Social studies teachers must think of alternative procedures for learning if students are not attending. Thus in the first item above with an asterisk, pupils might well be guided to identify a problem. The relevant problem takes indepth analysis for solving. Multiple resources are needed to arrive at a solution, including internet use. Assessment of the solution needs vital criteria which pinpoints its quality. This may require a teacher or student designed rubric. The problem solving activity needs to be shared with others in the classroom. A discussion might well follow. Other pupils may also wish to engage in a problem solving experience when noticing involved learners pursuing and persevering to the end. In the meantime, they also are involved in an alternative project in small groups, such as doing a mural, finalizing a class report, working at a chosen learning center, among others. Each pupil then needs to be actively engaged in learning vital subject matter and skills (See Hoyand Miskel, 2005).

Pupils do have preferences in how they progress and accomplish. The following are considerations in teaching pupils in the social studies:

* do they prefer individual or small group experiences?
* do pupils learn better through the use of visual aids or with more of abstract school work such as reading in the social studies?
* do pupils like to work more with their hands or prefer mental endeavours?
* do pupils learn best through deductive or inductive means?
* do learners do better with self chosen activities in a lesson/unit of study as compared to teacher directed learning?
* do pupils sequence their own school work or does the teacher sequence experiences?

Each of the above must be considered thoroughly when curricular decisions are made by the social studies teacher. For example in the first item with an asterisk, the teacher may have a pupil work on a unit report emphasizing soil conservation, such as making terraces, a grassed waterway, and/or area with planting trees to prevent soil erosion on hilly land. The report may have illustrations to show each procedure in preventing soil erosion. Reporting the results in a committee or class as a whole helps the learner in orally communicating ideas to listeners. Standards may be developed co-operatively, pupils with teacher guidance, to assess the quality of the activity.

Even if a pupil prizes individual endeavours as the preferred way of learning, he/she still needs to be able to work harmoniously with others. In society, individuals do things by the self as well as with others. The pupil who prefers co-operative work experiences also needs to learn to achieve on an individual basis (See Reeves, 2007).

In the second asterisked item above, all pupils need to learn to read well, however that still leaves room from learning from audio visual aids. Use of AV aids assist the pupil to understand better in terms of what was read. Meaningful background experiences assist in making abstract print understandable. This leaves leeway for learning from pictorial forms as well as from printed materials. A rational balance between the two media of learning must be stressed. Providing for individual differences must always be emphasized.

Adequate background experiences must always be emphasized to have learners engaged in an ensuing experience. In learning by discovery, for example, the pupil needs prerequisite activities in order to discover the new subject matter or skills. When attending a National Council for the Social Studies (NCSS) convention, a sectional meeting emphasized "learning by discovery". The presenter said, "I never answer a pupil's question, but, instead, raise another question or more which leads the pupil to discover his/her own answer to the question." This does stress a learning by discovery approach.

The third asterisk listing above, selected pupils do prefer a hands on approach in learning rather than strictly intellectual endeavourers. However, it is difficult to completely separate the two kinds of experiences. Project methods tend to stress hands on learning procedures, but thinking is involved. Thus, a committee of learners in an ongoing unit of study may prefer as a purpose to develop a model farm scene. Here, pupils with teacher guidance plan to fulfill the purpose. Research, using a variety of activities, is used to gather information as to the type of model farm to develop. It can be a feed lot for beef cattle, a hog complex, structures for laying hens, a broiler unit for raising chickens, and/or grain farm. Considerable knowledge is needed to develop the kind of farm desired. Careful planning is necessary. Various kinds of materials are needed to make the model farm. Each committee member has a significant role to play in working on the model; quality is salient when doing the specifics. The criteria used in terms of processes to do the model include everyone contributing and no one dominating the activity, politeness and consideration for each other being in evidence, as well as sharing ideas, skills, and materials. The processes are very important to emphasize within any project method of teaching/learning. When the project is completed, the following standards need to be in the offing for evaluation of the product:

* accurate workmanship is stressed
* neatness in appearance is reflected in the project
* co-operation in doing the project was in evidence
* self evaluation by each learner emphasized.

The social studies deals with people interacting with their environment. As they interact, there are changes within persons and their surroundings. The environment is modified through land use, as well as through buildings, roads, bridges, and housing areas being constructed, among others. The natural environment brings the social science area of geography in ongoing lessons and units of study.

The location of places is one theme in geography. Whatever is studied in the social studies emphasizes a specific location which may be pinpointed on a map and globe. The location is within a region and connects places such as nations, bodies of water, and continents. There is human interaction with the place of location in terms of trade and travel (Ediger, 2005). Being able to adjust to the natural environment as well as to human beings is inherent in the social studies as is the art of living. Thus, a study of civics must permeate the curriculum. Democracy as a way of life is salient in school and in society. It is not only a form of government, but also a way of life with the human population being able to work harmoniously together. This certainly is not the case in many nations with its wars, murders, kidnapping, destruction of property, among other forms of violence. People need to learn to co-operate and work together for the common good (See Hayes, 2002).

A good current events program assists pupils to be informed of and notice where people do and do not work harmoniously. It is important for pupils to be very knowledgeable about current events since it affects all people. Wars fought affect those who are killed/wounded as well as those who live in the home area where grief and sorrow are experienced. Borders of nations change and new governments are formed while the previous ones collapse or are voted out. It behooves the teacher to develop and maintain a high quality current events program. When children first enter school, they should be introduced to developmentally appropriate current events items. People in a democracy must be informed of what is transpiring on the local, state, and national scenes. Voting in elections can only be done effectively by an informed citizenry. There is no better time to start becoming informed, than when first entering the public school years. Current events instruction, as is true of all of education, is ongoing and never completed. There is much to learn within a short life span. Current events deal with issues which are somewhat persistent such as:

* need for different forms of energy to minimize dependance upon fossil fuels. Fossil fuels produce pollution in terms of green house gases.

* wind energy units and ethanol plants being developed as alternative sources of energy. There is a trade-off here in that ethanol depends upon corn products which are heavily dependent upon irrigation at a time when water sources are becoming more limited.

* fuel efficient vehicles needed to cut down on exhaust emissions.

* geothermal energy being useful where the earth's interior can be tapped for heat useful in heating buildings and homes. This involves much expense in having the heat piped and regulated to where it is needed. Reykjavik, Iceland is able to do much heating of structures with geothermal energy, a non-polluting source (Ediger, 7 (3),14-15).

Current events instruction keeps the social studies updated. A well informed citizenry should begin early in life and be ongoing throughout each individual's life span.

CONCLUSION

The psychology of learning when implemented and pupil learning are definitely related. However, teaching and learning must be focused upon helping each pupil to achieve well and succeed in school. These learnings should then transfer to doing well in society. Using principles of psychology in the socials studies should assist pupils to:

* attach meaning and understanding to what is being accomplished

* develop an inward desire for lifelong learning

* broaden the scope of learner interests

* achieve an attitude of feeling positive toward education, in general

* persevere until goals are accomplished
* obtain feedback from personal endeavours being successful in goal attainment.

Pertaining to attitudes in teaching, Leland *et al.* (2007) wrote the following:

> All participants in schools are learners. Yes, teachers and professors are learners, too. It takes attitudes to reject the traditional dichotomy that positions veteran teachers and professors as knowing it all and having little to learn from their students.

All learners deserve rich, multilayered learning experiences. It takes attitude to reject the assumption that low-level learning tasks are appropriate for low-income and low-achieving children.

Knowledge is social constructed and therefore subject to change. It takes attitude to reject the idea that knowledge is fixed and statements labelled as "facts" are necessarily true.

Quality teacher and student attitudes are important in all of learning. Learning from diverse people and sources may indeed stress multi-cultural education.

REFERENCES

Balu, A. (2006), *Effect of Metacognitive Orientation Among Teacher Trainees on Developing Competencies in Teaching Social Studies.* Alagappa University, India, Chapter Two. (Ph.D. thesis evaluated by the writer).

Ediger, Marlow (2001), "Themes to Emphasize in the Geography Curriculum", *Journal of Instructional Psychology*, 32 (2),160-163.

Ediger, Marlow (2007), "Current Events in the Social Studies", *Edutracks*, 7 (3), 14-15.

Ediger, Marlow, and D. Bhaskara (2002), *Teaching Social Studies Successfully. New Delhi,* India: Discovery Publishing House, Chapter Four.

Hayes, Michael T. (2002), "Assessment of a Field Based Teacher Education Program", *Education*, 122 (3), 581-586.

Hoy, Wayne K., and Cecil G. Miskel (2005), *Educational Administration, Theory, Research, and Practice*. New York: McGraw-Hill Companies, Inc., 65-78.

Leland, Christine H. *et al.*, (2007), "Literacy Education, Equity, and Attitude", *Language Arts*, 85 (2), 135.

Reeves, Douglas B. (2007), "How do You Sustain Excellence?" *Educational Leadership*, 65 (3), 86-88.

3

Objectives in Teaching Social Studies

Objectives serve as a compass for the teacher in that they point in the direction of changes to be made in the learner. What types of behaviours does the social studies teacher wish to develop within students? Democratic behaviours is a broad heading for goals to stress in student achievement. This is a broad category and needs to be more specific. Thus, from the general goal, the teacher needs to analyze this end to more specific objectives for student attainment.

OBJECTIVES AND THE SOCIAL STUDIES

A careful study of the literature in teaching the social studies needs to be made in determining which objectives should be emphasized. National Study Groups, such as the National Council for the Social Studies (NCSS), has developed reputable lists of objectives for teacher implementation. A second source for objectives selection stresses beliefs, aims, and standards emphasized by known competent social studies instructors. News accounts of salient topics also provide important information in objectives selection. Fourth, teacher education textbooks for university classes in teacher education are additional sources to read for the selection of educational objectives. Relevant and useful objectives must be in the offing. Also, developmentally appropriate objectives make for successful student learning when implemented. They must meet the needs, interests, and purposes of involved students in ongoing lessons and units of study. Actively engaged students in teaching and learning situations achieve more than the disengaged.

Major objectives to stress in social studies teaching and learning situations need to incorporate problems faced in the societal arena. First, students need to be highly knowledgeable of the natural environment and how it affects human beings. Clean air is a vital concern. Emission of green house gases from factories and vehicles pinpoint a possible change in climate. Among other things, these emissions might raise the ocean levels by melting the ice in the Polar regions. Already, floods from tsunamis and heavy rainfall has caused mudslides and damaged property much in many areas. In other places, droughts have occurred, together with flooded areas, have caused extensive crop damage. Carbon dioxide emissions, too, may well cause respiratory problems as well as decrease in resistance to different diseases (Ediger, 2007).

A corollary to air pollution is land pollution. With excess use of herbicides and pesticides, run offs into creeks, streams, and other bodies of water contaminate and kill fish and other important sea life. Then too, there are always possibilities for ground water contamination. Land fills also can greatly contribute to a polluted environment, unless they are properly maintained and managed. If human beings do not have clean air and water, they may not be able to maintain or make for progress in society. Thus, a major objective in the social studies should emphasize a healthy, clean environment.

Second, energy sources are truly necessary to operate a healthy, forward looking society. It takes energy to cool and heat homes and businesses as well as produce goods and services. But, pollution must be greatly minimized. Automobile standards should indicate that better mileage is obtained from fossil fuels. Excessive waste from exhausts should be taken care of with improved catalytic converters. Alternative sources for vehicle energy must include ethanol and electrical power. More effort should be given to promoting and using wind and bio-mass energy. Geothermal energy also must be used more extensively where possible (Parker, 2001).

Third, students need to learn much pertaining to institutions in society. There are important institutions which impinge upon and influence human behaviour. Religious institutions play a strong role in the lives of many. If students are studying a unit on the Middle East, they must understand basic beliefs pertaining to Islam, Judaism, and Orthodox Christianity. In Islam, for example, there are five pillars which devout Muslims believe in:

* saying the Creed which states, "There is no God, but God, and Mohammed is His prophet."
* making a pilgrimage once in a life time, at least if health permits, to Mecca, Saudi Arabia, the birth place of Mohammed. This is known as the *Hajj*.
* praying five times a day at designated times, facing Mecca
* giving alms to the poor which amounts to two and one half per cent of one's annual income.
* fasting from sunrise to sunset each year during *Ramadan*, the holiest month of the lunar year when the Hajj is being emphasized (Ediger, 1998).

Additional institutions which affect human behaviour include government with its rules and regulations. There are definite laws to abide by in any society. There are fines and other penalties for law violation. Most people abide by laws in society because of duty involved or fear of monetary penalties or prison possibilities, depending upon the severity of breaking the law. Formal means of control involves attorneys, judges, juries, sheriffs, and policemen in law violations, as contrasted within informal means such as in

Old Order Amish Society. The later stress working out problems within their own group. Thus, the deacon, Bishop, and the two ministers in an Old Order Amish community work out disagreements among their own congregation. There are approximately thirty families in a congregation. Informal means of control may involve enforcing no Sunday work, no dancing, and no commercial recreation.

Economic institutions affecting human behaviour include the free enterprise system, competition, the market economy, and a hands off of governmental control, in degrees, in regulating the economy. The latter does stress subsidies, tax breaks, as well as federal and state aid to selected businesses/ enterprises. Students with teacher guidance need to study which economic institutions and to what degree these affect individuals in society. Economic concepts such as massed production, goods, services, distribution, consumption, assembly lines, among others, might well become concepts stated as objectives for student attainment (National Council on Economic Education, 1999).

A fourth kind of objective, relevant in the social studies, for students to attain, emphasizes good citizenship (Political Science). Here, students need to understand and attach meaning to the federal and state constitutions. Their rights and responsibilities as citizens need much emphasis. Democratic behaviours need to be practiced. These include respecting the rights of others, not vandalizing property, as well as assisting others as necessary, Being able to live harmoniously with others in school and in society is highly relevant (National Standards for Civics and Government, 1994) .

Fifth, wise use of leisure time is salient presently as well as in the future. In school and in society, there are a plethora of opportunities for leisure experiences. Reading will always be important as a leisure time activity including library books, newspapers (internet) and reputable magazines. Social studies needs to stress students selecting and reading from diverse materials and resources which integrate with the present lessons and units of study bring taught. Library books must be periodically introduced to students to encourage interest and purpose in reading. For young children, story time can be an excellent occasion to read social studies library books aloud. Assistance in word recognition skills and comprehension strategies need to be in the offing for students to do meaningful reading. Word recognition skills may include students being taught in using phonics, syllabication, and context clues, among other techniques, to recognize unknown words. Student understanding of subject matter read requires careful monitoring, assessing, and evaluation (Ediger, 2006-2007).

Sixth, higher levels of cognition need to permeate the social studies. Solely, comprehending content read literally is inadequate. The student within small groups and the class as a whole needs to be challenged with interesting questions when reading critically. When reading critically, the learner separates the accurate from the inaccurate, the relevant from the irrelevant, as well as fact from opinion. Creatively, the student comes up with a new synthesis. Creativity involves unique, novel ideas emphasized in ongoing lessons and units of study. Also, problem solving stresses higher levels of cognition. Here, students with teacher guidance identify relevant questions and secure information from a variety of reference sources for possible solutions (See Dewey, 1933).

Seventh, metacognition skills need to be developed and honed. This involves thinking about thinking. For example, the student needs to reflect upon and monitor the self in making progress in an ongoing experience such as in:

* analyzing subject matter in a discussion. Thus, the learner may rehearse how he/she reached a certain conclusion. The inherent steps of thinking are then analyzed.
* self monitoring to ascertain reading comprehension of ideas gleaned
* determining steps involved in a previous problem solved.

* evaluating how a project might have been improved upon in the social studies.

Teachers, too, need to reflect upon how a social studies unit was initiated, developed, and then culminated, in order to improve teaching strategy in using the unit next school year (Ediger and Rao, 2001).

Students need to learn how people interact among themselves as well as with the natural environment. History, geography, political science (civics), economics, anthropology and sociology provide subject matter background for knowledge and skills in learning about society. Current events add to the list with recent vital happenings on the local, state, national, and international scenes. Integration of subject matter is to be emphasized rather than a separate subjects curriculum. There are times when a focus upon one academic discipline is needed to understand specific subject matter in a meaningful way. Social studies in diverse ways should assist students to adjust to societal trends, but keeping an open mind toward what needs improvement. Careful interpretation of societal trends must be in the offing with a critical evaluation of what might need to be changed. The past needs to be connected with the present, as well as the present with the future. A study of the past is necessary to identify problem areas which are related to the present. Solving these problems indicate what might accrue in the future. However, new problems continue to arise. At this writing, the writer is looking at an ice storm in which trees have broken branches. The fallen branches litter the yards surrounding the houses. Broken electrical lines make for power outages on cold days. Many homes depend upon electricity for heating the home and using different appliances. Individuals are no longer able to read by kerosene light, but need electricity for proper illumination. With ice storms, branches may litter the streets and slick streets make car driving dangerous. A city may then almost become barren of consumer activities.

The scope of social studies may indeed become broad with science and mathematics also being incorporated into the social studies curriculum. News of scientific and mathematical achievements abound in current events items. The National Council for the Social Studies (NCSS) developed ten themes, which are italic, and might well be considered as the scope of the social studies, but can also be the framework for stating objectives in ongoing lessons and units of study:

* *culture* such as studying the human made part of the environment as well as the aims, values, artifacts of a specific people and includes foods eaten, kinds of clothing worn, languages spoken, and architecture.
* *time, continuity, and change*, as in studying relevant events of the past and observe changes in states and nations. Historians, from leading universities and colleges, assist in determining relevancy.
* *people, places, and environment* in which geographical regions are identified, located, and studied indepth.
* *individual development, and identity* whereby the motivations, purposes, and interests of people are fostered.
* *power, authority, and governance* are studied in terms of local, state, and federal levels of government. Influences of each of these three levels of government are explored, critically examined, and attempts made at synthesis.
* *production, distribution, and consumption* are studied, as concepts, to notice each student's desires and purchases of goods and services.
* *science, technology, and society* and its impact on human beings. Machines, automation, and computers have made the world of work less dependent upon manual labour and more effort placed upon efficiency, massed production, automation, and personal accountability.

* *global connections* in which there is movement among people, manufactured items, and trade among different nations, continents, and regions. Among other ways, these connections may be shown on maps and globes. Current events news happenings indicate in the many ways how nations and human beings interact and are not islands unto themselves.

* *civic ideals and practices* are indicated in the political arenas and good/bad citizenship practiced. Criteria need to be developed to emphasize good citizenship.

Relevant objectives must be written for student attainment. The underlined concept of culture listed as the first item above with an asterisk, for example, may be analyzed in terms of the following objectives for student attainment:

1. the Old Order Amish, a rural people, have main centers of population in Holmes County, Ohio; Goshen, Indiana area; and Lancaster County, Pennsylvania.

2. they dress in unique ways which identifies then instantly from others in society. Thus, Amish women wear prayer caps, long dresses reaching toward the ankles, high necklines, and long sleeves reaching to the wrists. The dresses are of plain colours, not stripes nor checks.

3. they speak Pennsylvania Dutch in the home setting with high German being the language of church services. English is used in society.

4. horses pull buggies (carriages) for transporting their own people as well as goods and services purchased. Automobile, bus, and train service are used for distant travel to other Amish communities (Ediger, 1997).

5. less than 25 per cent of Old Order Amish farm to make a living. Otherwise, Amish men work as carpenters, on construction crews, and are self-employed as furniture makers, among other jobs which the church approves of.

6. Amish men and women marry within their own fold of church members. They are no longer members if they marry outsiders.
7. If they leave the Amish community and wish to come back in, an apology in front of the congregation must be made to be accepted for reinstatement.
8. the Bishop heads the congregation, usually made up of thirty families. There are two men who serve as ministers, and one deacon, making up the leadership of an Old Order Amish congregation. These leaders are chosen by lot.
9. Old Order Amish men are conscientious objectors during times of conscription. The serve in civilian work approved by the Federal government, instead of in the military.
10. Old Order Amish assist each other in times of hardship such as tilling farm land in case of illness or death of a congregation member. Or, they build a farm building in case of a fire or tornado, among other ways (Ediger, 2005).

Objectives need to be relevant in the academic are being studied. They need to be clear and meaningful so that the teacher knows what is to be taught. There is an issue pertaining to how specific an objective should be stated. Behaviourism stresses that objectives be stated in measurable terms. After instruction, the teacher may then be certain if a student has/has not been successful when being tested, in achieving the stated objective. Other schools of thought in education may feel that objectives be left more open ended so that a variety of outcomes are possible, and yet not so open that the objective is meaningless. Room should always be left for student questions and comments relevant to the unit being studied. Inquiry approaches in learning emphasize an open ended curriculum. One truly open ended procedure would be where a teacher answers no questions with specific answers. Instead the teacher responds to the student's question within another question which in sequence leads the learner to the necessary information.

A student teacher supervised by the writer used a kit of materials from a commercial company whereby pupils in the classroom would brainstorm the use of that item in an ancient society. Here, pupils worked as anthropologists who had unearthed these items. The branch of anthropology emphasized was archeology. The brainstorming was done to the point where no more uses were given. This was done for all five items in the kit. It does take time to do this as a classroom activity. Each hypothesized answer was printed on the chalkboard. No hints were given for the uses of any object and avoidance of duplications in answers was a rule. Respect for each answer was stressed. Thus, an inquiry approach was used here where responses as to the use of each item came from pupils. There was considerable enthusiasm for the inquiry approach with pupils eagerly participating. After the hypothesizing was completed, the student teacher mentioned how each item was used in the ancient society, as given in the manual. It was mentioned that the authors of the kit were not always certain how selected items were used. Pupils mentioned that they had to do much thinking to come up with additional hypotheses as to the use of each object. In inquiry approaches in learning, pupils are actively involved in making responses. No lecture or explanations are given, except at the end of the activity where the student teacher stated how the authors of the kit believed each object was used by the ancients.

This does stress good teaching where pupils are actively engaged in learning and time on task is observable. Inquiry learning has its many advocates. Selected educators recommend that explanations given as needed in teaching assist learners to move on to increasingly more complex ideas in the social studies. They believe that giving meaningful explanations, as necessary, might increase more optimal achievement among students (See Reeves, 200).

The complexities of teaching in contemporary classrooms are immense. With the limited number of hours available in most preservice education programs and the relatively short time preservice teachers spend in field placements prior to assuming their first teaching positions, looking outside of university classrooms for ways in which to support and extend preservice teaching becomes imperative. Economic realities would also seem to dictate the need to explore ways in which various stakeholders in public education can network to maximize the limited resources available (Siebert, 2005).

There are different groups and organizations in society with which educators might network to improve teaching and learning in the social studies. These always must be carefully assessed before being used. One way is to use online education courses. There are several that have seemingly reputable courses and degrees in teacher education. They even offer complete degree programs. These courses and degrees must meet quality standards and be accredited, for example, by the National Council for the Accreditation of Teacher Education (NCATE). The latter accredits most teacher education programs nationally. By taking these courses, in-service education may well be strengthened and improved teaching result.

The following provide sessions involving recommended ways of selecting objectives in the social studies as well as improving the school curriculum:

* *The National Council for the Social Studies (NCSS).* Sessions at their annual convention deal with all facets of teaching social studies as well as for all levels, kindergarden through graduate school.
* *The National Council for Teaching Mathematics (NCTM).* While these meetings emphasize mathematics teaching predominately, there are sectional meetings stressing an integrated curriculum as well as on specific methods in the psychology of teaching and learning.

* *International Reading Association (IRA).* Social studies teachers may' certainly benefit here from sectional meetings on reading such as applying these learnings to reading social studies content. The other language arts areas are also stressed including listening, speaking, and writing. The four language arts areas are very valuable to emphasize in the social studies.
* *The National Council Teachers of English (NCTE).* There are valuable sessions here for teaching listening, speaking, reading, and writing. Each of these areas might well apply to the teaching of the social studies. Pupils need to become good listeners, speak clearly in discussions, read subject matter accurately and comprehend subject matter well in reading in the social studies.
* *The National Science Teacher Association.* While this organization stresses the teaching of science, the latter and social studies may well be correlated or integrated. Sometimes, it is difficult to tell if a unit of study is science or social studies in subject matter and skills content: Minimizing Pollution in Our Environment; Preventing Soil Erosion; and Production and Distribution of Goods and Services.

CONCLUSION

Objectives for social studies teaching may come from a variety of sources. Social studies teachers need to stay abreast of these sources, as indicating in this writing. An updated social studies curriculum should be an end result.

REFERENCES

Curriculum Advice: Center for Civic Education (1994). Calabasas, California: National Standards for Civics and Government.

Dewey, John (1933), "Democracy and Education". New York: The Macmillan Company.

Ediger, Marlow (2007), "Developing an Appreciation for the Social Studies", *Edutracks*, 7(1), 5-7.

Ediger, Marlow (2005), "Old Order Philosophy of Education", *Education*, 125 (3), 422-425.

Ediger, Marlow (1997), "Examining the Merits of Old Order Amish Education", *Education*, 117 (3), 139-143.

Ediger, Marlow (1998), "The Holy Land", Kirksville, Missouri: Simpson Publishing Company.

Ediger, Marlow (2006-2007), "Exploring Poetry: The Reading and Writing Connection", *Primer*, 36 (1), 18-21.

Ediger, Marlow, and D. Bhaskara Rao (2001), "Teaching Social Studies Successfully". New Delhi, India: Discovery Publishing House.

National Council on Economic Education (1999), "The Standards in Economic Survey". Washington. DC: NCEE.

Parker, Walter (2001), "Social Studies in Elementary Education". Upper Saddle River, New Jersey: Prentice-Hall, Inc.

Reeves, Douglas B. (2007), "How Do You Sustain Excellence?" *Educational Leadership*, 65 (3), 86-88.

Siebert, Cathy J. (2005), "Promoting Preservice Teachers' Success in Classroom Management by Leveraging a Local Union's Resources: A Professional Development School Initiative", *Education*, 125(3), 385-392.

4

Scope in Social Studies

Scope refers to "what" is taught in the social studies. It then stresses the breadth of subject matter in this area of the curriculum. The academic disciplines involved may be one or more from the social sciences. A rather narrow scope, for example, might refer to history and geography only, whereas a broader scope may add and emphasize economics, among others. Generally, integration of subject matter is in evidence, differentiating it from a separate subjects curriculum in which each academic discipline is taught separately. What then should be the scope of content in the social studies? This will be elaborated upon in the ensuing discussion.

SCOPE IN THE SOCIAL STUDIES

Perhaps, the oldest academic discipline from the social sciences taught is history. History involves a study of selected events of the past which professional historians deem to be relevant. Over time, historians have studied and critically accepted vital items to be included. When lay people think of the social studies, they generally have the academic discipline of history in mind. But, units of study would be rather narrow if a single discipline were emphasized. All individuals have a historical background. They were born, for example, in a specific area and in a particular time. The ancestry of each goes back in succeeding generations. Any movement in history, for example, may be placed on a time line, such as colonization of a given society, establishment of guilds, manors, knighthood, and the events go on and on. Pupils studying relevant events in history is important and needs to be integrated with other academic disciplines (Ediger, 2002).

To broaden the scope of a social studies unit, geography may also be stressed. Thus, historical events take place within a region. Regions are generally defined as an area of land which tends to have homogeneous characteristics. The Mediterranean region is rather homogeneous in that it has many desert areas; low rainfall amounts; as well as unique agricultural crops produced such as olives, dates, figs, and different citrus fruits. Oil production, too, is a major source of income for several Middle East nations. Thus, human beings may also be studied from a geographic as were as historic focus (See National Council for Geographic Education, 1994).

Increasing the breadth of subject matter taught, economics may be brought into the social studies curriculum. There are selected concepts which are salient in economics. These are goods, services, production, distribution, consumption, massed production, standardized parts, assembly lines, inflation, depression, and recession, among others. Seemingly, the economic world affects individuals as much as does any other social science academic discipline. Incomes need to be earned so that goods and services may be purchased. These purchases involve necessities of life such as food, clothing, and shelter. In higher income homes, increased money will be spent on luxury items and leisure time activities. Voters may well vote pocket book issues in an election reflecting the concerns for making a living or not going downhill on items of comfort and recreation. Housing slumps and job losses causes anxiety and fear (See Dunn and Dunn, 1979).

To increase the scope of the social studies even further, political science (civics) might well be added. Political Science does stresses a study of government and how it affects people in society. Indepth study of local, state, and federal levels of government is necessary in order that individuals may know their rights and responsibilities. Governments need to be receptive to the will of the people. Students need to learn about democracy as a form of government and as a way of life. They must realize the importance of available freedoms and ways of upholding these ideals through laws, rules, and regulations. Arbitrary decisions are not a part of a democracy in society. An orderly society needs to be in evidence. Each person must be equal before the law. Sometimes, laws are very broadly written which lends to multiple interpretations law suits may then arise as to the meaning of these laws. The rule of just laws, not the thinking of few individuals, is necessary (Ediger, 2007).

Two more academic disciplines need inclusion in an integrated social studies curriculum. These are sociology and anthropology. Sociology, among other things stresses the role of institutions and how they affect society. Many institutions have their affect on human beings. These include religion, economic (such as the workplace), government, secular organizations and membership in clubs (those meeting personal needs), education, and recreational groups. Organizations and institutions fill vital roles and functions in society. Behaviour of human beings is influenced by these organizations. For example, each work place has its unique culture or culture(s) in terms of stressing language used, humour expressed, levels of politeness as well as caring for others, and degrees of acceptance.

Anthropology, too, emphasizes a study of culture, but also studying the remains of ancient civilizations. Anthropological digs fascinate learners. When actually visiting an excavation sight or viewing a video tape on the work of anthropologists, the student notices the care taken in mapping where each object and artifact was found as well as labelling it. Anthropologists are not always certain of how an artifact was used in earlier times, and they then develop educated hypotheses. The writer was teaching in Jericho on the West Bank of the Jordan when Archeologist Kathleen Kenyon and her team were excavating ancient remains of that city in 1952-1953. Scientifically, they examined each artifact, labelling it, and mapping the area it was discovered. Among many other things, they dug up the dirt around the wall of ancient Jericho. The wall dates back to 8000 BC and the limestone blocks are clearly visible and appear as a partial, rounded watch tower.

The different social science disciplines then provide subject matter for teaching the social studies. The social studies teacher needs to teach the contents as being related and fused whenever it is relevant to do so.

QUALIFICATIONS FOR TEACHING THE SOCIAL STUDIES

It is necessary for social studies teachers to have a good background of course work in the social sciences in undergraduate and, preferable, on the graduate level. Background experiences in these academic disciplines can indeed make for more competent and quality teaching. If a teacher is weak in these social science disciplines, he/she needs to do inservice education work to take care of deficiencies. A professional teacher is highly interested in strengthening areas of subject matter deficiencies as well as in methods of teaching students. To integrate subject matter beyond the social sciences, social studies teachers also need to bring into the student class discussion subject matter ideas from the general education curriculum including literature, writing skills, the different branches of science, and mathematics. Integration is not done for the sake of doing so, but rather to enrich the social studies.

Current events correlate well with a quality social studies curriculum. Current events very frequently emphasize Middle East items, for example. The Palestinian/Israeli disputes have festered for many decades and are far from being resolved. Palestinian refugees, border disagreements on the West Bank, the Israeli/Syrian disputes covering the Golan Heights area, and the status of the walled city of Jerusalem present a plethora of insurmountable problems which need to be addressed and attempts made at arriving at solutions.

A quality current events program also addresses other problems on the planet earth. Earthquakes, hurricanes, tornados, floods, mudslides, cyclones, tsunamis, among others, come from natural causes. Science may be brought in to explain the causes of each disaster. Human made disasters in current events include wars, violence, car bombings, kidnapping, robberies, and domestic crimes, in general. Major events should be reported upon in class; the insignificant should be avoided. Patterns then need to be observed in natural and human made disasters.

Solutions to problems need thorough discussion, analyzation, and synthesis. Brain storming may be used to ascertain the most viable, possible solutions. Solutions always need to be held tentative until further evidence arrives. Knowledge then is subject to change. Students with teacher guidance need to be aware of problematic situations and possible solutions in current events. Teacher interest and enthusiasm for current events is necessary. Hopefully, this will reflect upon students. Lifelong student leaning is salient.

Materials needed to teach current events include reputable daily newspapers and news magazines, the internet, and resource persons knowledgeable about a certain facet of current events being emphasized in the classroom. Foreign newspapers are relatively easy to access on the internet. For example, in reporting news pertaining to the Middle East, the following daily newspapers on the internet are easily readable:

* The Beirut, Lebanon Daily Star

* The Jerusalem Post

Innovative methods need to be used in teaching. Large and small group instruction, as well as individual endeavours should be in the offing. When the class as a whole is used in teaching, the teacher introduces a lesson or unit whereby a common body of knowledge is stressed. Audio-visual aids are used here so that students of all ability levels may benefit. The visual part makes it possible for all to see images of what is discussed in the abstract. In the unit on the Middle Ages, a picture of a knight, a guild member, and/or nobleman clarifies the appearance of each. Also, this stimulates students to do further thinking on the duties and responsibilities of each individual. Questions raised by students motivates learners to pursue interesting ideas. Problem solving might then be emphasized when securing information from a variety of reference sources in answer to the indepth question. Student interest and motivation in each social studies unit of study is important.

Construction activities may be emphasized when students make model puppets of knights, guild members, and nobleman to be used in a dramatic experience. Art work might be stressed when students make a mural pertaining to a village in the Middle Ages. For each construction and/or art activity, students need to perceive this as a worthwhile purpose. They accept reasons for their undertaking. Then students need to work to complete the purposeful project. Quality work is necessary. Ultimately, criteria must be used to appraise the project. Questions such as the following need to be answered pertaining to the completed project:

* did each person do the best possible work?
* was there co-operation among participants?
* did students share materials while doing the project?
* were planning sessions fruitful in that quality sequence was involved?
* did students truly see purpose for the construction/art project?

Social studies teachers need to identify personal competencies necessary for quality instruction which include the following:

* giving worthwhile assignments
* being able to read aloud in an interesting and enthusiastic manner
* asking interesting questions pertaining to vital subject matter
* initiating lessons in a motivating manner
* pacing ideas presented in an orderly way
* managing the classroom conducive to optimal learner achievement
* presenting meaningful verbal and audio-visual content
* clarifying content as needed for student understanding
* using reinforcement techniques properly
* achieving lesson closure
* probing for indepth student learning
* emphasizing critical and creative thinking
* guiding student improvement in reading social studies subject matter (See, Balu).

When reading social studies content, students with teacher assistance need to obtain an overview of what will be read. The overview provides readiness for reading and may consist of carefully viewing the inherent illustrations directly related to the ensuing subject matter. Bold topical headings assist the learner in obtaining structural ideas of what will be read. Advance organizers might well help students, too, in reading content with meaning. Thus, the social studies teacher may present clearly and in an understanding way selected major ideas pertaining to what will be read. Learners then possess a major generalization or generalizations relating to oncoming abstractions. It is appropriate for students to raise questions, at this point, about what has been discussed. Predictions given as possible answers to identified questions provide a framework for reading.

New vocabulary terms may be identified through context clues and phonic learnings. They may also be discussed meaningfully before the subject matter has been read. These vocabulary terms then need to be printed on the chalk board for students to see prior to the ensuing reading activity. As a result, students should have developed readiness experiences for reading.

Followup experiences include discussing what was read within the class as a whole or in small groups. Evaluating the quality of predictions made is important. Critical reading stresses separating facts from opinions as well as fantasy from reality. Creative reading emphasizes the student coming up with new, innovative ideas from text reading. A stimulating discussion involving ideas read must be in the offing (Ediger and Rao, 2001).

Scope in the social studies emphasizes "what" should be taught to indicate breadth of academic disciplines stressed in the curriculum. This needs to be clearly defined in an integrated social studies program. Learning activities stressed need to reflect the identified scope. Then too, quality criteria from the psychology of learning must be in evidence in teaching and learning situations.

REFERENCES

Balu, A. (2006), *Effectiveness of Metacognitive Orientation Among Teacher Trainees on Developing Competencies in Teaching Social Studies*. Ph.D. thesis evaluated by the writer for Alaggapa University (India), 21.

Dunn, Rita S., and Kenneth Dunn (1979), "Teaching Styles/Learning Styles", *Educational Leadership*, 36 (4), 238-244.

Ediger, Marlow (2002), "The Supervisor of the School", *Education*, 122(3), 602-604.

Ediger, Marlow (2007), "Learning Activities in the Curriculum", *College Student Journal*, 41(4), 967-969.

Ediger, Marlow, and D. Bhaskara Rao (2001), *Teaching Social Studies Successfully*. New Delhi, India: Discovery Publishing House.

"National Council for Geographic Education (1994), Geography for Life". Washington, DC: NCGE.

5

Sequence in Social Studies

It is highly significant to have quality sequence in teaching social studies. Why? If good sequence is being stressed in teaching, students should feel success in learning. New ideas obtained are then directly related to what was learned previously. Students retain learnings better if relationship of subject matter is perceived. Building upon content acquired previously makes for better retention of learnings since there is a foundation of subject matter already in the repertoire.

SEQUENCES IN SUBJECT MATTER ACQUISITION

There are several approaches in stressing sequential learnings in the social studies for students. A logical approach might stress the social studies teacher choosing learning activities for students to pursue. Thus, the order of activities as perceived by the teacher would build on past learnings of students and then proceed from the easier to those gradually more complex in terms of new facts, concepts, and generalizations for student acquisition. The teacher's judgement is involved here in determining logically in what makes for a quality sequence. Hopefully, students wilt also perceive this order of leaning activities as emphasizing increased achievement in knowledge, skills, and attitudes.

Meaningful learnings will then accrue. The social teacher, here, is the key person to arrange learning activities so that each student may learn as much as possible sequentially. This requires teacher knowledge and skill.

Toward the other end of the continuum, the beliefs are that sequence resides within the student, not the teacher. Students, involving teacher guidance, are then motivated with a variety of learning opportunities to raise questions and problems in ongoing units of study. The questions/problems may be used as a means of engaging students in doing projects. The ideas for project development come from students with teacher guidance. Students develop an interest in a purpose or reasons for doing a project. The project may be done individually or within a committee. Careful planning needs to be involved, followed by implementation of these plans. The processes of good committee work must be stressed such as all participating and no one dominating in an atmosphere of respect. Evaluation of the completed project needs quality standards to be used in the assessment. These standards should be developed by students with teacher assistance (Ediger and Rao, 2003).

Constructivism, as in the project method and in problem solving, stresses student/teacher planning and considerable learner input into teaching and learning situations. Sequence then involves student interests, purposes, and active involvement. The teacher helps, encourages, and motivates students.

For many social studies teachers, both teacher sequences and constructivism are emphasized. It is not one to the exclusion of the other. Students, however, should:

* raise questions pertaining to what is not understood
* be actively involved in planning selected learning experiences
* be challenged to come up with unique ideas in class discussions

* assist each other as the need arises
* emphasize good citizenship (See Hopkins and Stanley, 1991).

QUALITY SEQUENCE IN ONGOING LESSONS AND ACTIVITIES

To possess good sequence, new knowledge must be based upon what is already possessed in terms of facts, concepts, and generalizations. Jumping too far ahead of where students are presently leaves many learners behind. Once, students have revealed their present level of achievement, then the social studies teacher can move forward, gradually, with increased complexity of learnings, based on developmental characteristics of learners.

One unique approach in sequencing learnings is to use programmed learning for students. The programs are generally purchased from a commercial company. A few teachers have written and developed their own programs. Generally, commercial programs have been field tested to take out the kinks. Programmed learning tends to follow the following procedure for student learning:

* the student reads a short paragraph or even a few sentences on the monitor
* the learner responds to a test item, usually in multiple choice format
* he/she then checks his/her response with the correct one provided by the programmer
* if correct, the learner is rewarded; if incorrect the student knows the correct answer and then also moves on to the next sequential item with read, respond, and check being emphasized continuously (See Walsh and Betz, 1985).

With good, filled tested programs, students generally respond with, 95 per cent accuracy. That does indicate quality sequence. The programmer from a commercial company writes the complete program. There is no chance for student input, other than responding to multiple choice test items. Each small step of read, respond, and check moves forward very gradually in complexity of items to read. This is done so students make few errors in learning.

Programmed learning is rigid and formal. There are no opportunities of changing any ensuing items with no input from the social studies teacher or the students. Factual information is usually learned (Ediger, 2007a).

Compare programmed learning with more flexible procedures such as students with teacher guidance, within a unit of study, identifying open ended questions to discuss. Thus in a unit on The Middle East, students may experience a related audio-visual presentation and ask questions such as the following:

* why does the Mediterranean climate have no rain basically from April to November and then experience rainfall from November to April?
* what provides moisture during the dry season to produce figs, dates, olives, and citrus fruits as agricultural crops?
* which kinds of building materials are used to build homes and businesses?

Each of the above named questions may be used in problem solving. Students then gather information from a variety of reference sources including the internet, basal textbooks, library books, and resource personnel, among others. The information is then gathered to develop a tentative hypothesis. The hypothesis is tested with additional information from reputable reference sources. If the testing upholds the hypothesis, it is accepted. If not, the hypothesis (answer) may need additional information for evaluation.

Problem solving leaves much leeway for student initiative. There is much responsibility on the student's part and skilful teaching is necessary. Students will need assistance to move forward in developing an acceptable solution to the problem. Wise use of time and knowledge of reference sources is needed. The teacher's role is to assist in making suggestions as needed, monitoring the activity, praising work well done, and setting a model. Students with teacher assistance do much of their very own sequencing (Ediger, 2007b).

When students do an increasing amount of sequencing their learnings, the concept of "constructivism" is used. Individual constructivism was advocated by the late Jean Piaget of Switzerland who noticed in his research four levels of pupil maturation. These were

* sensori-motor which lasted basically from birth to eighteen months. Here, the infant begins to develop his/her five senses and muscle movement.
* preoperational, eighteen months to seven years of age, whereby the young child continues to develop from the sensori-motor stage, to perceiving one variable only in what is experienced, such as the length or width of an object, only.
* stage of concrete objects in which the learner needs to experience real objects and items, alongwith what is being learned in the abstract, such as in a discussion. This stage lasts until age eleven, basically
* the stage of abstract thought whereby the pupil learns much less from concrete experiences and more on abstract thought.

The above summary ideas provide a framework for further investigations by social studies teachers. These might then be developed in lesson plans/units of study and applied in teaching and leaning situations. Len Vygotsky, instead of individual constructivism, emphasized the social factor in which pupils worked and learned in small group/committee settings. As pupils collectively work together, ideas circulate among learners in a discussion. Learning from each other in a social setting assists pupils to modify their thinking and move toward higher levels of cognition. The interaction among committee members helps learners to test ideas and refine their thinking. Objects and items used together with abstract ideas during the discussion aids pupils to understand what is being discussed.

Mediation occurs between students and the objects/ideas in ongoing learning activities. Reasoning and problem solving, among other kinds of thinking, occur in these kinds of rich classroom experiences. Sequence then resides within the learner, not the teacher. However, the social studies teacher is there to encourage student responses. He/she assists in setting the stage for learning by discovery and intrinsic student motivation. From within, the student evaluates what is known and not known with attempts made to fill the gaps.

In contrasting Vygotsky with Piaget, the latter stressed individual maturation to sequence thinking and progress. Thus, Piaget, trained as a biologist, emphasized that changes in thinking come from biological maturation. But, the maturation process needs assistance with quality teaching. For example, in the sensori-motor stage of development, infants engage in much movement and play with appropriate objects. This is followed by young children focusing upon one variable basically. Thus, objects are viewed from one perspective only/largely, such as length and not width, or tallness, not diameter as in a tumbler. Maturation moves forward with the stage of concrete objects whereby abstract ideas may be understood, but with the related concrete objects generally being present. Later, the stage of abstract thought is developed and concrete objects need not be used, basically, in teaching and learning situations (See Hoy and Miskel, 2005).

With traditional methods of teaching, such as in a teacher determined social studies curriculum whereby he/she determines sequence in student learning or in teacher/student constructivism, the salient ideas are for learners being interested in learning and where meaningful subject matter is being studied. Content acquired needs to be understood by students.

Quality sequence in the social studies needs to lead students to achieve vital objectives. Balu (2006) lists the following:

* development of good human relations
* education in citizenship
* growth in thinking behaviours and decision making
* social competencies
* teaching the art of self-realization
* assist students to adjust to as well as modify the social/physical environment
* relevant use of economic competencies
* assist in developing his/her personality
* gain insight into spiritual and political values
* interest in life long and continuing education
* acquire feelings of belonging
* promotion of world peace.

Each of the above goals has important implications for students in the social studies. Lesson plans and units of study need to reflect these goals. For example, in the first listed goal above, the teacher may assist students when they work in small groups. These groups may consist of committee work, peer mediated instruction, and/or peer lead instruction, all with teacher supervision. With good human relations being practiced, students should have developed feelings of belonging. Bullying and rudeness need to be omitted. Instead quality human relations need to be in evidence. Esteem needs might well be met when negative feelings are omitted and good will is in the classroom, school, and surrounding environments.

To promote good sequence, several strategies may be used in teaching and learning. Scaffolding emphasizes that gaps between where the student is presently in achievement and a desired goal may be minimized/eliminated. Thus, the teacher in small steps provides learnings whereby the desired goals will be achieved and the gap taken care of. The gap is reasonable to achieve with quality sequence.

Also, problem solving needs to be implemented. Here, the student(s) in an ongoing lesson/unit of study identify a problem. The problem requires deliberation and effort of an unsolved situation. Indepth thinking will be involved. A variety of sources of information will be necessary in solving the problem. This results in a tentative answer. Tentativeness indicates the answer is subject to evaluation. The question which need to be answered is, "Does the answer hold water?" If the solution is unsatisfactory, learners with teacher guidance must keep digging. Selected problems have no true solutions; however, selected answers are better than others. Life would be easier if exact solutions to problems would be in the offing. The most exact science is mathematics which has precise answers for operations in addition, subtraction, multiplication, and division. It still has its own rules which brings in subjectivity.

In thinking of possible solutions to societal problems, there are many possibilities, but none with certainty. The Middle East is an example involving Palestinian versus Israel goals. Problems here have festered for a lengthy period of time and include:

* boundaries clarified by two separate nations
* water rights in an area which lack this precious commodity
* claims made by refugees of lost lands and the right of return to their former areas of habitation
* reimbursement for property lost.

Problem solving emphasizes a sequence whereby students tend to order their experiences in arriving at tentative solutions when using a variety of learning activities. Sequence resides within each learner. Compare this learning situation where sequence largely resides in the mind of the teacher. The social studies teacher:

* activates background information for the ensuing lesson
* writes the new words in manuscript style on the chalkboard
* discusses meanings attached to the new words through student participation and contextual use in obtaining learner readiness for reading from the basal social studies textbook
* assists students to raise questions in establishing a purpose for textbook reading
* helps students to analyze subject matter read, as followup activities. Followup activities need to include discussing content read with critical and creative thinking experiences. "Why" and "how" kinds of questions need discussion from subject matter read. Stimulating discussions need to be in the following (Ediger, 2005).

Quality sequence assists students to experience growth, achievement, and development. A major goal is to help students lead productive lives in society. Students need to live in harmony with others in the home, community, state, and nation. These ideals need extension to the world scene. Too much destruction and loss of lives occur in and among nations due to wars, tension, hatred, and competition.

Living harmoniously, also, with the environment is important. Clean air and water are needed for sustenance of human life. An excessive amount of green house gases are omitted from smoke stacks of factories. The soil needs protection from erosion, misuse, floods, as well as excessive use of pesticides, and herbicides.

Knowledge, and use of the different branches of the social sciences should help in curbing abuses. These social science disciplines in an integrated social studies curriculum include history, geography, political science (civics), economics, sociology, and anthropology.

To live more enriching lives, students need to learn to think effectively and flexibly in different types of situations. Critical thinking assists in separating the relevant from the irrelevant as well as synthesizing useful information. Creative thinking emphasizes learners coming up with unique solutions to identified problems areas. The level of application helps students to use what has been learned. Change is a key item in society. Situations never stay the same, but are subject to change. With changing situations, new problems arise and new solutions must be sought. Good sequence encompasses these changes.

REFERENCES

Balu, A. (2006). "Effectiveness of Metacognitive Orientation Among Teacher Trainees on Developing Competences in Teaching the Social Studies". Ph.D. thesis. Alagappa University: The writer appraised this Ph.D. thesis, and other theses for Alagappa University, India.

Ediger, Marlow (2007a), "The School and Students in Society", *Experiments in Education*, 35 (9),17-20.

Ediger, Marlow (207b), "Developing an Appreciation for the Social Studies", *Edutracks*, 7(1), 5-7.

Ediger, Marlow (2005), "Themes to Emphasize in the Geography Curriculum", *Journal of Instructional Psychology*, 32(2), 160-163.

Ediger, Marlow, and D. Bhaskara Rao (2003), *Psychology and Curriculum*. New Delhi, India: Discovery Publishing House, Chapter Six.

Hopkins, Kenneth, and Julian C. Stanley (1991), *Educational and Psychological Measurement and Evaluation*. Englewood Cliffs, New Jersey: Prentice-Hall, Inc.

Hoy, Wayne K., and Cecil G. Miskel (2005), *Educational Administration: Theory, Research, and Practice*. New York: McGraw-Hill, 66-68.

Walsh, Bruce W., and Nancy E. Betz (1985), *Tests and Assessment. Englewood Cliffs*, New Jersey: Prentice-Hall Inc.

6

Current Events and Social Studies

Current events should be an inherent part of the social studies. Learners need to stay abreast of what is transpiring in the world. Citizens in a democracy need to be well informed of happenings locally, state wide, nationally, and internationally.

Objectives in the current events must be meaningful and on the developmental level of students. They need to consist of knowledge, skills, and attitudinal goals. Balance among the three kinds of objectives need to be stressed in teaching. Relevant objectives for student attainment must be chosen. They should emphasize those events which are enduring, rather than being transitory. Teachers must use quality pedagogy and possess much knowledge of current events in order to do well in assisting learner progress (Ediger and Rao, 2001).

TEACHING CURRENT EVENTS

Current events may be brought in as they relate to an ongoing unit of study. Thus, if a unit is taught on India, then current events on that nation should be brought into teaching/ learning situations. But, not all salient events are related to the social studies being taught. These may be stressed separately such as happenings in Brazil or Argentina. Or an entire unit may be taught on a current events situation, if it possesses high importance, such as "The Middle East Dilemmas."

Relevancy and importance are salient in selecting current events items to be taught. Then too, they need to be on the understanding level of students. Meaning is vital to students when learning about current events. What is not meaningful must be identified and retaught. The current events items must be adjusted to where students understand the subject matter taught.

Scaffolding must be used when assisting students to achieve from where they are presently to a possible ideal level. This represents a gap which needs to be filled. Carefully sequencing within the gap assists students to achieve as optimally as possible. Concrete, semi-concrete, and abstract materials in teaching students must be used (Smith, 2006).

Learner engagement is salient in teaching current events. Passive students tend not to accomplish whereas active involvement is preferred. Each student must work diligently to attain vital objectives of instruction. Good work habits will assist students to achieve well presently as well as in the future as adults. Being prompt in completing assignments and doing the best work possible are two good habits to attain in current events instruction.

Quality attitudes toward current events need to be developed. Good attitudes assist in securing knowledge as well as skills. Attitudinal development is ongoing and is not developed in a short period of time. Feelings of adequacy, self fulfilment, and possessing a good self concept are necessary to achieve well. These objectives are being met when learning experiences are satisfying to the learner. To be satisfying means the experiences were interesting and new knowledge/skills were achieved.

Attitudes, too, are developed when recognition needs are being met. Each person desires to be recognized for doing well in some facet of life, depending upon talents possessed. The late A.H. Maslow (1954), listed the following sequential steps in developing desirable attitudes:

* having physiological needs met such as possessing adequate food, clothing, and shelter
* having safety needs met
* having love and belonging needs met
* having esteem needs met
* having knowledge needs met
* realizing self-actualization.

By viewing the above named needs of students, it is quite apparent that knowledge needs do not come first in importance, but are subject to prerequisites which need fulfilling. It might seem as if some of these are far removed from current events instruction, but it does indicate that hungry children will not achieve well in school. Physiological needs may be met, in part, with school breakfasts and lunches. However, there are too many days when a school is not in session to meet nutrition needs of students such as Saturdays and Sundays. In some areas, lunches are served free to children during selected summer months, but again there are loop holes here in students not being fed from among the needy, in particular, when these meals are not being served during intervals. Clothes closets and selected religious groups do provide clothing free of charge. Through contacts with these groups, schools are assisted in meeting clothing needs of students. Schools, in part, can meet love and belonging needs of children with teachers accepting and respecting each learner. A caring feeling by teachers and peers can go a long way in helping children do well in school.

Going back to specifically teaching current events, students need to communicate items clearly and accurately, orally and in writing. They need to check news-reports against each other to notice discrepancies. It is salient to notice who wrote an item since the nationality of the writer might well be subject to bias. News items need discussing to look at diverse points of view held by students. Readiness factors need to be considered in any type of learning opportunity including discussions.

Sources for current event items may come from the internet, newspapers and magazines, and radio news reports, among others. The student may learn much in current events from viewing illustrations in the news media, as in televised reports. The sense of hearing may be used solely (radio use) or collectively with the visual (pictorial) and print discourse. Whatever source is used, meaning needs to be inherent pertaining to that which is learned.

News items cover a broad scope including:

* changes in governmental officials within a nation and election disputes
* border disputes and boundary changes between/among nations
* wars, declared and undeclared
* natural disasters including earthquakes, floods, hurricanes and tornados (Ediger, 1995).

A variety of learning opportunities should be used in current events including debates, indepth analysis/synthesis of news items in a seminar procedure, committee deliberations, dramatization of selected news events, and reports by individuals or within small groups. Interest might well be developed through students making posters, charts, models, experience charts, giving oral reports on news happenings, keeping an ongoing log/ portfolio on current events, and murals.

Standards need to be developed and implemented pertaining to current events discussions. These include staying on the topic pursued, respecting the thinking of others, listening carefully to the ideas of peers and the teacher, each participating but no one dominating the discussion, presenting ideas clearly and accurately as well as evaluating them in an atmosphere of trust, drawing valid and accurate conclusions from discussions, and attaining feelings of motivation.

At one school in which the author supervised university student teachers in the public schools, a classroom of sixth graders wrote a newspaper of current event items discussed. They had an editor, an assistant editor for each category of news items, and proof readers, among other divisions of workers for the classroom newspaper. The small newspaper was received favourably among parents and served to communicate, in part, what the school was achieving (See Ediger, 2003).

A bulletin board of news clippings should be used to have students display current events items. The student who brought a news item may then briefly report to the class on subject matter in the clipping. A world map may be located adjacent to the news clippings with yarn connecting the item to the place of happening. This is a good time to bring into the unit on current events, important map and globe learnings such as meridians, parallels, latitude, longitude, hemispheres, the polar regions, and time zones, among others.

METHODS OF TEACHING CURRENT EVENTS

A variety of methods needs to be used in teaching/learning situations. Students may develop generalizations inductively, following a discussion of an important happening. The conclusion may be checked by having other learners present their summary statements.

In contrast, a deductive procedure may be used whereby the teacher provides the conclusion to a news item with students offering supporting statements.

Problem solving may be emphasized pertaining to current events items. Here, learners identify, in a contextual situation, a relevant problem/question. Based on knowledge possessed, an hypothesis or tentative answer, to the problem is suggested by learners. The hypothesis is evaluated through further study and research by learners. It is then revised and modified, if necessary.

Learners should be encouraged to develop and maintain a notebook of ideas gleaned from current events discussions. The notebook may be bound for review as well as for other uses in future situations. An electronic notebook, alternatively produced when students are ready for these kinds of experiences, might also be developed (See Supon, 2006).

Self-evaluation helps the teacher to think of additional learning activities which might assist learners to achieve objectives pertaining to current events in the social studies (See Hopkins and Stanley, 1991). The following are questions which the teacher may ask the self to improve instruction:

* do I have a learning environment which stimulates learner curiosity?
* are learning opportunities varied so that students will not lack motivation for learning?
* have I emphasized intrinsic motivation of students rather than continually stressing assigned work?
* what evidence is there that students are actively involved in ongoing learning activities?
* how often do students volunteer to do additional work?
* is the quality of work from each student the best that can be expected of him/her?
* do students have ample opportunities to do work on something which is relevant?
* do I praise students for doing better than formerly regardless ability levels?
* do I provide a learning environment whereby each feels he/she can achieve optimally?
* do I help each student to respect the thinking and rights of others?

* does it appear that students have a positive attitude toward current events?

* what can be done to assist each student in wanting to learn in current events?

When pondering over each of the above named questions, the teacher meditates on improving instruction, including the current events. Dialog needs to begin among teachers in working toward the best objectives, learning opportunities, and evaluation procedures possible for teaching and learning situations.

REFERENCES

Ediger, Marlow (1995), "Geography in the Social Studies", *Perspectives*, 27(1), 9-10.

Ediger, Marlow (2003), "Mentor Teachers", *Edutracks*, 2 (9), 915. Published in India.

Ediger, Marlow, and D. Bhaskara Rao (2001) *Teaching Social Studies Successfully*. New Delhi, India: Discovery Publishing House.

Hopkins, Kenneth D., and Julian C. Stanley (1991), *Educational and Psychological Measurement and Evaluation*, Sixth Edition, Englewood Cliffs, New Jersey: Prentice-Hall, Inc.

Maslow, A. H. (1954), *Motivation and Personality*. New York: Harper and Row.

Smith, Lynn Alleen (2006), "Think aloud Mysteries: Using Structured, Sentence by Sentence Text Passages to Teach Comprehension Strategies", *The Reading Teacher*, 59(8),764-773.

Supon, Viola (2006), "Using Digital Cameras for Multidimensional Learning in K-12 Classrooms", *Journal of Instructional Psychology*, 33(2), 154-156.

7

Learning Activities in Social Studies

Subject matter acquired in ongoing social studies units of study needs to be analyzed and synthesized in order to obtain meaningful content. Salient facts are important to achieve, but they need to be used in a variety of ways. One way to use ideas is through discussions. Discussions might well stress higher levels of cognition. The teacher must be able to steer away from the mundane and the routine by leading quality interactions among students. These discussions and other learning activities must be on the understanding level of learners in order to achieve objectives (Ediger and Rao, 2001).

CRITICAL THINKING IN ONGOING UNITS OF STUDY

To do well in critical thinking, there needs to be vital rules to optimize thought processes. Respect for the thinking of others is significant. Interrupting others is to be avoided. With practice and calling attention to this rule assists learners to be more respectful and caring. Rudeness decreases the effectiveness of committee endeavours and it hinders students from participating. Also bullying and harassing must be outlawed in schools. Careful monitoring of students decreases the likelihood of these two evils from occurring since they breed fear and resentment among learners.

All need to participate in a discussion with no one dominating. Ideas need to be expressed clearly and succinctly, Student voices need to emphasize proper pitch, stress, and juncture. A pleasant, well modulated voice encourages active participation in discussion settings.

The teacher needs to set the stage for interesting discussions based on students achieving objectives in ongoing relevant lessons and units of study. Adequate background information needs to be in the student's repertoire in order to be actively engaged in learning. Problems to be identified in large group sessions might include the following in a unit on the Middle East:

* What were selected causes for the Crusades during the Middle Ages?
* How did Great Britain and France gain dominance in the Middle East following World War I?
* What happened to the Ottoman Empire after their defeat in World War I?
* Why did Great Britain receive the Mandate to govern Palestine, Transjordan, and Iraq, while France secured the Mandate for ruling Lebanon and Syria?
* What importance did the Balfour Declaration of 1917 have for encouraging Jewish immigration to Palestine?
* How did the Arabs of Palestine react to Jewish immigration?
* What role did Adolph Hitler's persecution of Jews in Germany have for their settlement in Palestine?
* How does Islam, Judaism, and Christianity have their influence in Middle East affairs?
* What influence did the following have in the Middle East: King Hussein of Jordan. Yassir Arafat of the

Palestinian Arabs, Yitzak Rabin Shimon Peres of Israel, Hosni Mobarek of Egypt, and Hafez Assad of Syria (Ediger, 1998).

To obtain needed information for each of the above problem areas, students, with teacher guidance, need to use a variety of reference sources. These reference sources include the internet, textbooks, library books, and encyclopedias, among others.

Students may work in committees or individually. Problem areas may be assigned or learners may volunteer to secure necessary information individually or within committees. Information obtained needs to be compiled in a comprehensive manner followed by intensive. Analyzation emphasizes critical thinking in separation facts from opinions, accurate from inaccurate statements, as well as fantasy from reality. Higher order thinking skills are then involved. Students with indepth analyzation may well come up with valid and reliable conclusions (See Parker, 2001). Differences in thinking between Palestinian Arabs and Israelis will tend to be great. Thus, reading between the lines and creative thinking may well be necessary to reach conclusions in summarizing information obtained.

Information secured and conclusions realized may be presented to the class in a variety of ways including:

* oral reports whereby each student takes a segment of the total report
* debates in which team A debates team B when representing Palestinian Arab versus Israeli views
* seminars to present information obtained in its totality to the entire class, followed by a question/answer session from the audience for elaboration
* written reports placed in a binder, for all to read and study. This approach works well in harmony with other procedures listed above. Drawings, diagrams, illustrations, and time lines may be incorporated into the folder.

* issues resulting from information obtained need to be listed and studied indepth. Discussions may follow in attempting to secure a synthesis.

EVALUATION OF THE ACTIVITIES

A quality program of evaluation is necessary to determine the worth of each activity as well as provide information for ensuing learning opportunities. Teachers as well as students need to assess the unit of study in answering the following questions:

* did the learning activities assist in meeting the objectives of the course?
* how well was indepth discussions emphasized in ongoing lessons and unit of study?
* did everyone participate actively in the different, ongoing learning opportunities?
* what needs to be improved upon to make the unit comprehensive in scope when acquiring worthwhile subject matter?
* how effectively was the subject matter obtained in answer to problems and questions?
* might more subject matter have been secured in answer to issues identified?
* how well were the committee reports presented to others?
* what else might students want to learn about the Middle East (See Stiggins, 2007)?

Social studies units of study should encourage interest and engagement in learning. Intrinsically, learners must feel an inward desire to learn and achieve. Motivation to learn salient facts, concepts, and generalizations should be in the offing. The teacher sets the stage for student learning for students being wholeheartedly involved in each lesson and unit of study. There is much to learn in a unit on the Middle East; newscasts on radio and television tend to be filled with tense reports from the Middle East. The United Nations as well as the United States have innumerable problems to solve in the Middle East such as:

* finding a solution to the lengthy Iraqi war
* Israeli occupation of the West Bank and the Golan Heights
* Lebanese self determination
* nuclear ambitions of Iran.

Each of the above extends the study on the Middle East, including vital concerns in that area of the world. A good current events program might well assist students to understand the Middle East in increasing depth.

REFERENCES

Ediger, Marlow (1999), *The Holy Land*. Kirksville, Missouri: Simpson Publishing Company.

Ediger, Marlow, and D. Bhaskara Rao (2001), *Teaching Social Studies Successfully*. New Delhi, India: Discovery Publishing House.

Parker, Walter C. (2001), *Social Studies in Elementary Education*. Upper Saddle River New Jersey: Merrill, Prentice-Hall.

Stiggins, Rick (2007), "Assessment Through the Student's Eyes", *Educational Leadership*, 64(8), 22-26.

8

Student Learning in Social Studies

Social studies teachers are always seeking innovative methods to assist student learning in the social studies. History and the social sciences (geography, economics, political science, anthropolgy/sociology) provide subject matter for the social studies. Subject matter to be acquired by students must be reflected in relevant, salient objectives. Meticulous selection of objectives is needed so that students achieve what is important. Learning opportunities to achieve objectives must be engaging and purposeful. How might teachers assist students to achieve more optimally?

PROMOTING LEARNING IN THE SOCIAL STUDIES

There are selected guidelines which social studies teachers need to follow in guiding learner progress. A behavioural approach might assist in learning lower level objectives. Major facts are important for students to learn. Thus, in a unit on the Middle East, Past and Present, learners may be guided to attain the following measurably stated objectives:

* The student will outline the configuration of the Ottoman Empire on a map.

* The student will locate the British mandated areas of Iraq, Jordan, and Palestine

* The student will point out the French mandates of Lebanon and Syria.

Behavioural psychologists advocate using specific objectives in teaching and learning situations. Little/no leeway exists for teacher interpretation as to what is to be learned by students. Learning activities are to be aligned with these specific ends of instruction. Tests measure if the objectives have been achieved by students. To reinforce learnings acquired, success in goal achievement is one reward. Others may include praise and small, inexpensive prizes given at intervals for correct responses.

How much students will learn and remember each of the above, with an asterisk, will depend upon seeing these places on a map of World War I. Each area and region must be carefully noticed. Elaboration on each learning will assist in achievement and retention. For example, the Ottoman Empire had become increasingly weak over the years, prior to World War I with inherent nations (Romania and Bulgaria, among other Balkan areas) breaking away. However, Greater Syria, as it was then called, had remained intact which included the British and French mandated areas (Ediger and Rao, 2003).

The late B.F. Skinner was a leading exponent of behaviourism as a psychology of learning. Programmed learning is emphasized here. Skinner pioneered operant conditioning whereby the student responds to a *Stimulus* in SR theory of learning after reading a small bit of information, perhaps a few sentences. The *Response* by the learner is given covering the small amount of content just read. Generally, there are four possible responses for the student to choose in answer to the question. The student then checks his/her own response by viewing the correct answer provided by the writer of the program. If the answer is correct, the student is rewarded. If incorrect, the learner now knows the correct answer and is ready for the next sequential programmed item. The method of learning here is rather repetitious with read, respond, and check, used sequentially as well as continuously (See Skinner, 1950).

In quality programs, students tend to respond correctly, due to closely sequenced items in pilot tested programs. Programs are written by programmers and are generally provided on TV screens in the classroom for learner interaction. The correctness of responses is what Dr. Skinner emphasized in operant conditioning. Reinforcement of correct answers is a major belief in programmed learning. Operant conditioning psychology of B.F. Skinner may be compared with the well known Russian late psychologist Ivan Pavlov and his emphasis placed upon the Stimulus. The classic experiment of Pavlov involved his work on dogs when the stimulus was changed. For example, the dog salivated when meat was being presented. This is natural and normal. When the sound of a bell accompanied the meat, the dog was conditioned to accept the meat and the sound of the bell as one related incident. Later, the dog salivated with the sound of the bell only. Ultimately, the response to the sound of the bell faded away. However, stimuli can be substituted, from an unconditioned to a conditioned stimulus, to obtain a response in Pavlov's stimulus/response theory of learning. Thus, in gaining the attention of students, a bell, together with the teacher's voice calling the children to order, may be sounded to secure engagement of learners. Ultimately, the ringing of the bell may, by itself, have conditioned children to attention for the new learning activity to be pursued such as in the unit on the Middle East.

Direct instruction, as another method of teaching, may be used for students whose favourite learning style is subject matter presented by the teacher to students in a relatively one way street of communication (Searson and Dunn, 2001). Thus, there is some leeway for teacher directed student interaction. The direct teaching model may be viewed with six teaching functions in the Middle East unit of study:

* review and check the previous day's work. If students had studied The Hussein/MacMahon Correspondence

of 1916, they would review its essential provisions. It promised the Arabs independence in the Middle East if they supported Great Britain in the war against Germany. This would have given the Middle East areas of Greater Syria independence as a nation and not divided into small states.

* present new materials in small steps. The teacher teaches about the Balfour Declaration of 1917, issued by Great Britain. Ideas are presented sequentially. The provisions of the Declaration contradicted those of the Hussein/McMahon correspondence in that Jews would be provided a homeland in Palestine. The provisions also included not hindering Arab goals in Palestine nor affect Jews living in other lands or nations.
* provide guided practice. Here, students are asked questions and their mis-conceptions corrected, if any. There should be 80 per cent correctness of learner responses.
* give feedback and corrections based on student responses. This helps to keep the teaching act focused.
* provide independent practice. Let students apply learnings on their own, either in seat work, co-operative groups, or homework.
* review weekly and monthly (See Rosenshine, 1988).

Direct instruction should be varied and used with other methods of teaching. The variation provides for individual differences and prevents loss of interest. The direct teaching model, listed above, may be modified to meet learner needs. It may well be one approach which might be used in the instructional arena to up learner achievement and progress.

INQUIRY LEARNING AND PROBLEM SOLVING

For those students who prefer to discover knowledge, inquiry learning and problem solving are major procedures which benefit students in this style of achievement. However, all students need to experience different approaches in learning. To emphasize discovery learning, students may view a series of illustrations on Jerusalem, for example, and state what they have viewed. Each comment, stated as a single word or phrase, may be recorded as a concept. Concepts given should not be duplicated. This makes for higher levels of cognition. Ultimately, learners will not be able to come up with additional ideas. Similar concepts might then be grouped together. Now, students need to come up with viable generalizations in discovery learning. There may be disagreements which will need to be ironed out.

In discovery learning, students do the responding with the teacher's role being to encourage, motivate, and keep learners on track. Discovery learning can be exciting and interesting due to challenges involved in coming up with new concepts. Students in many ways own the learning activity due to their heavy involvement. It is important to respect each other's thinking. Ridiculing a response discourages creative thinking. Rather, students' comments need to be valued so that cognitive responses are increasingly complex. Inquiry learning stresses the importance of:

* involving students, heavily, in learning
* emphasizing the interests of learners
* challenging students to come up with new ideas
* creativity as a learning experience (See Ediger and Rao, 2000).

Problem solving has similarities to discovery learning. It is strongly student orientated in that learners identify and solve problems with teacher guidance. Thus in the ongoing Middle East unit of study, students may identify a problem which requires deliberation. The problem is of personal interest and requires the use of a variety of information sources for a solution. Thus, the question may arise as to why Jerusalem is Holy to both Arabs and Jews. The solution requires thought, critical and creative thinking. An hypothesis or tentative answer needs to be formed. Many reference sources may well need to be used. Encyclopedias, library books, specialists on the Middle East area of the world, and computer data information need to be used to gather information. The information must be analyzed and synthesized to test the hypothesis. New hypotheses may arise requiring additional information. The hypothesis may stand as is, be modified, or refuted.

Problem solving begins as inductive learning with identifying the problem as well as developing an hypothesis. To assess the hypothesis emphasizes deduction in that it is being evaluated against specific cases. Problem solving is salient in that it:

* may be used in school and in society, rather continuously, for its practicality
* emphasizes the use of higher levels of cognition
* is student centered due to students being heavily involved in its procedures
* promotes learner curiosity in identifying and solving problems
* stresses co-operative learning in that students work in committees (See Dewey, 1916).

Problems such as the following, if developmentally appropriate, might well be fascinating for students to locate information:

* why do both Arabs and Jews want the land of Palestine?
* what is the significance of the Dome of the Rock to devout Muslims, and the Western Wall to devout Jews?
* why is the Church of the Holy Sepulcher holy to devout believers in Christianity?
* what were selected major goals of the Crusades, 1099- 1187?

Discovery learning and problem solving should emphasize active learner involvement in the ongoing experience. Interest in either activity is important when stressing higher levels of cognition. Purpose in learning is inherent when students respond to questions as well as in selecting/solving problems.

Social studies teachers need to try out a variety of psychologies and philosophies of instruction to assist learners to achieve more optimally. The best of objectives, learning opportunities, and evaluation procedures must be in the offing. That which assists students to attain as well as possible must be implemented.

REFERENCES

Dewey, John (1916), *Democracy and Education*. New York: Macmillan Company.

Ediger, Marlow, and D.B. Rao (2003), *Teaching Social Studies Successfully*. New Delhi, India: Discovery Publishing House.

Ediger, Marlow, and D.B. Rao (2001), *Philosophy and Curriculum*. New Delhi, India: Discovery Publishing House.

Rosenshine, B. (1988), *Explicit Teaching, in D. Berliner and B. Rosenshine* (Eds.), Talks to Teachers (pp. 75-92). New York: Random House.

Searson, Robert, and Rita Dunn (2001), "The Learning Style Teaching Model", *Science and Children*, 38(5), 22-36.

Skinner, B.F. (1950), "Are Theories of Learning Necessary", *Psychological Review*, 57, 193-216.

9

Learning Activities in Social Studies

Learning activities assist students to achieve objectives. They need to be varied to provide for students of different styles of learning. The following styles of learning need to be considered when choosing those experiences which assist students to attain relevant ends of instruction:

* working individually versus working co-operatively with classmates in ongoing lessons and units of study
* wanting open ended activities as compared to those possessing more structure
* favouring teacher directed as compared to peer involvement in activities being considered
* desiring more formal as contrasted with creative experiences
* preferring a separate subjects as compared to an integrated social studies curriculum (See Searson and Dunn, 2001).

SELECTING LEARNING ACTIVITIES

Pupils differ from each other in talents and abilities possessed. There are multiple categories then which need to be considered. These categories of talents/abilities include:

* creativity as in art experiences. Art correlates well with social studies in that it can be emphasized in portraying ideas in ongoing lessons and units
* eye/hand co-ordination as in manual endeavours. Construction experiences to develop concepts and generalizations might well assist students to achieve meaning in the social studies.
* abstract skills as in reading and writing. Much knowledge is acquired through reading diverse social studies materials.
* objective thinking as in possessing unbiased attitudes when participating in problem solving activities.
* logical thinking as in the social studies
* abilities in music as in composing musical scores and tunes directly related to the unit being taught.
* working well with others to maximize achievement or optimizing achievement through individual endeavours, depending upon the personal preference of the individual (See Gardner, 1993).

Thus, learning activities need to be selected with each student's capabilities and interests in mind. Quality teaching should make for effective learning. The lives of children may be enriched to live more fully, wisely, and humanely. Stimulating learning activities need to be in the offing to challenge students, and yet these activities must provide for successful learning.

Multimedia technology should be emphasized whenever it assists optimal learner achievement. In this approach, students view visuals as well as hear the spoken voice to make learnings meaningful. Pacing of presentations may be adjusted to accommodate each student's abilities. Increasingly, schools are providing students individually with lap tops on the middle/senior high school years. Instruction is needed in how to use the lap top in ongoing activities and experiences. On task behaviours are necessary to avoid misuse.

Multimedia experiences should assist students to achieve relevant objectives in the social studies. Alignment of learning activities to the chosen objectives is needed to make for more optimal progress. The interests of learners are piqued when diverse senses are involved in learning. There are activities which use all senses at one time, basically, such as seeing, hearing, smelling, tasting, and touching.

Second, hands on experiences provide many students with a feeling of accomplishment when purpose is involved. There are a plethora of construction activities possible on the developmental level of the learner. These include making models, puppets, background scenery, and realia. Each task needs to be chosen within an ongoing experience in the social studies. Careful planning of each project needs to be in evidence. Quality work implements the plan for construction work. Recommended criteria need to be in the rubric to assess the total project. Conscientious efforts and self-discipline are necessary for learners to develop good projects. The teacher is a guide and motivates students to do the best work possible. Projects may be made individually or within a committee setting. Projects, when completed, may be displayed in the classroom for parents and other classrooms of students to observe. Snapshots or digital photos may be taken of these projects and placed into the portfolio of each respective student. Digital photos may become an inherent part of a power point presentation to be shown to parents, in an all school assembly, or parent/teacher organization meeting.

Artistic experiences correlate well with each social studies unit. Uniqueness and novelty in thinking is to be emphasized here. Well planned creative experiences assist students to develop concepts and generalizations in depth. Doing murals, for example, help students to think more deeply about a topic. The following are examples of murals: a zoo scene, a fruit orchard, a desert, and a cattle ranch. What to put into a mural and why needs careful consideration. How to do the specifics in a mural assesses learner thinking about what is known about a topic as well as what is left to learn. Colours and media to be used in the mural emphasizes further problems to be solved. Continuous evaluation of the mural must be in evidence. Developing criteria for the assessments provides rich evaluative experiences for learners (Ediger and Rao, 2001).

Third, developing time lines stresses meaningful approaches in studying historical concepts. As each event is being studied, it can be placed on a time line. Thus, in studying a unit on Colonies in the New World, students may place Jamestown (1607), Plymouth Rock (1620), and Massachusetts Bay (1630), among others, on the time line as they are being studied sequentially. An illustration for each date on the time line should be drawn such as a drawing of Jamestown Colony of 1607. Important information about each colony will be learned as the unit progresses. It is salient to understand salient time concepts when studying historical units.

Fourth, charts made of concepts and generalizations studied aid in understanding abstract ideas. The following charts may be made:

* a diagram showing lines of organization of city, state, and federal governments
* changes at specific points, such as in petroleum which is heated and gives off gasoline, kerosene, or diesel fuel at respective temperatures
* a data chart showing capitol cities and population figures of nations/states being studied. Art designs and decorations may accompany each chart
* line, bar, pictorial, and circle graphs may be placed in a chart showing statistical information in ongoing social studies units.
* a categories chart showing how cultural items in a unit may be classified such as illustrations drawn of food, clothing, farming methodology, religions, and homes.

* a story chart such as the sequence of steps involved in coal mining (Parker, 2001).

Each chart made by students individually or within a committee should serve a purpose and make subject matter increasingly understandable.

Fifth, reading is another valuable way to learn social studies content. There are multiple approaches in emphasizing reading. When reading from the basal, students should posses adequate background information to read the ensuing subject matter. Some will need assistance in recognizing new words. Phonics and context clues may be taught as word recognition techniques. Also, reasons or questions identified for reading the selection need to be in the offing. The actual reading activity should provide answers to the identified questions. Follcwup activities should culminate the reading experience. Additional reading experiences in the social studies include:

* sustained silent reading
* individualized reading and book reports
* reciprocal reading (Palincsar and Brown, 1984).
* questioning the author (McKeown, et. al., 1993).

Sixth, a good current events program must be stressed in the social studies. There are happenings which might well be covered in daily world news such as the Palestinian/Israeli conflict, the war in Iraq and Afghanistan, as well as new nuclear powers including Iran and North Korea. News in a nation should also receive attention including the borders between the United States and Mexico. Local news is a salient part of a good current events program. Thus, current events include border disputes, crime, newly elected leaders, the environment, inflation, and taxation problems. It should stress what is salient, enduring, as well as who is affected by the events (Ediger, 1995).

Map and globe learnings relate well to current events instruction. They also provide salient learning activities when social studies textbooks are used in teaching and learning situations. Students might then locate places on maps/globes depending upon where the events took place. It is important for students to learn more than place location, but also what kinds of vegetation and community surround the place and what kind of interactions exist with other nearby places. Major reference lines to use include meridians, parallels, latitude, longitude, Tropic of Cancer, Tropic of Capricorn, North Pole, and South Pole. Application of learnings are important so that they are retained and remain functional.

Seventh, citizenship education should be inclusive in teaching/learning situations. High standards of knowledge and good conduct should be in evidence. These include:

* respect and caring for others in a democracy
* possession of civic rules, duties, and responsibilities
* application of civic learnings to everyday situations in life
* assistance provided to others as needed.

Students with teacher guidance should appraise the self to ascertain if the above named citizenship goals are being attained. These goals are not there for the sake of being, but rather to emphasize in teaching and learning situations as well as notice their degree of achievement.

Eighth, vocabulary development is very important in order to understand the language of the social studies. A subject should not be considered as simply a body of content, which is often the mistake made in social studies. There are ways of thinking which govern the disciplined study of social studies concepts, ranging from causes and effects and thesis and proof to comparisons and chronology. As with any other subject, comprehension of social studies depends on the effective integration of appropriate ways of thinking and the appropriate degree of scaffolding by the teacher to support student's attainment of the intellectual outcomes. Preserving social studies instruction in the threatened area of elementary curriculum may depend upon the extent to which committed teachers employ survival skills that link the discipline to the accountability favoured subjects of reading and writing. We believe that effective instructional practice geared to cross disciplinary skill development can be a vital link between curriculum areas as well as a life line for an underserved curriculum area (Jones and Thomas, 2006).

There are additional learning activities to numerous to mention. The social studies teacher needs to be creative and be on the lookout for new experiences which assist students to achieve well in school and in society. The social studies should provide knowledge and help students to become good citizens in the societal arena.

REFERENCES

Ediger, Marlow (1995), "Geography in the Social Studies", *Perspectives* 27(1), 9-10.

Ediger, Marlow, and D. Bhaskara Rao (2001), "Teaching Social Studies Successfully". New Delhi, India: Discovery Publishing House.

Jones, Raymand C., and Timothy G. Thomas (2006), "Leave No Discipline Behind", *The Reading Teacher*, 60(1), 58-64.

Gardner, Howard (1993), "Multiple Intelligences: Theory Into Practice". New York: Basic Books.

Mc Keown *et al.*, "Grappling With Text Ideas: Questioning the Author", *The Reading Teacher*, 45: 560-566.

Palincsar, A.S., and A.L. Brown (1984), "Reciprocal Teaching of Comprehension Fostering and Comprehension Monitoring Activities". *Cognition and Instruction*, 1: 117-175.

Parker, Walter C. (2001), *Social Studies in Elementary Education*. Upper Saddle River, New Jersey: Prentice-Hall, Inc.

Searson, Robert, and Rita Dunn (2001), "The Learning Styles Teaching . Model", *Science and Children*, 38(5), 22-36.

10

Maps and Globes in Social Studies

Maps and globes are valuable devices to locate important places on the planet earth. In the home setting, maps and globes should be available to locate significant places when listening to news broadcasts or reading current events in newspapers. Places mentioned in the news may then be located on a map/globe. It becomes more meaningful when listening to the news when an unknown place can be located.

The writer feels it enjoyable to study maps/globes to notice the relationship in distance of different places. It is surprising how little one may know of where a place is in relation to another such as Iraq and Iran or why the time may be nine hours earlier in Baghdad as compared to the central part of the United States.

There are a plethora of rich learning experiences for students in the social studies when incorporating the study of maps and globes (Ediger, 1990).

WHICH OBJECTIVES SHOULD STUDENTS ACHIEVE?

Objectives should be chosen carefully so that relevance is involved in student learning. Knowledge objectives, as a first category to be discussed, need to emphasize vital subject matter learnings. These kinds of objectives stress major generalizations and concepts, key ideas, as well as structural content. They emphasize rational balance among the academic disciplines of history, geography, political science, economics, anthropology, and sociology. Each academic discipline contains subject matter which occurred in a geographical place, located on a map/globe.

The following, among others, are salient map/globe knowledge objectives for pupils to achieve:

* distances between places may be measured by using the scale of miles given on the legend
* specific places may be located on the planet earth by using two imaginary lines—latitude and longitude
* north latitude indicates distance in degrees north of the Equator whereas south latitude refers to distance in degrees south of the equator
* east longitude indicates distance in degrees east of the Prime Meridian whereas west longitude has to do with distance in degrees west of the Prime Meridian
* distances north and south of the equator are measured along a meridian while distances east or west of the Prime Meridian are measured along a parallel (Ediger and Rao, 2001).

Knowledge objectives need indepth teaching, using a variety of materials. Methods of instruction should include problem solving in that students identify a contextual problem requiring thought and deliberation. An hypothesis is developed. The hypothesis is tentative and subject to change if evidence warrants. Information is gathered from diverse sources directly related to the hypothesis. The hypothesis is tested against the information secured and might then be modified, revised, or refuted. A new hypothesis might then need to be developed and/or a new problem identified. Steps in problem solving are flexible and open ended. Inquiry learning, inductive, as well as deductive thought is inherent in problem solving activities (Dewey, 1918).

With No Child Left Behind (NCLB) law of 2002, students are tested in grades three through eight and an exit test given in the high school years. These tests must be passed by students in order to be promoted. The present law is for passing tests in reading and mathematics as well as science. There are selected states which require testing in the social studies, such as the state of Kansas. Map and globe learnings might well be a part of these tests. The specific objectives for these tests are to be in the hands of teachers to gauge their teaching, prior to testing. This may make for direct teaching of subject matter, outside the framework of problem solving. Much good teaching has been done outside the framework of solving problems. When viewing the above listed map/globe objectives, it is quite obvious that direct teaching will be involved for students to understand the intricacies of using diverse reference lines in studying maps and globes.

A second type of objectives stresses skills. Skills emphasize using acquired knowledge objectives in numerous ways. Thus, writing a report on what has been learned emphasizes the use of knowledge. The following also stress skills for learners to attain:

* making drawings of the rotation of the earth on its axis and the revolution of the earth around the sun
* doing a model solar system using play dough or clay
* writing a report on the influence of geography on human life styles
* discussing how climate affects agricultural crops grown (See, NCSS, 1994).

Teaching metacognition skills aids the learner in monitoring the self in terms of subject matter and skills acquired. For example, when reading content pertaining to geography within a social studies unit of study, the pupil monitors his/her own comprehension of subject matter. The learner then is aware if word calling occurs in reading without attending to ideas read. Comprehension of ideas is the reason for reading. The pupil also monitors word recognition skills to notice if they are effective. These skills may involve phonics, syllabication, and/or use of configuration clues. Good readers, eventually learn to analyze, synthesize, and evaluate subject matter read. Main ideas are identified, supported by those which are subordinate; details are noticed which support the subordinate thoughts. Thus, metacognition pertains to thinking about thinking. This involves thinking about the best way to recognize new words in reading as well as how to organize information obtained (Balu, 2006).

Attainable goals must be stressed when learners are to achieve skills ends. At the same time, students need to be successful achievers with challenging learning activities on maps/globes.

A third category of objectives for students to achieve is attitudinal ends. These are generally an end result of acquiring knowledge and skills objectives. Quality attitudes help students attain future knowledge and skills ends more thoroughly. Good attitudes are always desirable in school and in society. The following attitudinal objectives are worthy for students to achieve:

* desiring to learn more about maps/globes
* participating actively in discussions related to map/globe learnings
* wanting to improve reading information from maps/globes
* listening carefully to ongoing ideas presented in class
* desiring to present ideas clearly and accurately in small and large group activities (See, Edmunds and Bauserman, 2006).

Objectives chosen determine the direction of student learnings in ongoing lesson plans and units of study. Activities to achieve the objectives should be interesting and engage learners in goal attainment. Students need to perceive purpose or reasons for leaning. Perceiving purpose is indeed a motivator to grow, develop, and accomplish. Motivated learners do better than the non-motivated in the curriculum.

ORGANIZING THE MAP AND GLOBE CURRICULUM

There are several means of organizing the map/globe curriculum, one being to have a separate unit of study on that title. Thus, a separate subjects approach is emphasized specifically on maps/globes. This provides time for the teacher to teach specific learnings on a particular topic, with depth teaching involved. For example, intensified instruction might well be stressed in having students achieve the following generalizations:

* the earth rotates on its axis once every twenty four hours (causes of day and night may be shown by using a flashlight, a darkened room, and a globe which represents a model of the planet earth)
* the earth revolves around the sun, approximately once every 365 and one/fourth days. On March 1 and September 21, approximately, the sun is directly overhead at noon on the equator. Whereas on June 21, approximately, the sun is directly overhead at noon on the Tropic of Cancer, located twenty three and one half degrees north of the equator. At noon, the sun is directly overhead on the Tropic of Capricorn, located twenty three and one half degrees south of the equator. Other factors in determining temperature reading include elevation of land above sea level, ocean currents, and nearness to bodies of water.
* the axis of the earth points toward the North Star. On a bright, sunny day, each student may look at his/her shadow and is then facing north. The direction of the North Star may be pointed out by the teacher with students noticing in the late evening where that constellation is located.

* maps do not represent as accurately the surface of the earth as do globes. A globe is a more accurate example of the planet earth. With the use of maps, however, a certain continent, or nation, may be noted more conveniently on a flat surface since it will represent a larger land area on a single map (Ediger, 1995).

Map/globe learnings contain many specifics which might well make for a broader *scope* in an ongoing unit of study. Thus, there are a plethora of symbols used such as those for capitol cities, seaports, bodies of water, mountains, hills, elevation, railroad tracks, legends, and hospitals, among others.

There are also many types of maps for students to learn to read including highway or road, city, park, agricultural products, natural resources, contour maps of a given agricultural region, national maps, world, and rainfall maps. Each of these maps has its relevance. For example, highway maps stress practicality when used in planning a trip or when actually travelling a distance (See, Michaelius, 1980).

A separate unit on maps/globes certainly could stress a rather broad scope of subject matter to be taught. However, it still provides time to cover selected concepts and generalizations in depth.

In addition to a separate subjects curriculum consisting of map and globe learnings only, a correlated procedure may be implemented. Here, when a social studies unit is taught, related map/globe learnings may be brought in. For example, if a unit on Argentina and Brazil is taught, relevant map and globe generalizations may be brought in to the ongoing unit of study. Boehm and Peterson (1995), elaborate on "The Fundamental Themes in Geography", which include the following:

* *Location.* Absolute location such as using grids (latitude and longitude), different types of maps and globes (thematic maps showing population, economic systems, climate zones, political divisions, and settlement

patterns), map projections (to show the spherical earth on a two dimensional map sheet), as well as earth-sun relations (to determine climate, seasons, and time zones). Relative location, such as locations having geographical explanations as well as the importance of a location can change with history.

* *Place*. Physical characteristics (land forms, climate, soils, natural vegetation, and animal life). Human characteristics including religion, language, population factors, settlements, and economic activities.
* *Human-environmental system*. These include relationships between humans and environment, the role of technology (humans apply technology to modify the environment), problems of technology (air and water pollution, waste disposal, and toxic materials), environmental hazards (earth quakes, hurricanes, floods, volcanoes; human induced -nuclear disasters, oil spills, and heat pollution of water bodies), environmental limits (water, land, and natural resources), and adaptations (influence of the environment in making a living, house types, ways of life, and the appearance of the human landscape.
* movement of people.
* regions as defined by culture or physical characteristics.

Pertaining to the above Fundamental Themes in Geography, the first item stresses place. In any social studies unit of study, students learn that places may be located though a grid system emphasizing latitude and longitude. Also learners achieve objectives, for example, through the use of maps/globes stressing themes such as population figures. Thematic maps stress, not only population data, but might also include mining, agriculture, and natural resources information.

A third way of organizing the social studies is to emphasize the integrated curriculum whereby maps/globes are taught as the need arises, which moves away rather thoroughly from a separate subjects unit of study. There are fewer opportunities to stress in depth map/globe learnings with the correlated and integrated procedures as compared to complete units in a separate subjects curriculum (Ediger, 1995).

The geography teacher needs to matter subject matter as well as use appropriate methods of teaching. Thus, he/she needs to engage students actively in ongoing learning opportunities.

If students are making relief maps, each must be thoroughly involved. Students, here, may work individually or within a committee, preferable meeting their own unique styles of learning. As a result of these activities, students should become increasingly interested in place location and other related information containing relevant concepts and generalizations. For example, placing the Dead Sea (1300 feet below sea level), the Sea of Galilee (660 feet below sea level), and the Jordan River as a connector, assists students to use knowledge in making a relief map.

Second, students need to perceive reasons for learning. Mere busy work is not a purpose, but assisting students to sense reasons for making a products map may clarify for learners why specific farm crops are grown in that particular area. The learning activity should help students to acquire information on *why* the agricultural crops are grown in that particular area. Information on citrus fruits and vegetables grown in the Middle East can be placed on a products map in pictorial form.

Third, students should experience quality sequence in learning. Each idea gained should provide background information for the new objective to be achieved. With objectives to be achieved being related, the student should perceive connections in the geography curriculum. Thus, knowledge about agricultural products grown should provide necessary information on marketing and selling consumer items. Related knowledge and skills are retained for a longer period of time as compared to isolated learnings.

Fourth, students should perceive meaning in teaching and learning situations. Learners who understand subject matter taught are better able to apply what has been learned as compared to meaningless content acquired. Depth learning should be stressed. A variety of learning activities pertaining to a concept or to a generalization should assist students to attach meaning to ongoing objectives.

Fifth, individual differences should be provided for in the multi-cultural geography curriculum. Students individually possess multiple intelligences (Gardner, 1999). The strengths of each student must be respected/accepted and use positively in the classroom setting. For example, a student who does not read well may work within a committee where there is a proficient reader. Those who need assistance in reading may receive help in word recognition. Thus, the good reader may work harmoniously with other committee members in doing art work, construction experiences, creative dramatics, and the making of models which directly relate to the ongoing unit of study involving geography (Ediger, 2005).

It is vital that students achieve relevant objectives in the social studies. News reports of happenings around the world indicate the importance of humans being able to locate places on maps/globes and have much knowledge of happenings in these critical areas. Learning activities need to be of interest in order to motivate learner achievement. Engaging students in map/globe learnings is important.

A student centred geography, geography curriculum needs to contain essential elements. These elements, among others, include quality, challenging objectives which are attainable by learners. Learning opportunities need to assist students individually to achieve the chosen objectives. Assessment helps to determine if the objectives have been achieved, as well as provide feedback to students and teachers for further needed learnings.

Personalized learning should be a major goal in assisting student achievement. There needs to be a match between the characteristics of the learner and the curriculum. This stresses:

* active involvement of the student in learning, not a passive recipient of knowledge
* student choice in learning opportunities pursued
* the teacher being a facilitator of learning, not a lecturer
* an effective school climate for learning, not an autocratic situation
* an integrated curriculum
* peer committee work as well as peer teaching
* positive attitudes and feelings toward learning (See Keefe, 2007).

REFERENCES

Balu, A. (2006), *Effectiveness of Metacognitive Orientation Among Teacher Trainees on Developing Competencies in Teaching Social Studies*. Ph.D thesis appraised by the writer for Alagappa University, Karaiku, India, Chapter Two—Review of Literature.

Boehm, Richard G., and James F. Peterson (1994), "An Exploration of the Five Fundamental Themes of Geography", *Social Education*, 58(4), 214-218.

Dewey, John (1918), *Democracy and Education*. New York: The Macmillan Company.

Ediger, Marlow (1990), "Maps and Globes in the Social Studies in the Elementary School", *Geografia w Szkole*, 43(217), 21-36, published in Poland.

Ediger, Marlow (1995), "Geography in the Social Studies", *Perspectives*, 27 (10), 9-10.

Ediger, Marlow, and D. Bhaskara Rao (2001), "Teaching Social Studies Successfully", New Delhi, India: Discovery Publishing House.

Ediger, Marlow (1995), "Subject Centered vs. An Activity Centered Curriculum", *Education*, 116(2), 268-271.

Ediger, Marlow (2005), "Themes to Emphasize in the Geography Curriculum", *Journal of Instructional Psychology*. 32(2), 160-163.

Edmunds, Kathryn M., and Kathryn L. Bauserman (2006), "What Teachers Can Learn About Reading Motivation Through Conversations With Children", *The Reading Teacher*, 59(5), 414-425.

Gardner, Howard (1999), *The Disciplined Mind*. New York: Simon and Schuster.

Keefe, James W. (2007), "What is Personalization?" *Phi Delta Kappan*, 89(3), 217-228.

Michaelius, John (1980), *Social Studies for Children—A Guide to Basic Instruction*. Englewood Cliffs, New Jersey: Prentice-Hall, Inc.

NCSS (1994), *Expectations of Excellence—Curriculum Standards for the Social Studies*, Developed by the Task Force for the National Council for the Social Studies and approved by the NCSS Board of Directors.

11

Pen Pals and Social Studies

Social studies teachers are always on the lookout for innovative ideas in teaching pupils. A variety of activities are necessary for pupil interest to thrive and motivation to occur. Readiness for new learnings must be in evidence for learners to achieve, grow, and develop well. Relevant objectives then need to be in the offing. Also, vital subject matter, appropriate skills, and wholesome attitudes must be achieved in ongoing units of study. As a learning opportunity, pen pal activities might well be challenging and encourage learner progress.

INFORMATION TO SECURE FROM PEN PALS

Depending upon the title of the unit of study being emphasized, there is considerable information to obtain from a pen pal. If a social studies unit on the Middle East is in the offing, the pupil with teacher guidance may study a listing of possible pen pals. Rapport must be established with the pen pal. Skills need to be developed by the pupil in order to correspond clearly and effectively. Thus, the following mechanics of writing, using the word processor, need to be sequentially achieved:

* correct spelling of words with assistance from spell checkers

* margins for the hard copy being adjusted properly
* use of correct punctuation, capitalization of letters, and indentations
* emphasis placed upon use of complete sentences as well as variety in kinds of sentences

If a pupil lacks skill in using a word processor, he/she should practice its use under the guidance of a skilled operator. This involves utilization of proper key boarding skills. Sequential achievement must be emphasized.

The kinds of information to be acquired depends upon the specific knowledge desired in the ongoing unit of study. If, for example, the walled city of Jerusalem is being pursued, the pupil may want to know from the pen pal the dimensions of the wall such as being two and one-half miles to encircle it as well as being forty feet tall. It is good to make comparisons with something near to the school which has similar dimensions. Inside the walled city, pupils in pen pal correspondence may learn about The Dome of the Rock, an octagonal mosque built in 691 AD which is located over Mount Moriah, the identified Biblical place where the Patriarch Abraham was tempted to sacrifice his son Isaac, or the Koran emphasis of the possible sacrificing of Ishmael, also a son of Abraham. The base of the Dome of the Rock is octagonal. The walled city of Jerusalem contains much history, religion, geography, and cultural anthropology. From these learnings alone, the pupil might ask the following questions of the pen pal:

* why was the wall built around old Jerusalem?
* why does Jerusalem contain many holy sights?
* why is Jerusalem set on a rocky hill?
* how does the geography of Jerusalem compare with that of the surrounding area?

The feelings/affective dimension will be involved in pen pal correspondence as will the every day experiences.

Charron (2007), wrote the following pertaining to pen pal learning activities:

> "Teacher and student comments indicate that the internet pen pal program facilitates communication through the use of authentic tasks and teaches about different cultures. Enthusiasm generated by the program translated into student written language production. Special needs pupils, second language learners, and general education students reported enjoying writing to an authentic audience. The program facilitates problem solving and supports critical thinking in written language acquisition and the social nature of learning is evident in the correspondence between pen pals."

Electronic communication is the wave of the present and of the future. Students seemingly are fascinated in learning through the internet and writing through e-mail use. The internet contains an abundance of information on a plethora of topics. Students can certainly become motivated to seek, search, and use sought after information. Practical use then may be made of authentic information from pen pals. There is purpose in seeking information since it will be used to communicate. It is not learned for its own sake or for reasons of it being tested upon. Rather, purpose involves a feeling of significance to learn and achieve. In the digital age, Prensky (20052006) wrote the following:

> "Our students are no longer 'little versions of us', as they may have been in the past. In fact, they are so different from us that we can no longer use either our 20th century knowledge or our training as a guide to what is best for them educationally.
>
> I've coined the term digital native to refer to today's students. They are native speakers of technology, fluent in the digital language of computers, video games and the internet. I refer to those who were not born into the digital world as digital immigrants. We have adopted many aspects of the technology, but just like those who

learned another language later in life, we retain an "accent" because we still have one foot in the past. We will read a manual, for example, to understand a program before we think to let the program teach itself. Our accent from the predigital world often makes it difficult for us to effectively communicate with our students."

Background information is necessary to understand subject matter acquired from pen pals. The teacher must assist and guide students to obtain the needed prerequisites. For example, to understand why there is a wall built around old Jerusalem, students need to attach meaning to the necessity of keeping enemies out of a city. The importance of the wall around old Jerusalem becomes more vivid when this was the third wall built in the history of this city. King Solomon in approximately 970 BC had the first wall built. This wall was destroyed by the Babylonians in 586 BC. The second wall was built by Nehemiah in 530 BC when selected Jews returned to Jerusalem from the Babylonian captivity. The present and third wall was completed in 1542 after the Ottoman Empire captured the land of Palestine.

Interest in the subject matter, to be acquired from pen pals, might well be secured since the student is curious in learning of other cultures. A two way street of communication is involved between the pen pal and the student in seeking more information. Curiosity breeds interest in a project such as obtaining relevant facts, concepts, and generalizations through a pen pal. Interest is a powerful factor in learning since it propels the student to achieve objectives of instruction.

In all of learning, students seek meaning. Thus, in learning that the Dome of the Rock was built over Mount Moriah brings on a plethora of questions and problems. The following become salient:

* what was the importance of Mount Moriah?
* what is a mosque and what is its significance to Islam?
* why was the Dome of the Rock built over Mount Moriah?

Students desire to make sense of knowledge and skills acquired. Vague, hazy understandings present dilemmas to be resolved. Closure needs to be sought here in that meaningful learnings accrue. Through pen pals, knowledge and skills might well become filled with thought, information, conclusions, and main ideas. The learner seeks meaning, not the teacher per se, in these situations. The teacher's role is to assist pupils to clarify, to think critically, and creatively pertaining to ideas acquired from pen pals.

The project method (Ediger and Rao, 2003), might well be emphasized within a pen pal activity. Thus, a relief map of the land of Palestine (Israel and the occupied territories) may be developed by mixing equal amounts of salt and flour and adding enough water to make a thick paste. The modeling material may be poured over an outline map of this area. The land of Palestine is unique with its many geographical features such as the following, among others, to be shown with the use of the modelling materials:

* Jerusalem being about 2500 feet above sea level
* Jericho, located eighteen miles to the east, being 800 feet below sea level
* the Dead Sea, 1300 feet below sea level, located four miles southeast of Jericho
* Haifa, located in the northwestern part, is on sea level
* the Plains of Esdraelen, the only truly level area of land, being thirty by thirty by twenty miles in circumference, located east of Haifa
* the wavy Jordan River, 600 feet below sea level in the north where the Sea of Galilee ends flowing southward to the Dead Sea entrance, 1300 feet below sea level.

Each of the cities/geographical areas listed above on the relief map may be extended through research by obtaining related information from pen pals, the internet and other reference sources. Thus, inside the walled city of Jerusalem, the following vital information might well be secured in extending the project method:

* The Church of the Holy Sepulcher where, according to devout Christians, Christ was entombed

* The Western Wall, a holy site to devout Jews, the only remains of the ancient Jewish temple

* The Mosque EI Aksa, built in 712 AD and near to the Dome of the' Rock, from where, according to devout Muslims, the Prophet Mohammed, ascended into heaven and came back to earth again (Ediger, 1999).

Corresponding with pen pals can be a fascinating way to learn about other cultures, nations, and geographical regions. Students need interesting and purposeful learning experiences to achieve objectives of instruction. Pen pal correspondence might well offer these kinds of opportunities. To initiate pen pal references sources, using the internet, the following may provide needed information:

(www.iecc.org)

(www.epals.com)

(www.gaggle.net)

REFERENCES

Charron, Nancy Necora (2007), "I Learned That There's a State Called Victoria and He Has Six Blue-tongued Lizards!", *The Reading Teacher*, 60 (8),762-769.

Ediger, Marlow (1999), *The Holy Land*. Kirksville, Missouri: Simpson Publishing Company.

Ediger, Marlow, and D. Bhaskara Rao (2003), *Philosophy and Curriculum*. New Delhi, India: Discovery Publishing House, 69-85.

Prensky, Marc (2005-2006), "Listen to the Natives", *Educational Leadership*, 63(4), 8-13.

12

Psychology of Teaching Mathematics

It is important to emphasize the psychology of learning when teaching mathematics. With No Child Left Behind (NCLB), more is expected of students than ever before. Students are to pass mandated tests in grades three through eight and an exit test in high school. Then too, Adequate Yearly Progress (AYP) means that learners in any category, be it English Language Learners (ELL) or special education students, must pass requirements for at least two years in a row or be labelled as a failing school. To optimize achievement in mathematics, the teacher must use salient principles of learning to meet federal mandate requirements in mathematics as well as in reading.

TEACHING AND LEARNING IN MATHEMATICS

Which principles of learning should be emphasized in mathematics instruction? Students should be assisted to perceive purpose in an ongoing lesson. Thus, there needs to be reasons for students engaging in any ensuing topic. The mathematics teacher may state the reason(s) deductively. Many times, students accept these reasons as being purposeful. It may be necessary to state questions for learners to arrive at purposes inductively. In society, individuals like to sense acceptable reasons for doing things. Students are no different, they, too, like to feel that purpose is there for doing mathematics.

Students need to possess background information for an ensuing learning activity. Prior to finding the area of a circle, for example, students need to look at and discuss scenes where circular designs are used such as circular driveways and circular windows on buildings. Students, too, need to understand the following prerequisites in finding the area of a circle:

* what is meant by the concept "radius". This teacher may show this by drawing a circle on the chalkboard and showing half the distance through that circle. He/she needs to verbalize the procedure involved.
* what is meant by squaring the radius, and showing this meaningfully, to learners on a drawn circle. The Greek symbol "pi" should accompany the explanation.
* indicating why the square must be multiplied by 3.14 to determine the area of a circle. A square may be cut out from construction paper and placed inside the circle to indicate the ratio of the square to the circle.
* asking students to verbalize how to find the area of a circle and, with clarity, tell about each involved step. Understanding what has been learned is important (See National Council Teachers of Mathematics, 1989).

Rote learning and memorization occur when students understand partially that which is taught. To do well on a mandated test, students need to attach meaning to each ordered concept being studied. If present learnings are not understood, it will become increasingly difficult to attach meaning to ensuing learnings.

Vocabulary development is important in the mathematics curriculum. It assists students to comprehend and apply knowledge. Many times when students do not know how to work a mathematics problem, they fail to identify vocabulary terms in print and are hesitant about their implied meaning(s). Identifying the meaning of a vocabulary terms has to fit a contextual situation. Mathematics has its very own terminology. As students progress through the grades, they will encounter new vocabulary. Each must be mastered as foundational learnings for new lessons and units of study. If students miss out on understanding a vocabulary term, the chances are that readiness for new learnings will abate. Beginning with young children, the teacher needs to make certain that learners understand meanings and relationship of the following vocabulary terms: addition, subtraction, greater than, less than, carrying, borrowing, place value, commutative, and associative properties, among others. They provide background information for multiplication, division, regrouping, renaming, ratio, proportion, decimals, per cents, as well as more complex understandings of commutative and associative properties (See Tiedt, 1983).

With good teaching, vocabulary development increases and intensified learning makes for increased indepth meanings. Rich listening, speaking, reading, and writing vocabularies must be in the offing to meet NCLB standards as well as in doing mathematics in real life situations in society. Teachers need to use and to encourage students to use mathematics vocabulary terms properly in every day classroom discussions.

A good reader also does well in reading mathematics subject matter. Thus, teachers must help students to identify unknown words in word problems. Context clues definitely assist in identifying the unknown. An unknown word must make sense with the rest of the words in the sentence or paragraph. This may not be adequate. Thus, the student must look at the beginning consonant of the unknown word for additional help in its identification.

Then too, phonics is very useful in reading mathematics content. When decoding a word, many times there is consistency between symbol and sound. Each letter might well then be decoded to form a meaningful word. Sometimes, a part of a word may be spelled phonetically. There are words spelled irregularly which require the sight method for its identification and remembrance.

There are useful prefixes (un) and suffixes (ly) which may be memorized to decode the unknown. Good readers attach meaning to ongoing words in order to read fluently (See Dekonty, *et al.*, 2006).

A variety of methods should be used by the teacher in teaching and learning situations. This adds interest in ongoing lessons and units of study. Learning inductively and deductively are two useful approaches in assisting students to learn subject matter. Concrete and semi-concrete materials serve as models in making mathematics meaningful. Audio visual aids may be used to clarify ideas. Above all, mathematics needs to be used again and again involving the level of application. Mathematics needs to be useful in school and in society.

Securing student attention is salient in the teaching of mathematics. In a classroom of twenty five students, the teacher needs to have a teaching strategy with diverse kinds of materials to obtain learner interests. Thus, to have young children learn to identify a set of ten, the teacher must have ten large sticks to show in concept development. It is better if each student has ten sticks to count in one to one correspondence. Students may then see, concretely, how members of a set are determined. All new learnings in mathematics must be presented in this way.

Constructivism is a relatively new concept, useful in appraising learner achievement. Appraising is done in a contextual situation, not by external procedures. External procedures involve using of standardized tests written by specialists, removed from the local classroom setting. Then too, standardized tests are administered once a year, such as in No Child Left Behind (NCLB). Thus, a one shot approach is used in evaluating student achievement. With constructivism, the mathematics teacher assesses continuously. Errors made by students may be identified at once. Assistance can then be given to improve in mathematics learning. Constructivism is:

* student centered, in that the focal point is the learner in determining how well he/she is doing
* sequential, in that the student is assisted when difficulties are faced at a specific moment
* continuous in observing achievement, not a one shot yearly procedure in evaluating learner progress
* contextual, and relates to what has happened previously in the ongoing lesson and unit of study
* emphasizes that the mathematics teacher is available at the time of need
* personal, in that the appraisal is valid for a given student.

With constructivism, if a student does not understand place value such as ones, tens, and hundreds, the teacher at the specific time might well provide needed assistance (Ediger and Rao, 2000).

Students should be motivated to achieve as optimally as possible. There are numerous psychologists in education who have excellent suggestions for motivating learners. Teachers and supervisors need to study and analyze diverse schools of thought in educational psychology to ascertain which procedures work best and with which children in mathematics. They need to do much reading, studying, and discussing to notice which trends in motivation and teaching pupils are in vogue. Students are different from each other in a plethora of ways. They vary in learning styles possessed as well as in preferred intelligences.

Very briefly, the author will provide a synopsis of salient ideas of selected leading psychologists in ways of motivating students:

* the late Carl Rogers (1983), advocated self-directed learning. Here, students pursue their individual

interests. Learning centers in mathematics emphasizes one approach in self-directed learning in which the learner selects tasks sequentially from different stations in the classroom. There are enough centers and tasks to stress time on task so that those not desired may be omitted.

* Robert Gagne (1985), stressed a hierarchy of learnings to achieve objectives in mathematics. Thus, if a student does not understand how to solve a problem, the teacher may go back to a preceding level. Thus, the teacher helps the student to understand the related generalization necessary in problem solving. For example, if a student is to find the area of a rectangle as a problem, the teacher checks to see if the learner understands the generalization "length time width". If not, going back a step, the teacher must determine if the student attaches meaning to the concept of "length" as well as the concept of "width". If the learner understands these two terms, the student is ready to learn the related generalization and solve the problem. Gagne' has five steps previous to a student not understanding a "concept" in diagnosis of problems to solve in mathematics. Gagne's psychology may also be used, not only in diagnosis, but also in developmental teaching when assisting students to achieve an objective. Perhaps, helping students first in concept development pertaining to what is being studied in mathematics followed by develop a generalization, and the solving the problems is adequate in most cases in quality sequence.

* the late B.F. Skinner's reinforcement theory also needs attention here. He advocated rewarding the response if it is correct. Thus, in learning the basic addition facts, a child is asked in context pertaining to what 5+8 is. The child responds with "13". The teacher says "correct". Being correct reinforces that 5+8=13. Some teachers have used additional reinforces such as inexpensive prizes to reward a series of correct responses (Ediger and Rao, 2003).

Mathematics teachers need to study and analyze diverse psychologies to ascertain which might well assist students to achieve more optimally in ongoing mathematics lessons and units of study.

REFERENCES

Dekonty, *et al.*, (2006), "Profiles in Comprehension". *The Reading Teacher*, 60(1), 48-57.

Ediger, Marlow, and D.B. Rao (2000), *Teaching Mathematics Successfully*. New Delhi, India: Discovery Publishing House.

Ediger, Marlow, and D.B. Rao (2003), *Psychology and Curriculum*. New Delhi, India: Discovery Publishing House.

Gagne', Robert (1985), *The Conditions of Learning and Theory of Instruction*. New York: Holt Rinehart and Winston.

National Council Teachers of Mathematics (1989), *Curriculum and Evaluation Standards for School Mathematics*. Reston, Virginia: NCTM.

Rogers, Carl (1983), *Freedom to Learn in the Eighties.*

Tiedt, Iris M. (1983), *The Language Arts Handbook*. Englewood Cliffs, New Jersey: Prentice-Hall, Inc.

13

Mathematics Curriculum and Psychology of Learning

How might the mathematics teacher optimize pupil achievement in mathematics? This is a continual question for any professional. What may assist pupils to focus more on the objectives being stressed in mathematics? Mathematics is one of the basics in the curriculum and needs quality teaching and learning procedures.

TEACHING IN A PUPIL CENTERED MATHEMATICS PROGRAM

Mathematics teachers must meet salient needs of pupils in ongoing lessons and units of study. Which principles of learning will assist in guiding optimal pupil achievement? First, teachers need to provide adequate background experiences in order for pupils to benefit from the ensuing lesson. Thus, pupils need to achieve necessary knowledge and skills related to new learning opportunities to be presented. If pupils then are to learn about borrowing in subtraction, do they possess needed concepts and generalizations pertaining to place value? If the answer is in the negative, the mathematics teacher must assist pupils to understand place value by using the needed materials such as place value charts and manipulative objects. This activity should lead to success in learning about borrowing in subtraction (Ediger and Rao, 2003).

Second, teachers need to provide quality sequence in pupil learning. Covering subject matter too rapidly may make for too many pupils left behind in achieving. Good sequence stresses challenging learning opportunities for pupils and yet success in achievement is an end result. Success generally is a motivator to involved pupils to tackle new learnings. With quality sequence, pupils perceive relationships in ideas, and not focus upon isolated subject matter. If, for example, addition and subtraction are viewed in isolation from each other, it takes longer for pupils to acquire new ideas being presented in ongoing lessons. However, if subtraction is perceived as the inverse operation of addition, pupils will progress sooner to increasingly more complex learnings. Clarity of ideas in these relationships may be shown with markers to indicate addition and then subtraction (Ediger, 2007).

Third, teachers need to be certain that pupils attach meaning to what is being taught. This means that learners must understand what is in the objective being emphasized. For example, if pupils are studying congruent geometric figures, they need to demonstrate from the ongoing lesson that they can explain and show congruency. Being able to do these things will provide feedback to the teacher as to what is understood. Pupils always need to understand the present objective before they are taught more complex ideas. If they do not understand, this will be shown in future learnings being pursued. Meaning attached to concepts and generalizations taught makes for increased retention. Retained learnings may then be used to provide readiness for the ensuing lesson. Success in learning is then more likely to accrue (Sridevi, 2007).

Fourth, mathematics teachers need to emphasize purpose in having pupils achieve new ideas pertaining to the subject matter to be presented. Having pupils perceive reasons for attaining new objectives in the ongoing lesson in mathematics, assists in accepting the goals being stressed. There should be reasons for having pupils, for example, finding the area of a square or rectangle. Practical situations abound such as finding the area of a classroom for putting in a new carpet or installing it in a home setting. Flexible thinking by the teacher in developing purposeful, practical learning situations helps pupils to perceive purpose for achieving. It also facilitates motivation to learn.

Fifth, Higher Order Thinking Skills (HOTS) must be stressed, particularly when pupils work on word problems. These problems may come from the basal textbook or be teacher designed. As a university supervisor of student teachers in the public schools, the writer observed selected fifth and sixth grade pupils write clearly worded story problems, challenging for others to solve. Creative thinking was definitely in evidence. Student teachers and co-operating teachers wrote some excellent, realistic story problems which supplemented the basal textbook. Critical thinking was necessary to find needed answers. Here, pupils separated necessary information from that which was not needed to solve problems (Ediger and Rao, 2006).

Sixth, inductive learning must be a salient objective in the mathematics curriculum. Learning by discovery then becomes important in teaching and learning. There are selected approaches which might be used to implement a strategy for pupil inductive learning. Learners do need appropriate background information in order to learn inductively, but not to the point whereby the activity will be routine. There is excitement in learning by discovery. Pupils need opportunities to hypothesize and try out educated guesses on solving a new process in mathematics. For example, pupils may offer solutions on how to solve a new type of word problem involving three steps. The word problem is written on the chalkboard or presented in a duplicated paper. In either case, a small number of pupils (four or five) should be on a committee so that more frequent participation is possible as compared to the class as a whole. As pupils interact with each other in an atmosphere of respect, brain storming is being stressed. Duplication of ideas may not be emphasized unless this is needed for problem solution. Pupils find this activity to be exciting and interesting. It does make pupils do indepth thinking to offer solutions. The mathematics teacher may need to offer some clues along the way to keep the activity moving forward. Clues given should be as limited as possible. The writer has noticed several of these highly successful learning by discovery activities when supervising university student teachers (Ediger, 2005).

Mathematics is the most exact science and its conclusions are capable of exact proof. All mathematics truths are relative and conditional. Mathematics may be regarded either as a body of achievements or as an intellectual enterprise. Mathematics draws its main strength from the following features: 1. abstractness, 2. generalization, 3. logical consistency, 4. depth, 5. precision, 6. seriousness, 7. elegance, 8. economy of thought, 9. thoroughness, 10. significance, 11. clarity, and 12. permanence (Savithiri, 2006).

The above enumerated items might well provide objectives of instruction such as in # 1 above—abstractness. There are indeed a plethora of abstract symbols such as the written/typed numerals, symbols used for operations on number, algebraic formulas for determining perimeter and area of geometrical figures, as well as lines, points, rays, among others. These learnings provide activities and opportunities for vocabulary development. Reading in mathematics, also, has its abstractness from which pupils need to perceive meaning. Also, #2 above stresses pupils developing generalizations from subject matter acquired in mathematics including the commutative/associative properties of addition and multiplication as well as the inverse operations of subtraction and division.

METACOGNITION NEEDS TO BE STRESSED IN MATHEMATICS

Metacognition emphasizes that pupils think about thinking. It is a highly relevant tool of instruction.

Mathematics with its emphasis upon logical thinking, as well as creative thought involved in problem solving must stress a developmentally appropriate set of metacognitive strategies. It is very important for pupils to think about how they added, subtracted, multiplied, and divided a given of numerals. When doing this, the learner rehearses strategies which were successful and those which were not appropriate to use. When engaged in problem solving, the pupil thinks about useful versus non-useful strategies and how the ensuing problem may be solved. Rote learning is not involved when thinking about thinking, but indepth analysis is in evidence. Intensive thought prevails.

Monitoring one's own progress is involved in metacognition. When reading mathematical subject matter, the pupil monitors achievement in ascertaining if he/she is comprehending needed content or merely pronouncing words. Understanding what has been read requires careful monitoring. The pupil may also monitor if he/she is reading at higher levels of cognition, rather than the recall level only or largely. Additional items in monitoring reading of mathematical content emphasizes the following:

* techniques to use in identifying unknown words including phonics, syllabication, and the use of context clues. Readiness factors are salient in being able to recognize new words which comes from maturation and previous rich experiences.

* making predictions pertaining to what the ensuing selection will be about. This is done by viewing the related illustrations in the basal textbook as well as in the library book. Good predictions assist in comprehension of subject matter to be read.

* knowledge of semantics helps pupils to attach meaning to what is being read. There may be several meanings possible for sentences read and these need to be contextually clarified. Semantics guide pupils to read subject matter meaningfully (See Griffin, 2004).

GUIDING PUPILS' MATHEMATICS LEARNINGS

Mathematics teachers need to monitor their own teaching to notice what pupils need to achieve objectives successfully. Very frequently, entry behaviours of pupils is inadequate to benefit fully from instruction. A lack of quality entry behaviours will show up in not understanding an ensuing process being stressed. Readiness for the new leanings was then not in evidence. Teachers need to evaluate if pupils individually possess the necessary facts, concepts, and generalizations to benefit from ongoing instruction. Planning for teaching a new lesson should incorporate which prerequisites are needed. Thus, a new objective of instruction must be analyzed to determine which knowledge and skills are to be taught so that the learner understands the new learnings. If pupils have made certain computational errors, these need to be retaught. Diagnosis, as to why these errors in computation occurred, must be made.

Vocabulary development in mathematics is very important. Pupils must understand thoroughly the vocabulary necessary to do good work in mathematics. Pre-kindergarden to grade twelve, vocabulary development needs to receive proper emphasis. Failure to achieve an objective might well be a lack of vocabulary development. For each lesson taught, the teacher needs to be certain that pupils attach meaning to the contextual meaning of words.

Pupils sometimes do not compute effectively due to a lack of meaning attached to what is being emphasized in teaching and learning situations. Knowing and understanding the meaning of basic addition, subtraction, multiplication, and division facts provides foundational learnings for increasingly complex computation skills. Among other things, they also provide foundational learnings for solving word problems correctly. Learners need to understand prerequisites for ensuing sequential abstract ideas. Possessing necessary entry behaviours is a must for achieving new objectives of instruction.

Mathematics teachers need to realize that all learning activities are developmentally appropriate for pupils. Forcing pupils to achieve an objective in mathematics for which he/she is not ready is unproductive. Objectives need to be realistic and pupils have reasonable expectations of achieving them. Jean Piaget (1950), who studied pupil behaviour for over fifty years and in his research came up with different maturational stages which pupils go through. His research indicated that maturation is a key factor in learning and that children go through different stages as in the following:

* sensori-motor in which the use of the muscles and physical interaction with objects predominate. This stage lasts from birth to eighteen months/two years.
* preoperational stage (ages two to seven) whereby the child perceives one variable only, in physical objectives. The one variable may be length only or width only of objects and items perceived.
* stage of concrete operations, ages seven to eleven, in which the learner perceives several dimensions in concrete objects (length, width, and height) and is able to learn from the abstract as well as from the physical items being discussed
* stage of abstract thought whereby the learner can now discuss ideas in the abstract without reference to real objects and items.

The above research of Piaget has salient implications for mathematics teachers. Pupils then may not have matured adequately to benefit from the ensuing lesson taught. There are stages of maturation which pupils go through in life which determines what can be achieved and learned. If learnings are too complex, failure to achieve will be in evidence. Maturation is related to the age level of the child. Hurrying in teaching with stress placed upon covering much subject matter is defeating. What matters is that pupils are ready maturation wise to benefit from the ensuing lesson taught.

Vygotsky (1934, 1986), Russian psychologist, in his studies came up with the concept of scaffolding in assisting learner progress. He advocated the zone of proximal development in viewing what should be taught to pupils. The zone dealt with a gap between what a pupil knows presently and what is to be acquired in the new learning. This gap, if reasonable, may be filled with sequential subject matter, requiring ordered content. Thus, the gap may be too wide, but, if reasonable, may be narrowed by ordering learning experiences. Scaffolding then emphasizes viewing what has been learned with what is desired, and if reasonable, the difference may be minimized with good teaching.

REFERENCES

Ediger, Marlow (2007), "Learning Activities in the Curriculum", *College Student Journal*, 41(4), 967-969.

Ediger, Marlow, and D. Bhaskara Rao (2003), *Teaching Mathematics Successfully*. New Delhi, India: Discovery Publishing House.

Ediger, Marlow, and D. Bhaskara Rao (2006), *Quality School Education*. New Delhi, India: Discovery Publishing House.

Ediger, Marlow (2005), "Teaching Mathematics in the High School Setting", *College Student Journal*, 39(4), 711-715.

Griffin, Sharon (2004), "Teaching Number Sense", *Educational Leadership*, 61(5), 39-42.

Piaget, Jean (1950), *The Psychology of Intelligence*. New York: Harcourt Brace Jovanovich.

Savithiri, V. (2006), "Impact of Metacognition Strategies in Enhancing Perceptual Skills Among High School Students on Learning Geometry". Ph.D. Thesis, Alagappa University, Alagappa. India, Page Four. Evaluated by the writer for Alagappa University.

Sredevi, K.V. (2007), "Constructivism: A Shift in the Teaching-Learning Process". *Edutracks*, 7(4), 9- 13. Published in India.

Vygotsky, L.S. (1934, 1986), *Thought and Language*. Cambridge, Massachusetts: the MIT Press.

14

Meaning in Mathematics Curriculum

Students attaching meaning to learnings achieved in mathematics is vital. Already in the pre-school/kindergarden years, children need to attach meaning to ongoing experiences in mathematics. Each experiences provides background information for each new lesson and unit of study. Mathematics teachers need to observe and evaluate if pupils understand what is being taught. Understanding mathematical ideas emphasizes the acquisition prerequisites for future subject matter objectives to be achieved.

MATHEMATICS AND THE STUDENT

Young children being' introduced to mathematics must attach meaning to each learning activity. Thus, in counting objects, a pupils needs to touch each object being counted and say the appropriate number, realizing that the last number pronounced represents the total number of objects. A variety of kinds of objects should be counted such as marbles, congruent sticks, and pencils, among others. The proper counting numerals need to be printed for each identified set.

Poster cards may be placed on a wall to indicate to pupils the number of members in each set such as card #1 showing one cat, card #2 showing two cats, and card #3 showing three cats, and so on. Looking around in the classroom or outside the classroom window, pupils may identify one, two, or three objects, depending upon the numerical value being studied. Thus, practical use is being made of what is being learned. Indepth teaching is advocated, but meaning must always be stressed. Later on in sequential learning, pupils will realize that readiness for achieving new objectives is being emphasized. Ausubel (1963), emphasized that good sequence is probably the single most important ingredient in teaching. To have quality sequence, pupils need to understand each previous process taught.

Showing and studying relationships are important in the mathematics curriculum. Once selected basic skills in counting have been developed, pupils need to learn to add amounts such as two cats plus three cats equal five cats. Changing the order of addends, or the commutative property of addition, should also be stressed. Meaning is then being attached to mathematical operations. A related learning is subtraction which undoes addition, such as five cats minus three cats equals two cats. This can be shown in the semi-concrete (illustrations), followed by the abstract together with the semi-concrete. These examples indicate that once meaning is attached to ongoing learnings, then sequential ideas may be presented. No matter how large the addends are in value in addition, or the minuend and subtrahend are in subtraction, the learning activities need to provide meaning to pupils. Learners then understand what is being taught and readiness for the new ideas to be presented are in the offing. The same can be said about multiplication and division (Ediger and Rao, 2002).

Inductive learning in mathematics might well be used if pupils understand necessary background knowledge. With induction, questions are raised of pupils to arrive at answers to problems. Thus, in sequence, if pupils are asked what the difference is in temperature readings from a high of 60 degrees at noon yesterday, and today's high of 48 degrees, there may be a variety of correct, as well as incorrect, responses. For correct responses, a child may count upwards from 48 to 60, making for a 12 degree difference. Another child may count backwards from 60 to 48, also making for a 12 degree difference. Both answers are correct and indicate meaningful understandings. Might it also be that a pupil reasons changing the 60 to five tens and 10 ones and then subtracting as usual? Thus, 10 minus 8 leaves two in the one's column and five minus four in the ten's column leaves one, resulting also in 12 degree difference. It might be necessary, too, for the teacher to demonstrate how the subtracting is done by thinking aloud in providing background information for future subtraction problems involving the concept of "borrowing". Demonstrating in subtraction involves deductive thinking since the teacher provides the necessary subject matter meaningfully to pupils. What is important is that learners attach meaning to renaming and regrouping in subtraction to show the concept of borrowing. These meanings provide the building blocks for more complex learnings.

If pupils attach meaning to ongoing learning experiences, they will be able to use these ideas in new lessons and units of study. Being able to apply new facts, concepts, and generalizations provide opportunities for learners to retain subject matter acquired. When engaging in problem solving, pupils need to be able to recall relevant ideas to secure solutions. Novel solutions to problem solving require creativity. Originality and uniqueness might well be emphasized in solving problems. Creativity then becomes salient in the problem solving arena. Achieving meaning in each step of problem solving is important. Thus, in problem solving pupils need to possess clarity in stating the problem. Vague, hazy problems do not lend themselves to finding solutions. When gathering information for solutions, ideas therein must be understood, resulting in an hypothesis. The mathematical hypothesis is tentative, comprehensive, and subject to testing. The hypothesis is then tried out in a concrete, abstract situation. If the hypothesis does not pan out in the level of application, additional information needs to be gathered. Meaning is very important to the pupils in each flexible step of problems solving (Ediger, 2003).

Robert Gagne' (1984), a former mathematics instructor, developed a system of task analysis which might well be quite helpful in the hierarchy of objectives. Of his eight levels, the last three are especially significant here. If a pupil is not able to solve the mathematical problem being considered, the teacher needs to assist the pupil in considering the previous level in task analysis and that being understanding the appropriate necessary generalization(s) or rule. Perhaps the pupil reveals he/she does not understand dividing a four place dividend by a two place divisor with the quotient having a remainder. If this is not understood by the pupil, a preceding level of task analysis involves teaching the appropriate concepts not understood. This might emphasize attaching meaning to the concept of place value in division. Once the necessary concepts are understood, then the generalization may be developed, followed by its use in problems solving. In task analysis, the mathematics teacher assists the student to move to the previous earlier level from what is not understood, that is from problem solving to understanding needed generalizations. If the pupil does not understand the generalization, then the teacher must assist the pupil to understand the necessary prerequisite concepts.

Pertaining to strategies in teaching and learning situations, Mary (2007) wrote that teachers, in problem solving activities, should:

* have a range from which to choose
* practice using new strategies until they are comfortable with them
* explain why learning strategies are important as they teacher them to motivate pupils
* match strategies with teaching materials

* model a variety of strategies in each class; different pupils may be more successful with one as compared to the other

* consistently encourage students to use learning strategies in ongoing situations

* mentor students' use of learning strategies to ensure they are using them correctly

* encourage strategy use to other curriculum areas.

As teachers model these problem solving strategies, monitor their use by pupils, and encourage learners to use them in a variety of ways, pupils learn to generalize these strategies to become independent learners.

Meaning in problem solving is emphasized when teachers assist pupils to systematically experience each strategy with the use of concrete, semi-concrete, and abstract experiences. Pupils should be encouraged to ask questions pertaining to what is not understood. This provides opportunities for the teacher to help learners synthesize the unknown and the known. Feedback from pupils is important for the teacher to provide sequential learnings in ongoing lessons and units of study.

Learnings for pupils need to possess perceived purpose. They need to understand the reasons for participating in an ongoing mathematical lesson. The lesson should not be presented for the sake of doing so, but rather to assist pupils to achieve worthwhile objectives. Developmentally appropriate experiences must be in the offing, and individual differences provided for. Positive feelings through successful achievement assists pupils to develop an inward desire to learn.

The preferred learning styles of pupils need thorough consideration. Preferred styles may consist of individual and/or co-operative procedures in the mathematics curriculum. Meaningful learnings may occur through either approach. In society, individuals work by the self as well as work co-operatively to solve problems.

The total classroom environment should be conducive to optimal achievement and progress. Thus, the noise level should not be excessive to hinder achievement, nor expectations of pin drop quietness to make for pupil anxiety. A busy, constructive learning environment will produce some noise, but not be disruptive. Pupils with teacher guidance should develop standards of classroom conduct. These need to be reasonable and understood by all pupils. Periodic evaluation to ascertain of the standards have been met need to be stressed. The standards are there for a purpose and that is to increase learner achievement through meaningful learnings.

Methods of instruction might be direct or open ended. Direct methods emphasize a teacher determine curriculum whereas an open ended approach stresses pupils input and choice in terms of learning activities provided. For a direct approach, the teacher may rely upon a carefully chosen mathematics textbook. Each step in teaching must involve meaningful learnings for pupils. An open ended approach might well involve mathematics learning centers whereby the pupil individually may select the center and sequential tasks to complete. The tasks chosen may involve individual as well as collaborative learning activities. A teacher at Boston Academy used a computer program to stimulate high school students in using inquiry procedures (Wiske, 2004).

Her students constructed geometric figures and then analyzed such data as angles, side lengths, and ratios, among other different measures. They developed and tested their own conjectures for measuring, dragging, reshaping, and comparing geometric objects. The software which records and displays the mathematical relationships of objects, allowed students to examine a similar set of cases, observe patterns, and make generalizations. The accuracy and speed of the computer programs freed students from the tedium of construction with traditional tools and yet enabled them to experience the process of arranging and analyzing shapes.

New technologies help students understand concepts, methods of reasoning, and effective ways of presenting ideas in many subject areas. Graphic calculators that instantly relate the graphic and symbolic representations of mathematical expressions might well assist pupils to appreciate the nature of variables and functions. Computer based simulations enable students to see and manipulate abstract concepts.

Computer programs in mathematics may well provide new experiences for many students. The excitement of challenge and high expectations may indeed stimulate pupils to achieve at higher levels in mathematics. It might well assist pupils to see relationships in subject matter. Interest factors are powerful factors to consider in teaching. The fascination which many pupils have with computers encourages increased levels of learning. Quality programs need to be selected which guide the student to become increasingly independent in mathematical learnings (Ediger, 2006).

REFERENCES

Ausubel, D.P. (1963), *The Psychology of Meaningful Verbal Learning*. New York: Grune and Stratton.

Ediger, Marlow (2006), "Writing in the Mathematics Curriculum", *The Journal of Instructional Psychology*, 33(2),120-123.

Ediger, Marlow (2003), "Data driven decision making", *College Student Journal*, 37(1), 9-15.

Ediger, Marlow, and D. Bhaskara Rao (2002). *Teaching Mathematics Successfully*. New Delhi, India: Discovery Publishing House.

Gagne', Robert (1984), *"The Conditions of Learning"*. New York: Holt, Rinehart and Winston.

Mary, Sr. K.A. Susai (2007), "Learning Strategies and Mathematics", Edutracks 6(12), 23 and 25. Published in India.

Wiske, S. (2004), *Use Technology to Dig for Meaning, Educational Leadership*, 63(1), 478.

15

Modern School Mathematics

There was much enthusiasm when the phrase "Modern School Mathematics" was coined shortly after the 1958 National Defense Education Act was passed. Many federally funded study groups such as the The Greater Cleveland Mathematics Project, The School Mathematics Study Group, as well as the The University Illinois Arithmetic Project came into being. University mathematicians were employed to provide leadership and innovations into the mathematics curriculum. Mathematics textbooks were soon revised in terms of recommendations from the above named study groups. Schools ordered approved mathematics, science, and foreign language teaching materials. If approved by the state, the school district paid one-half and the federal government paid the other one-half. Many teachers received their master's degrees in mathematics or science through federally funded stipends. Teachers received university credit and stipends for attending approved classes, courses, and workshops in mathematics. This was the Golden Age of Education. It sounded as if this was the cure all for an improved mathematics curriculum.

Presently, criticisms in secondary teaching are just as great as it was in 1958. The criticisms are quite similar. The innovations recommended by federally funded study groups has had little impact in teaching mathematics in particular.

The high school level of schooling receives rather continuous criticism, These criticisms are quite obvious when reading professional journal articles. Authors of these articles frequently are far apart on what is being recommended for secondary students. The elementary level of schooling does not receive nearly as much criticism as compared to the secondary level. This is surprising since the elementary level of schooling provides the foundation for later school years. An interesting and provocative comment for elementary teachers in the US was made by Xiaoxia Newton (2007), who received her formal years of schooling in Mainland China:

* The K-5 institutional design must free elementary teachers from being generalists. They need to become experts in specific subjects and will need opportunities to practicing teaching a single subject curriculum, to reflect, and to continue developing their content knowledge.
* The K-12 institutional design must free both elementary and secondary teachers from -spending every second of their time in teaching. The system must build in time for other equally important activities, such as lesson planning, collaborating with colleagues, grading student work, and provide high quality feedback to students. The allocation of time to teaching and to other activities must reflect the complex demands of teaching.

CRITICISMS OF THE HIGH SCHOOL CURRICULUM

Innovations coming from the 1958 NDEA funded groups and soon appearing in mathematics textbooks were numerous. Rate learning and memorization of subject matter was heavily criticized, then as well as now. Why is it so difficult to make changes in the high school curriculum?

Much emphasis by the federally funded NDEA study groups focused on selected key ideas. First, the structure of knowledge was to be identified, generally by university mathematics professors, and these were to be made available to teachers to be used in teaching. Then too, structural ideas from the federally funded study groups were incorporated into mathematics textbooks. Presently, the term "structural ideas" is not used; however salient ideas are identified, perhaps, as mandated objectives of instruction. The writer believes "structural ideas" should be again be studied, not only by university mathematicians, but also with the involvement of elementary as well as secondary public school math teachers. By involving all three of these categories, the structural ideas may become more developmentally appropriate for implementation in the public schools. Parents, too, need to be involved since they felt frustrated in helping their offspring with homework in the new "modern school mathematics". Much stress was placed upon providing for individual differences in any classroom. The following structural ideas, among others, were frequently written about in teacher education journals in what was then called "modern school mathematics":

* the commutative property of addition and multiplication
* the associative property of addition and multiplication
* the distributive property of multiplication over addition
* the inverse property of subtraction and division
* the property of closure.

Set theory and venn diagrams received much emphasis, also, as did the concept of number systems as well as other bases than base ten. These are a few of the concepts stressed in modern school mathematics and are important presently also, except other bases. Separation of what is recommend today in the mathematics curriculum from what is actually practiced in the classroom makes for a wide divide.

Modern school måthematics stressed the importance of discovery learning. This tended to make mathematics exciting and emphasize thinking about number. Presently, there is much criticism of mathematics being boring with its emphasis being placed upon memorizing for annual mandated tests. The accountability movement has advocated pupils being tested in grades three through eight and an exit test on the high school level. Pupils need to pass the grade level tests to be promoted and the exit test to receive a high school diploma.

Modern school mathematics emphasized that learnings be meaningful. Pupils then are to understand what is taught. It is salient to make sense of mathematical content. With mandated test preparations, it appears that meaning theory is being neglected. Drill does not stress meaningful learnings. Much stress must be placed upon higher levels of thinking in the curriculum. Logic and critical thinking needs to be in evidence and should be at the heart of the curriculum. Creative thought too is needed in that new procedures of doing algorithms need to be found by pupils. There are generally several ways to perform an operation on numbers. Creative discovery of new procedures is important. Creativity in determining novel, unique ways of doing things is salient in the school curriculum as well as in society. Myers (2007), wrote:

> We must de-emphasize answers and correctness as the only worthy goals in mathematics. Sure, "right answers" are an important part of mathematics, but they aren't always the bottom line. Instead of always asking, "What's the right answer?" we should also wonder, "What's the right question?" and "What's the most interesting way to find the answer?" Mathematics is about bold, adventure some ideas and the history of the subject is therefore fraught with mistakes, confusion, and invalid convictions. Let's make the classroom a bit more like the discipline and allow our students to revere in the "wrong" while they pursue the "right".

New technologies help students understand concepts, methods of reasoning, and effective ways of presenting their ideas in mathematics. Wiske (2004), wrote the following pertaining to a Boston Academy teacher using a computer program called the Geometer's Sketchbook to stimulate high school students in inquiry approaches:

> "Her students constructed geometric figures and then analyzed such data as angles, side lengths, and ratios, among other different measures. They developed and tested their own conjectures for measuring, dragging, reshaping and comparing geometric shapes. The software, which records and displays the mathematical relationships allowed students to examine similar set of cases, observe patterns, and make generalizations. The accuracy and speed of the computer program freed students from the tedium of construction with traditional tools yet enabled them to experience the process of arranging and analyzing shapes".

Among other materials of instruction, technology might well assist students to attach meaning and understand in what is being experienced. Then too, varying activities can develop interest in learning.

Stimulating experiences may be a motivating factor in students achieving mathematical objectives of instruction. Students should work individually as well as collectively in ongoing learning activities. A preferred learning style for some is to work by the self in assignments to complete, as well as doing voluntary work at an interest center. Others like to work collectively. In society, people work at things individually as well as within a group setting. Students should have opportunities to follow personal preferences in the preferred style of learning. Maximum learning from a student may accrue from the style of learning preferred (Ediger, 2006).

The mathematics supervisor or lead teacher can do much to assist teachers to improve instruction. The following means of inservice education might well be provided mathematics teachers to assist student achievement and progress:

1. talk to teachers about innovative ideas in teaching. The supervisor and teacher must learn from each other in improving the curriculum.
2. visit classrooms to guide in curriculum improvement.
3. read current literature on trends and developments in the curriculum.
4. attend state and national teacher education conventions.
5. meet with supervisors in the district.
6. conduct research to improve the curriculum for each student (Ediger, 2002).

REFERENCES

Ediger, Marlow (2007), "Writing in the Mathematics Curriculum", *Journal of Instructional Psychology*, 33(2), 121.

Ediger, Marlow, 2002), "The Supervisor of the School", Education, 122 (3), 604.

Myers, Perla, "Why? Why? Why? Future Teachers Discover Mathematical Depth", *Phi Delta Kappan*, 88(9), 696.

Newton, Xiaoxia (2007), "Reflections on Math Reforms in the U.S.", *Phi Delta Kappan*, 88(9), 685.

Wiske, S. (2004), "Using Technology to Dig for Meaning", *Educational Leadership*, 62(1), 8.

16

Mathematics Curriculum

There are different schools cf thought on how the mathematics curriculum should be organized. The objectives of instruction would then vary also, as would the learning opportunities to achieve the objectives. One or more of these schools of thought in teaching may be emphasized. Each student should achieve as optimally as possible, regardless of the philosophical school of thought involved.

PLANS OF ORGANIZING THE MATHEMATICS CURRICULUM

Plan number one stresses the practical or utilitarian curriculum. Each activity to achieve objectives emphasizes what is useful in society. The mathematics curriculum is then not separated from society. Planners of the curriculum must ascertain which learnings are most useful in the societal arena. These need to be developmentally sequenced. Challenging and yet achievable objectives need to be in the offing. Objectives to include the following need to be emphasized:

* buying needed goods and services
* purchasing needed appliances such as an electric/gas range, a dishwasher, a micro-wave oven, a refrigerator, among other items

* paying for water, light, heat, and other electrical bills
* paying for these items from a salary or wages earned
* using cash, checks, or credit cards, among others, to make payments
* shopping around and comparing prices for the best buys with equivalent quality involved
* making a loan, borrowing money, and establishing equity
* buying car, home and property/life insurance
* making safe investments
* paying sales, property, social security, and state/federal income taxes (Ediger and Rao (2001), Teaching Mathematics Successfully. New Delhi, India: Discovery Publishing House.

Learning opportunities to achieve objectives need to be varied to provide for individual difference. There should be entire class experiences whereby necessary information for all pupils should be presented such as in the topic "buying needed goods and services" as listed in the above first listed asterisk items. Information provided should clarify the concept "goods" as compared to "services". Actual objects or illustrations may show suits, dresses, cereal, and milk, among others. Illustrations of common services purchased include a service person repairing an appliance, a mechanic working on a car, and a truck driver hauling milk.

Teachers provide a service of teaching pupils and not one who deals in "goods". To achieve each item above with an asterisk, pupils should have learning opportunities which are challenging and yet success in achievement is possible. Providing interesting activities which are purposeful motivate learner achievement and progress (Ediger, 2006).

In addition to entire class activities, small group or committee endeavours should be emphasized. Within a committee then of four to five pupils, learners can experience concepts and generalizations indepth. Thus in asterisk item number two above, pupils may view a power point presentation showing the appliances listed. A discussion may follow on what to look for in a quality appliance. This might involve everything from comparing prices, choosing desired features, and related warranties. No doubt, pupil~ will want to extend this activity to the home setting whereby parents provide input and ideas.

In addition to large group and committee endeavours, pupils may also work on individual projects. Depending upon the developmental level of the learner, he/she, for example, may do a scrapbook on goods and services. Illustrations may be cut out from newspapers and magazines, as well as pictures from the internet with one part of the scrapbook dealing with labelled goods and the other with labelled services performed. Comparison of prices of prices, if possible, is salient in the project.

A utilitarian mathematics curriculum emphasizes:

* that which is useful in the societal arena. School and society are not to be separated.
* comparison of costs involving goods and services
* the use of everyday mathematics
* pupils bring in problems dealing with personal purchases made
* mathematics being learned within a practical situation
* a flexible scope and sequence depending upon ongoing situations (See National Council Teachers of Mathematics, 1989).

A psychological mathematics curriculum might then be developed in that learner input is salient, particularly in small group and individual endeavours.

Plan number two stresses a basics, subject matter approach in learning mathematics. Here, the scope and sequence in mathematics for pupils depends upon challenging subject matter. Mathematics contains its own inherent scope and sequence. Units of study for pupils are pre-planned by mathematics teachers and based upon a sound knowledge of key, structural ideas in the different branches of mathematics. Essential knowledge is to be achieved by students in preparation for the college/university level of schooling. Thus, a pre-kindergarten grade twelve sequence is planned. A logical order is then developed in that mathematics teachers determine the sequence of objectives for pupil attainment.

The following content in the mathematics curriculum needs indepth teaching, with the inclusion of technology, so that pupils understand the related underlying principles:

* addition and subtraction, including extension of numbers and numeration.
* multiplication and division, estimation, regrouping and renaming.
* informal geometry with emphasis upon plane figures, points, lines, rays, and line segments. Transformational geometry, symmetry, congruence and similarity, along with coordinate geometry should also be taught as needed subject matter in mathematics.
* common fractions, fractional numbers, equivalent fractions, including four operations on fractions such as addition, subtraction, multiplication, and division.
* decimal fractions and per cents related to fractions
* computing with decimals
* extending place value of decimals
* measurement of temperature, time, and money
* developing tables, charts, graphs
* use of statistics and probability (See Peressini, 1997).

Each of the above items in asterisks may be stated as one or more objectives for pupils to achieve sequentially.

They need to be emphasized on the developmental level of the learner. Students need to be successful in learning that which is challenging. Learning opportunities for pupils to achieve each objective need to be determined. Criteria to follow in teaching should stress meaningful learnings, active engagement of the learner, as well as involved purpose in acquiring basic subject matter. Reputable basal mathematics textbooks may well be the heart of the basics curriculum in mathematics. Workbooks accompanying the basal text supplements subject matter being discussed. Related worksheets reinforces what students have acquired from the basal textbook and the accompanying workbook. The learning activities assist students to achieve objectives of instruction. Methods of instruction include discussions, small group work, individual tutoring and monitoring, review of previous learnings, deductive, and inductive learning. Computers and technology need to be used to vary and supplement as well as provide new experiences for learners to achieve objectives in an essentialist mathematics curriculum (See S. Wiske, 2004).

Plan number three stresses the use of learning stations and student choice in mathematics. An adequate number of stations need to be set up by the teacher in the classroom. For twenty two students, there should be approximately five stations. At each station, there is a task card which lists possible learning activities for pupils to choose from. From the approximate five tasks on a card and with five stations, the student may select which learning activities to pursue sequentially. All tasks relate to the stated objectives. There are more tasks than what a learner can complete. The following characteristics are inherent developing the task cards:

* individual differences are provided for among learners
* choices may be made for individual, dyads, or small group work
* abstract and/or concrete experiences may be chosen

* tasks which harmonize with the student's present level of achievement are in the offing
* the mathematics teacher serves as a guide and stimulates optimal student achievement (See Thangarajathi and Viola, 2007).

Plan number four emphasizes students achieving predetermined, mandated objectives. These objectives are precise in that either a student does/does not achieve the desired outcome as a result of instruction. The mathematics teacher chooses learning opportunities for students which align with the precise, mandated objectives. Mandated standardized tests also align with the stated objectives. These tests are pilot tested to take out weaknesses in test items. The standardized tests are used in selected grade levels and must be passed by the student in order to be promoted to the next grade level. An exit test is given during the high school years and must be passed by the learner in order to receive a high school diploma.

Measurability is very significant here and all students are tested under the same conditions. The directions for test taking are the same for each age group as are the test items. Test results are machine scored, resulting in percentiles or grade equivalents for each student.

Data driven decision-making relates well to the measurability concept. Machine scored tests provide data or information in making curricular decisions. Thus, for example, if students are weak in understanding place value in mathematics, feedback is then available to teachers to emphasize place value as an objective of instruction (See Guilfoyle, 2006).

In closing, the four plans discussed in teaching mathematics may be used individually or in harmony with the other plans and procedures. Thus, a few learning stations may be used as enrichment in the other three plans of teaching mathematics. Or, a utilitarian mathematics curriculum might well be integrated with a basics or measurement driven philosophy of teaching. That which assists the learner to achieve most optimally should be stressed.

REFERENCES

Ediger, Marlow (2006), "Writing in the Mathematics Curriculum", *Journal of Instructional Psychology*, 33(2), 120-123.

Ediger, Marlow, and D. Bhaskara Rao (2001), *Teaching Mathematics Successfully*. New Delhi, India: Discovery Publishing House.

Guilfoyle, Christy (2006), "NCLB: Is There Life Beyond Testing?" *Educational Leadership*, 64(3), 8-13.

National Council Teachers of Mathematics (1989), *Curriculum and Evaluation Standards for School Mathematics*. Reston, Virginia: NCTM.

Peressini, D. (1997), "Parental Reform of Mathematics Education", *The Mathematics Teacher*, 90(6), 423-427.

Thangarajathi and Adlin Viola (2007), "Co-operative Learning Approach in Learning Mathematics", *Edutracks*, 6(9), 27-30. Published in India.

Wiske, S. (2004), "Use Technology to Dig for Meaning", *Educational Leadership*, 62(1), 478.

17

Designing Mathematics Curriculum

Careful attention needs to be given to designing the mathematics curriculum. Each part of the design is salient to aid learner achievement. Students need to experience challenging objectives and yet be successful achievers. They need adequate supervision to achieve well. Students need to be ready to do mathematics well in school and in society. A carefully designed mathematics curriculum provides for quality sequence for each student. No student should fail to understand and master basic leanings; he/she also needs to be able to use what has been learned in practical situations.

DESIGN IN MATHEMATICAL LEARNINGS

The objectives of mathematics instruction need meticulous selection. Each objective chosen must be relevant in the life of the student. Cognitive objectives are one category. They represent subject matter ends pertaining to a vital unit of study. Relevant learnings for a specific level of student achievement might include finding the area, perimeter, volume, and/or estimation. Clarity of each objective is needed so that agreement is there pertaining to what a student is to achieve as a result of instruction. There should not be guesswork in terms of what a student is to learn (See National Council Teachers of Mathematics, 1989).

Skill objectives to be selected emphasize students applying that which has been achieved in each cognitive end of instruction. Higher levels of thinking are involved here including critical thought when separating important from the insignificant in problem solving. Creative thought must be stressed when novel, unique ways are devised in arriving at mathematical solutions. Certainly, the level of application is also salient in that students use what has been acquired in diverse ways. Pertaining to Computer use, Wiske (2004), wrote the following pertaining to a teacher at Boston Academy using a computer program called the Geometer's Sketchboard to stimulate high school student in inquiry procedures:

> "Her students constructed geometric figures and then analyzed such data as angles, side lengths, and ratios, among other measures. They developed and tested their own conjectures for measuring, dragging, reshaping, and comparing geometric objects. The software, which records and displays the mathematical relationships of objects, allowed students to examine a similar set of cases, observe patterns, and make generalizations. The accuracy and speed of the computer program freed students from the tedium of construction with traditional tools yet enabled them to experience the process of arranging and analyzing shapes".

Attitudinal objectives need careful consideration in designing the mathematics curriculum. Quality attitudes for student development include the following:

* appreciating the role of mathematics in solving problems in society
* enjoying mathematics for its own sake
* desiring to learn more in the area of mathematics
* wanting to use mathematics in personal and in practical situations

* feeling challenged with indepth learning in mathematics
* wanting to work co-operatively with others
* assisting others as needed to be successful in mathematical learnings.

LEARNING OPPORTUNITIES IN MATHEMATICS

Learning opportunities need to harmonize with the present developmental level of a learner. They should not be too complex to for ordain failure, nor so easy that boredom settles in on the part of the learner. Thus, challenging and yet successful learning experiences need to be in the offing. Scaffolding might then be used. Developmentally appropriate activities need to be provided for each student. Concrete materials of instruction such as markers, small disks, checkers, marbles, among others, need to be used so that students attach meaning to what is being learned. Semi-concrete materials include place value charts, diagrams, use of compasses and protractors, drawings, graphs, and charts need to be used to move from the concrete to the semi-concrete, followed by the abstract. Abstract leanings include the use of numerals, operation signs, mathematical symbols, representation of plane and solid figures, as well as other representations of the concrete and the semi-concrete. Technology should definitely enhance learner achievement. Warschauer (2007), wrote:

> "Just as pencils, pens, papers, and books were the predominate tools for learning and knowledge production during much of the last century, computers and the Internet are the tools for learning and knowledge production in the 21st century. As computer-to-student ratios approach one to one, some educators are advocating Pam Pilots or hand held computers for the classroom. But the growth of these devices in schools has flattened out (Market Date Retrieval, 2004). This trend is not surprising because

the small screens on heldhands make them unsatisfactory for the kind of writing, research, and multimedia tasks that laptop computers are so well suited for...Laptops are not an instant panacea, but they are a powerful tool for the kinds of learning experiences that will prepare students for the future. Schools and districts that can meet the financial challenge while focusing on broad educational goals will find one-to-one computing an exciting and worthwhile venture".

Learning opportunities provided to students need to follow definite criteria for teaching and learning situations. They need to:

* stimulate interest in mathematics
* arouse purpose for learning
* engage students in achieving objectives of instruction
* understand indepth what is being learned
* provide for individual differences in the classroom
* emphasize small group and individual activities
* stress co-operative endeavours as well as wholesome competition
* develop quality affective behaviours such as politeness and caring.

Formative evaluation must be stressed to provide guidance and direction in assisting students to achieve objectives of instruction. Thus in an ongoing mathematics unit, discussions, teacher written test items, student self-evaluation, and daily work of learners, among other procedures, might well be used by the teacher to ascertain progress and growth of learners. Summative or end of unit assessments may include those mentioned above in formative evaluations, as well as mandated and district test results. The best procedures of evaluation need to be used in formative and summative evaluations (Ediger and Rao, 2000).

Observing excellent teachers teach provides models in innovations. A teacher may be able to refine methods of student inquiry learning by observing model situations of instruction. Critical and creative thinking, along with problem solving, are salient methods of instruction to use.

Mathematics teachers need to use the best objectives, methods of instruction, and assessment procedures possible, in teaching and learning situations. Hopefully, students will achieve well under these implemented plans (Ediger, 2006).

REFERENCES

Ediger, Marlow (2006), "Writing in the Mathematics Curriculum", *Journal of Instructional Psychology*, 33(2), 120-123.

Ediger, Marlow, and D. Bhaskara Rao (2000), *Teaching Mathematics Successfully*. New Delhi, India: Discovery Publishing House.

National Council Teachers of Mathematics (1989), *Curriculum and Evaluation Standards for School Mathematics*. Reston, Virginia: NCTM.

Warschauer, Mark (2007), "Going One-to-One", *Educational Leadership*, 63(4), 34-38.

Wiske, S. (2004, "Using Technology to Dig for Meaning", *Educational Leadership*, 62(1), 478.

18

Readiness for Mathematics Learning

The readiness concept is important for mathematics teachers to consider in teaching students. The writer has noticed in supervising university student teachers that public school learners are often hurried through different lessons in a mathematics textbook without understanding what is being taught. Leanings need to make sense to students. If meaning is not there for the student, he/she will fail to understand ensuing facts, concepts and generalizations. What is salient is that students attach indepth meaning to ongoing mathematical ideas acquired, not how many pages were covered in a mathematics textbook.

Student readiness for new learnings indicate the previous subject matter studied was mastered and meaningful. The learner is then ready to pursue challenging sequential content and yet be successful in achievement.

READINESS FOR LEARNING IN MATHEMATICS

Specific readiness is necessary for learning a new process in mathematics. Thus, if students are to understand how to rename and regroup in subtraction such as in 45 minus 28, they must attach meaning to forty five as representing "four tens and five ones", as well twenty five representing "two tens and eight ones". The concept of *place value* is very important here such as in ones and tens. Eight ones cannot be taken from five ones which then makes regrouping necessary. From forty five, one ten in a place value chart may be taken from four tens and this results in the regrouped three tens and fifteen ones, making it possible to take eight from fifteen, leaving seven ones. Two tens may then be taken from three tens leaving one ten. Minuend minus subtrahend, leaves a difference of 17. There are a plethora of understandings and skills needed to benefit from new learnings to be acquired in the mathematics curriculum. The mathematics teacher may observe to ascertain if a student is ready to benefit from achieving new subject matter or skills in an ongoing lesson or unit of study. Teacher observation is an excellent tool to use in assessing learner achievement as well as readiness for ensuing learnings (Ediger and Rao, 2007).

Second, attitudinal readiness is important for students. Thus, a student needs to possess quality attitudes toward mathematics and the use of quantities. The attitude needs to reveal a desire to learn and use mathematics in a variety of situations. These situations might well be practical in learning to use mathematics in life like situations. Mathematics is to be used in school and in society. Also, mathematics should be enjoyable as a curriculum area to pursue for its own sake. Too frequently, mathematics has become an area for drilling students for test-taking. Rather, the study of mathematics should involve enjoyment, discovery, and positive feelings. A variety of experiences assists students to develop feelings of enjoyment and appreciation. There is much to appreciate in learning mathematics with its emphasis upon progress in societal improvement. Modern machines have made the world of work easier and less of a burden. In farm operations, manufacturing, and the service sector, back-breaking work has been greatly minimized or eliminated. Also, in medical practices, for example, accuracy is salient such as in blood pressure readings, cholesterol levels (good and bad cholesterol), pulse rate, and medications prescribed with precise chemical readings. Quantities are used in almost all facets of living such in calories in food, per cent of each ingredient in food items, and ounces/pounds of selected products. Use of the metric system of measurement might well be substituted for the English system of measurement. Computers and technology have certainly taken over in different plans and systems of accounting procedures (See March, 2005).

Third, student readiness for responding to and using diverse methods of mathematical instruction need to be in the offing. Large group, committees, and individualized instruction need to be used to provide for individual differences in the classrooms. The use of learning centers, the project method, basal textbooks and workbooks, audio-visual approaches, among other materials and techniques of instruction need to be in the offing. Critical and creative thinking, problem solving, inquiry methods, and learning by discovery need to be used along with the different media and materials of instruction. Concrete materials (markers, fact finders, objects and items), Semi-concrete materials (Graphs, charts, illustrations, place value charts, measurement instruments, games, and number lines, among others), as well as abstract materials (numerals, symbols, formulas, and drawings) generally follow in sequence (See Smith, *et. al.*, 2006).

Methods of instruction need to be developmentally appropriate for involved learners. Students need to be engaged in ongoing activities. Active learners rather than passive students need to be in the offing. They need to perceive purpose in learning and accept reasons for participating in curricular experiences. Quality sequence must be inherent in ongoing lessons and units of study. With good sequence, student success in achievement is more likely to be in evidence. Individual differences and needs among students must be met.

Fourth, developmental readiness makes for salient considerations in teaching and learning situations.

Developmental readiness looks at stages of growth in each human being. Thus, the attention span of an individual increases much from the primary school years to the secondary level of schooling. Secondary students then might pursue a mathematical topic for a much longer period of time as compared to primary grade learners. Young children may become exhausted from a school day of learning activities as compared to older students whose bodies can manage longer periods of time in academic learnings. They, also, are able to concentrate on a task for a longer period of time. Developmentally appropriate activities then should harmonize with the learner's present attention span, interests, physical prowess and skills, as well as endurance (See Boyd-Batstone, 2004).

Fifth, the mathematics teacher must ascertain specific subject matter readiness within an ongoing lesson or unit of study. Adequate background information needs to precede achieving a new objective. Thus, the teacher must determine what a student needs as prerequisites to be able, for example, to multiply 56 times 345 within the context of a lesson. This multiplication problem emphasizes a set of 345 objects to be multiplied by 56 which requires as minimal prerequisites:

* knowledge of place value
* knowledge of multiplication facts
* knowledge of regrouping and renaming
* knowledge of partial products

Each of the above requires meaning in learning. Rote learning is inadequate since, among other things, meaning and understanding will be necessary for increased complexity of sequential mathematical learnings. Thus, students need to know the "why" of each step in algorithms performed. Indepth learning of underlying principles are needed in performing operations on number. Time spent on quality instruction is time well spent in teaching mathematics.

There are selected principles of instruction which assist students in developing readiness for learning. Scaffolding becomes salient in achieving necessary knowledge and skills. If a student then seemingly is unable to accomplish the next sequential step of learning, the mathematics teacher may close the gap between where the learner is presently and the desired goal in an ongoing lesson. Thus, the teacher uses small sequential steps of teaching which guides the learner to close the gap. The gaps generally are small between the present level of attainment and the ideal which the learner is unable to achieve unless scaffolding is used in teaching.

Second, the student needs to focus carefully on what is being taught. Too frequently, a student may turn off, day dream, or think of an oncoming weekend without paying attention to the subject matter and skills being taught. The student's attention needs to be refocused through the use of challenging, fascinating learning opportunities. Careful teacher observation needs to be used to notice when students are inattentive and when the kinds of materials used in teaching need to be changed within a lesson. Interest is a powerful factor to use in teaching and learning situations within the scaffolding process (Ediger, 1989).

Third, adequate attention needs to be paid to processes and not products only, in learning. Testing tends to stress the importance of right answers or the products of learning. Students do take many tests in a school year such as mandated tests, district wide tests, and teacher written tests. Correct answers, only, then may count. And yet, students may engage in correct processes and miss the correct answer due to a minor computation error. Mathematics teachers need to assist students to perform operations or processes correctly. This indicates understanding of the "how" and the "why" of doing mathematics. Each intricate step of a process is salient when meaning, not rote learning, is attached to ongoing experiences. Students need encouragement to ask why a procedure is done in a certain way and how a new procedure makes sense in the mathematics curriculum. Correct processes used should assist in making for accurate products.

Fourth, variety in appraisal techniques must be used to provide feedback to the teacher. The feedback aids the teacher in improving the mathematics curriculum. Specific feedback helps the teacher to diagnose and remediate difficulties experienced by students in ongoing lessons. Assisting students in overcoming difficulties helps to make for improved sequential progress on the part of the learner.

Appraisal procedures to be used include teacher observation, conferences with learners and with parents, as well as diverse teacher written, district wide, and mandated standardized tests. Results from each test should provide information on how to assist students to achieve more optimally. Student readiness for acquiring new facts, concepts, and generalizations should then be in the offing (See National Council Teachers of Mathematics, 1989).

Mathematics teachers need to provide for optimal achievement on the part of each student. To do this, one factor important in teaching and learning situations is to provide readiness for new learnings on the part of students. With readiness, sequence is harmonized between previously acquired learnings with the new facts, concepts, and generalizations to be achieved.

REFERENCES

Boyd-Batstone, Paul (2004), "Focused Anecdotal Records Assessment: A Tool for Standards Based Authentic Assessment", *The Reading Teacher*, 58(3), 230-239.

Ediger, Marlow (1989), "Psychology in Teaching Mathematics", *Delta K.*, 27(4), 20-23.

Ediger, Marlow, and D. Bhaskara Rao (2007), *Curriculum of School Subjects*. New Delhi, India: Discovery Publishing House, Chapter Five.

March, Tom (2005), "The New WWW: Whatever, Whenever, Wherever," *Educational Leadership*, 65(4),14- 19.

National Council Teachers of Mathematics (1989), *Curriculum and Evaluation Standards for School Mathematics*. Reston, Virginia: NCTM.

Smith, Lorraine A., *et al.*, "Activities that Really Measure Up", *Science and Children*, 44(2), 30-33.

19

Improving Mathematics Instruction

Much emphasis is being placed on drilling students to do well on the mathematics section of the No Child Left Behind annual tests for grades there through eight. Teachers are pressured for students to pass their individual grade level tests for promotion purposes. They also feel the pressure to have students meet Adequate Yearly Progress (AYP). AYP standards, if not met two years in a row labels a school as failing. There are penalties then for low student performance on the annual NCLB tests. Beliefs seemingly exist that students may succeed if drill is stressed as a method of teaching to up test scores. However, drill, as a method of teaching, robs students of being motivated individuals in teaching and learning situations. (Ediger and Rao, 2003). What can be done to increase enthusiasm for learning in mathematics?

TEACHING MATHEMATICS SUCCESSFULLY

The psychology of learning emphasizes selected trends in assisting students to do well in ongoing lessons and units of study. First of all, mathematics teachers need to engage students in learning. This means that the learning activities are being presented in an interesting manner which captures learner attention. The learning activities are centered around students achieving objectives of instruction. If students do not attend, the chances are little will be learned.

Second, students need assistance to perceive purpose in ongoing learning activities. Many times, students do not put forth effort in learning because they feel there is little value in the ongoing lesson. Students need to understand why something is salient to learn. It may take the teacher very little time to state a reason to assist students in seeing value in what is being presented. What is taught must be useful in school and in society. At intervals, students may brain storm how new learnings might be useful, presently as well as in the future. Intrinsic acceptance of purpose is salient. With drilling students in mathematics for state mandated testing, there is little perceived use for rote learning of subject matter.

Third, attaching meaning to what is being learned is essential. Unless mathematics content is intelligible to the learner, he/she may not possess foundational learnings to benefit from more complex mathematical procedures. New learnings acquired are based upon previous facts, concepts, and generalizations in mathematics in the curriculum. What is being learned must make sense to the student, otherwise use and application cannot be made of new ideas achieved in mathematics.

Appropriate sequence in lessons and units of study must be stressed. A teacher determined sequence may be emphasized whereby learnings are ordered from the simple to the complex. However, this may not meet the needs of selected students in the classroom. Thus, the teacher needs to also use open ended approaches in teaching such as students learning by discovery, through problem solving, through logic, as well as inductively. The student's style of learning must be considered in teaching and learning situations. Individual differences among learners then need to be provided for in mathematics. Ultimately, sequence resides within the student. He/she must order and organize subject matter which is applicable in school and in society.

Mathematics teachers need to plan for and implement diverse kinds of experiences for students. Concrete experiences or the use of real objects is important. In counting experiences for young children, objects may be counted. Or in addition, subtraction, multiplication and division, concrete materials need to be used in teaching. Number sentences need to be written when student readiness is in evidence. They relate to what was experienced or demonstrated through the use of concrete materials. In sequence, the commutative and associative properties for addition and multiplication need to be stressed. Structural ideas for subtraction and division need to follow in appropriate order. These foundational learnings for students provide the opportunity for relating the abstract with the concrete or the numerals and symbols, with reality. Students, sequentially, need to experience and understand concrete learnings so that increasingly complex ideas may accrue sequentially in the abstract for more complex ideas. Semi-concrete materials (pictures, drawings, diagrams, felt cutouts and a flannel board, number lines, and place value charts) for example, might well substitute for or follow ordered concrete phases in learning.

Technology is the continued wave of the future. It is used in all endeavours involving written communication. Thus, students should have ample learning activities in computer use. These experiences should be on the developmental level of the student in that they:

* are diagnostic and pin-point vital errors for remediation
* provide meaningful practice for learners
* provide for individual differences among learners
* possess ordered experiences for student success
* assist students to achieve important objectives of instruction
* relate directly to the present mathematics lessons and units of study being stressed
* are perceived as being worthwhile (Ediger and Rao, 2000).

Pertaining to multimedia and its use in mathematics, Hatfield and Bitter (1994), list the following characteristics:

1. promotes active versus passive learning.
2. offers models or examples of exemplary and non-exemplary instruction.
3. is illustrative and interactive.
4. facilitates the development of decision-making and problem solving abilities.
5. provides user control and multiple pathways for assessing information.
6. provides motivation and allows for variability of learning styles.
7. facilitates the development of perceptual and interpretational abilities.
8. offers efficient management of time for learning and less instructional training time.
9. allows for numerous data types, e.g., animation, graphics, voice, texts, and motion video.
10. offers multi-lingual presentation. The technology exists whereby programs and units can be presented in different languages.

The above named guidelines provide direction for using diverse media, including computers. Careful consideration needs to be given to quality in all learning opportunities provided to students, otherwise less interest will be in evidence in the mathematics curriculum.

Technology must be integrated within the inherent mathematics curriculum. It should assist learners to achieve more optimally. Student appreciation for mathematics should definitely be a goal. Quality attitudes assist students to become increasingly interested in the cognitive and psychomotor domain of mathematics objectives. Positive attitudes help students to do more complex thinking abut vital mathematical facts, concepts, and generalizations.

Logical thinking, analytic thought, synthesizing information, inferential thinking, and creative ideas need to be in the offing in ongoing lessons and units of study. Application in practical and abstract situations must follow achieved objectives. Use made of mathematical facts, concepts, and generalizations provide students with the opportunities of perceiving values of what was learned. Mathematics then becomes practical in everyday living.

MATHEMATICAL LITERACY

A major objective in the curriculum is to develop mathematical literacy within all individuals. That is indeed a difficult objective to attain. The word "all" indicates that not all can do something, whatever that goal is. However, objectives need to be established for mathematics literacy which are challenging, and yet there is hope they can be achieved. With effort and motivation, objectives can be attained. What is mathematics literacy? It is more comprehensive than being able to take care of every day activities involving number. There needs to be indepth understanding of what is inherent in operations on number. Thus, for example, there needs to be understanding of place value, regrouping and renaming. Being able to do the routine calculating is not adequate. Or being able to divide fractions meaningfully is different than merely revealing answers. Too frequently, students, here, have leaned to invert the divisor and multiply rather than indicating understandings of why this is done. The "why" of performing different operations on number or on any learning in mathematics needs to be in evidence. Above all, there needs to be developed within individuals an appreciation for the different branches of mathematics being pursued. This appreciation should assist learners to possess lifelong students of mathematics.

The irony of post-modern instruction is that preparing children for a high tech future requires us to focus our attention more then ever on the task of understanding what it means to be human, to be alive, to be part of both social and biological communities—a quest for which technology is increasingly becoming not the solution, but the problem (Monke, 2005-2006).

REFERENCES

Ediger, Marlow, and D. Bhaskara Rao (2003), *Teaching Mathematics in Elementary Schools*. New Delhi, India: Discovery Publishing House, Chapter Five.

Ediger, Marlow, and D. Bhaskara Rao (2000), *Teaching Mathematics Successfully*. New Delhi, India: Discovery Publishing House, Chapter One.

Hatfield, Mary M., and Gary G. Bitter (1994), *A Multi-media Approach to the Professional Development of Teachers: A Virtual Classroom, Professional Development of Teachers in Mathematics*, Reston, Virginia: Yearbook of the National Council Teachers of Mathematics.

Monke, Lowell W. (2005-2006), "The Overdominance of Computers", *Educational Leadership*, 63(4), 23.

20

Improving Mathematics Curriculum

There are a plethora of criticisms pertaining to a lack of student achievement in the Public Schools. Much of the criticism comes from low test scores. Test results from the Trends in International Mathematics and Science Study (TIMSS), and The National Assessment of Educational Progress (NAEP), have caused furor from selected observers in terms of student achievement. Mathematics, as one academic discipline, has been tested in each of these two tests.

Those who justify student achievement in mathematics state that the following make for differences among international student achievement in the TIMSS:

* cultural differences among nations whereby academic achievement has extreme value in some nations
* selected nations having aligned their mathematics curriculum more with the objectives of TIMSS as compared to the United States
* sampling errors of students within nations in statistics when making these comparisons
* TIMSS test items favouring particular nations in validity (See Ediger and Rao 2000).

Dissatisfaction of NAEP test results may be due to the following according to a few educators:

* test items written on too complex a level, especially for secondary students
* test items favouring those states which have highly qualified mathematics teachers
* possibility of sampling errors among students being tested
* cohort groups being tested rather than valued added situations (See Kennedy and Tipps, 1991).

Whatever the reasons, there are ways of improving mathematics instruction in the public schools. The balance of this paper will present means to strengthen teaching and learning situations.

EVALUATING MATHEMATICS TEACHERS

Teachers need to possess much knowledge in the area they are teaching. For example, an algebra teacher must be highly competent in subject matter being taught. He/she cannot just be one or two lessons ahead of students. Specializing is a key concept. Algebra teachers who are highly qualified have increased opportunities to assist learners as needed when subject matter propensities are in the offing. Subject matter knowledge possessed by the teacher is essential here. Then too in remedial instruction, the algebra teacher who can diagnose student difficulties may well possess essential subject matter to remedy difficulties.

Specializing not only in knowledge, but also in methods of teaching are needed to optimize learner progress. If one method has not worked in assisting students, a different procedure may. Too strengthen mathematics teaching then, the following are offered as suggestions:

* encourage teachers to take graduate courses in mathematics online or at a nearby university

* guide teachers, in an inservice activity, to diagnose the kinds of errors students make and assist in overcoming these problem areas
* provide time for mathematics teachers to share ideas on what works in teaching/learning situations
* conduct workshops on improving mathematics instruction, using the assistance of highly qualified instructors
* establish a professional library for the teaching of mathematics. Introduce and encourage its use.
* establish personal goals in writing at the beginning of a new school year to improve mathematics instruction and follow through with their achievement. The goals of the project need to be shared with other mathematics instructors (See Science and Children, October, 2006 Issue on Measurement).

Improving the quality of mathematics instruction is always possible. Innovative ways must be found to provide for the growth and development of mathematical instruction. Time should be given to teachers to observe each other's teaching and diagnose the quality of instruction, based on recommended standards. If direct observation is not possible, then video-taping of a lesson also provides opportunities for observation, as well as for critiquing. Lesson plan evaluation has become quite popular in Japan and has been introduced in selected schools in the United States. A committee of mathematics teachers assesses indepth a lesson plan which results in modification and change. The lesson is then taught, evaluated and need changes made, if any. If changes are made, then reteaching is in evidence.

What is salient is that mathematics teachers work together in devising the best curriculum possible.

SUMMATIVE AND FORMATIVE EVALUATION

A good mathematics teacher is a good evaluator. He/she observes rather continuously to notice if students are actively engaged in each lesson. The following learner traits are also observed:

* kinds and types of errors made in daily work
* remediation for mistakes made
* responsibility of the student for task completion
* interest shown in mathematics
* behaviour exhibited making for a learner centered classroom (Ediger, 1997).

New learnings to be presented are built upon what has been learned previously. Thus background information is being furnished for ensuing objectives to be attained. Readiness for achieving the new learnings are then in evidence. Quality sequence is salient in student learning. With improved sequence or order in learning activities, the learner is more likely to experience success. Careful listening to each step of learning must also be encouraged by the teacher.

Summative evaluation occurs within an ongoing unit of study. Summative evaluation may well involve the following:

* teacher written tests such as multiple choice and essay
* discussions within the class as well as in small groups
* teacher and student self-evaluation in terms of desired criteria
* student attentiveness in class (National Council Teachers of Mathematics, 1989).

Based on formative evaluation results, the teacher is better able to assist students where needed. Understanding mathematical concepts is necessary for meaningful leaning. Specific errors may be noticed to help students achieve as optimally as possible. From that point of diagnosis and remediation, each student should be ready to attain the next objective successfully. Being accurate and responsible are needed traits for students to achieve continuously in on ongoing lessons in mathematics. Adequate teacher attention must be given to formative evaluation results to notice the kinds of errors made and to overcome the making of each. Palanivasan (2006), lists the following common causes of errors made by students in mathematics:

* Computation
* Lack of reasoning ability
* Poor procedure or complete absence of a systematic approach
* Difficulty in selecting a procedure
* Failure to comprehend the problem
* Insufficient and ineffective reading skills
* Vocabulary difficulties
* Short attention span
* Inability to select essential data
* Carelessness in reading the data
* Lack of interest
* Prevalence of vague guesswork in an attempt to secure a quick answer.

It is necessary for mathematics teachers to study the kinds of errors students make in order to strengthen teaching and learning situations. Formative evaluation provides opportunities for teachers to make changes in an ongoing unit of study.

Summative evaluation is used to observe end of unit progress of each learner. The teacher needs to notice how much progress each student has made since the beginning of the now completed unit of study. Which changes might the teacher make in teaching this unit to the next encountered group? There will be changes which need to be made to help ensuing students to progress more optimally. This means objectives stressed, the sequence of learning activities in mathematics, problems faced by students, explanations provided by the teacher in diagnosis and remediation, grouping procedures, and the securing of learner attention, among others. The purpose is to get the mathematics unit ready for the next set of students to be taught (See Peressini, 1997).

It is salient for the teacher to use psychological principles of learning appropriately in teaching and learning situations. Thus, each student must perceive:

* purpose in each sequential step of learning. Accepted reasons for working on each problem needs to be in the offing. It is difficult for learners to be serious about purposeless work.
* interest in mathematics problems. If student interest is lacking, the teacher must devise approaches to stimulate learner achievement.
* meaning theory needs to be emphasized continuously. If students do not attach understanding to any specific aspect of study in mathematics, the teacher needs to use a strategy of instruction which assists each student to perceive meaning so that learning makes sense.

The mathematics teacher must be well prepared in teaching subject matter. He/she needs to grow continually in being a professional teacher. Relevant objectives, quality learning activities for students to achieve the stated ends of instruction must be in the offing. Evaluation procedures which are diagnostic need to be used. It is salient to use tenets of educational psychology in teaching and learning situations.

REFERENCES

Ediger, Marlow (1997), *Teaching Mathematics in the Elementary School*. Kirksville, Missouri: Simpson Publishing Company.

Ediger, Marlow, and D.B. Rao (2000), *Teaching Mathematics Successfully*. New Delhi, India: Discovery Publishing House.

Kennedy, Leonard M., and Steve Tipps (1991). *Guiding Children's Learning of Mathematics.* Belmont, California: Wadsworth Publishing Company, 525.

National Council Teachers of Mathematics (1989), *Curriculum and Evaluation Standards for School Mathematics.* Reston, Virginia: National Council Teachers of Mathematics.

Palvanivassan, M. (2006), *Analysis of Errors Committed by Higher Secondary Students in Calculus.* Ph.D. thesis evaluated by the author for the University of Madras, Chennai, India.

Peressini, Dominic (1997), "Parental Reform of Mathematics Education", *The Mathematics Teacher,* 90(6).

Science and Children, October, 2006 "Issue on Measurement", (44 (2), Arlington, Virginia, National Science Teachers Association.

21

Grouping for Instruction in Mathematics

A great deal of work goes into building learning experiences for pre-service teachers of mathematics. This effort involves identifying and sequencing core mathematical tasks and concepts to be explored and investigating instructional strategies and related research on student thinking. It also involves examining technologies and new teaching materials. So teachers can build on their own knowledge of mathematics. It involves planning discussions and practice with mathematical problems ranging from simple to complex. It also involves designing tasks that hone pre-service teachers' skills in listening and noticing, assessment, reflection and lesson design (Grundau *et al.*, 2007). The same skills also need to be in the repertoire of experienced teachers.

In addition, the mathematics teacher needs to study each learner's achievement carefully in order to ascertain which pattern of grouping in teaching/learning should be followed to make for more optimal achievement. There are a plethora of plans for grouping to assist each student to do well in class. The teacher needs to do well in planning when placing learner's into a specific group. The needs of the student need careful consideration.

PLANNING FOR GROUPING

There are times when students may be taught within a whole class setting. When students in the primary grades, for example, are studying sequencing a set of sticks from small to large in ascending order of length, the teacher may first demonstrate, in a meaningful manner, how this is done. Each should be able to clearly see the process involved. Then with the objects on each desk, the learner may arrange the sticks in ascending or descending size as wanted. The teacher may observe how well students individually are progressing. A few students may need additional assistance in ordering the sticks. This may be done until mastery learning has occurred. Hopefully, the class size is small enough to do large group instruction. The writer supervised a university student teacher in which there were thirty three students in a class with inadequate space between the rows to evaluate how weilleamers were doing seat work in a mathematics assignment. Teaching the class as a whole is more difficult, then, unless there is at least one responsible aid to assist students in ordering a set of sticks or other objects (Ediger and Rao, 2000).

As a second method of grouping for instruction, small group work may follow the large class session. Here, students may be grouped, according to identified needs. Thus, if primary grade students experience difficulty in classifying geometrical shapes in terms of squares, rectangles, triangles, rhombuses, and parallelograms, among others, they may receive teacher assistance within the small group. A variation of this approach would be to have peer centered teaching whereby a knowledgeable student assists others who need help in classifying objects.

If the geometrical shapes are made from different colours of construction paper, they may be used in geometrical art work. Thus, each geometrical shape needs to be correctly identified before using it to make persons, animals, buildings, and/or other structures. Geometrical shapes might also then be sorted in terms of colour, size, and thickness if made from diverse kinds of wood.

There are a plethora of learnings accruing from any set of objects for primary age students such as counting, addition, subtraction, multiplication, and division. These may be adapted in terms of what is developmentally appropriate for the learner. Small group work also has implications for stressing good human relations, politeness, and assisting each other when needed (Ediger, 1997).

Third, in an ongoing mathematics/social studies unit of study, a project method may be emphasized. Thus, a set of intermediate grade students might volunteer to do a series of graphs showing population, gross national product, agricultural products, among others items of a given nation or set of nations. These may include bar, picture, line, and/or circle graphs. Each graph needs to be labelled and be done accurately. Graphs should involve inaccuracy in their final form. Inaccuracies need identification and remediation. Graphs in newspapers and news magazines may be distorted to show a biased perspective. These need to be analyzed and discussed. This activity assists students to avoid weaknesses in developing graphic materials. Accurate information, only, should be projected in developing diverse types of graphs.

In working together on a project in graph development, Students need to plan the ensuing graphs carefully. There are a plethora of specifics that go into the making of a picture, bar, line, or circle graph. Each involved student needs to have an engaging role. The plans developed need to be implemented. Evaluation of each graph must be assessed in terms of desired criteria. The following criteria may be used:

* neatness and appeal to viewers. It is good to display each graph for classmate viewing, as well as for other students to see the completed products
* accuracy and possessing direct relationship to the ongoing unit and lessons being studied

* processes being fully implemented including all participating actively in project development with no one dominating others
* time on task being important with digressions minimized (See Parker, 2001).

Project members need to be able to explain each graph succinctly to classmates and visitors with the display drawing attention to the project.

Fourth, learning stations may be used as enrichment experiences and involve a procedure used in grouping students. Each center needs to possess purposeful mathematics tasks for learners. Approximately, four tasks need to be neatly typed on a task card for each center. The number of centers may vary and be as few as one or two. Students may choose which sequential tasks to complete voluntarily. Materials for completing each task need to be available at each center. Completed work needs to be handed in to the mathematics teacher for evaluation.

Since each student self-selects sequential tasks to complete, developmentally appropriate tasks are generally chosen. Enrichment experiences, here, challenge and extend mathematical knowledge and skills on each students ability level. Extra work needs to be available in mathematics for those who are motivated learners. Tasks involve individual endeavours as well as small group choices as learning activities (Shepherd and Ragan, 1982).

Fifth, homogeneous grouping may be used with a particular purpose in mind. Thus, a set of identified sixth graders may need additional assistance in understanding division using a two place divisor with a remainder in the quotient. Understanding of the problem must be in evidence when using these abstract numerals such as providing a practical situation whereby there are 725 oranges, for example, representing the dividend. Twenty four oranges are to go into each sack. The 24 represents the divisor. Following through with a meaningful discussion and computation, there would be thirty sacks of oranges with five as a remainder.

Homogeneous groups may be used when diagnosing a mathematical problem whereby students having a similar difficulty and may benefit from remedial work. Students then need to understand indepth what is involved in dividing a certain number of oranges (dividend) by a divisor (oranges per sack), resulting in a quotient (the number of sacks of oranges) and a remainder in this case.

Homogeneous groups may also be used in introducing a new process in mathematics to a somewhat uniform group of learners.

Sixth, lessons might well be taught, in many cases, in heterogeneous groups. Large group instruction, such as in team teaching, may use selected basal textbooks in teaching and learning situations. The basal might then be used as a point of departure for the total group. If fifth grade students, for example, are studying how to determine the perimeter of a selected geometric figure, such as a parallelogram, the teacher may first show for review purposes a square and a rectangle, both large enough for all to see clearly, asking how the distance around the square and the rectangle are determined. With a measurement instrument, students may measure to ascertain the perimeter of each geometrical figure. The formula for ascertaining the perimeter of each may be discussed. Now, previously acquired knowledge may be applied to the determination of the perimeter of the parallelogram. A large parallelogram, made of construction paper, may be held up for clarity in viewing. Now, there will be several hypotheses in determining its perimeter. The formula for finding its perimeter may then be discussed (2L + 2W). Students need to perceive relationships between the old and the new learnings. Application of each acquired concept needs to be practiced in abstract and in practical situations. With the use of visual aids, heterogeneously grouped students may be taught concepts meaningfully and in an interesting manner.

From the large group session, committees may be formed to discuss and elaborate on what was presented in the large group session. With opportunities to interact with peers, students may reflect upon and analyze difficulties in understanding the new learnings. In a committee, students feel more free to participate as compared to the larger group. Meaning needs to be attached to facts, concepts, and generalizations achieved in mathematics (See, National Council Teachers of Mathematics, 1989).

Seventh, a contract system may be used. A student may desire to complete an agreement whereby certain tasks in mathematics are fulfilled. Extras credit may be given for successful completion of the contract. The agreement lists specific items to be completed and is signed by both student and teacher with a listed due date.

Seven methods of grouping students for instructional purposes were discussed. Each plan may be used profitably in selected situations. The purpose of grouping students is to improve teaching and learning. Mathematics teachers need to be open to ascertaining additional approaches. Each lesson taught is vital to sequence new leanings in order to scaffold to higher levels of successful student progress.

REFERENCES

Ediger, Marlow (1997), *Teaching Mathematics in the Elementary School*. Kirksville Missouri: Simpson Publishing Company.

Ediger, Marlow, and D. Bhaskara Rao (2000), *Teaching Mathematics Successfully*. New Delhi, India: Discovery Publishing House.

Grandau, et. al. (2007), "On Location - Using School Classrooms as Sites for Preparing Teachers of Mathematics", Phi Delta Kappan, 88 (9), 686-690.

National Council Teachers of Mathematics (1989), *Curriculum and Evaluation Standards for School Mathematics*. Reston, Virginia: NCTM.

Parker, Walter (2001), *Social Studies in Elementary Education*. Eleventh Edition. Upper Saddle River, New Jersey: Merrill, Prentice Hall.

Shepherd, Gene, and William Ragan (1982), *Modern Elementary Curriculum*. New York: Holt, Rinehart and Winston.

22

Student Purpose in Mathematics Achievement

A very important factor in student learning is perceived purpose. Students then need to understand reasons for pursuing what is being taught. If they believe that what is being studied is busy work or unimportant, learner achievement will tend to go downhill. It behooves the mathematics teacher to assist students to realize that lessons and units of study have purpose. Establishing purpose for each lesson may not take long. The teacher may state the purpose clearly to primary grade pupils, such as, "The reason for studying subtraction is that you will want to know how much of allowance money is left if certain items are bought." Language used here must be developmentally appropriate and the example being used is relevant. The example can be clearly demonstrated with coins or other concrete objects. It becomes increasingly difficult to develop purpose within older students with the goal being to ascertain the area of a circle, for example, and why the computation is used in the teacher devised demonstration. Concrete and semi-concrete materials should be used for meaningful learning. Purpose in learning here is indicated by looking at illustrations of circular drives and circular windows in buildings. The circles here take up space and the area must be ascertained to secure correct window size as well as materials necessary for completing a circular drive.

PURPOSEFUL EXPERIENCES

Purposeful experiences emphasize what is relevant to the involved learner. Relevancy means that subject matter in mathematics is useful in school and in society. Thus, for example, counting experiences for young children may stress the following purposeful activities:

* counting the number of children who want milk today in the school milk program
* counting the raised hands for those wanting menu one, two, or three in school lunches at noon
* counting the number of children seated in each row in the classroom
* counting the number of plates, plastic utensils, and cups for four children in a role playing activity seated at the kitchen center

Creative teachers use every day lifelike experiences to involve children in mathematical activities. These experiences are seized upon as the necessary situation arises. With practical uses for counting, the child's growth in enumeration provides situations for sequential growth. It also makes children more aware of relevant uses in mathematics. They love to count objects intrinsically when opportunities arise. Each experience provides occasions for increasingly more complex uses of number. Thus, seeing the abstract numeral for each ordered set of objects might well bring in addition as in joining two sets together to make for one set, 3 plus 2 equals 5, or subtraction with $5–2 = 3$ as well as $5 - 3 = 2$. The commutative property for addition is learned as well as subtraction undoing addition. Perceiving purpose in number relationships is highly important. With quality sequence, the learner is able to perceive purpose in increasingly complex uses of number in mathematics (Ediger, 2006).

INTEREST FACTORS AND RELEVANCY

Interest is a powerful ingredient in achievement. With developed interest, the student is able to hurdle more complex learnings. If interest is not there to begin instruction in a new process, the teacher must develop it within learners. There are several ways of doing this, such as:

* varying the kinds of materials used involving concrete (using objects and items), semi-concrete (illustrations, drawings, graphic items, pictorial representations, and diverse charts), and abstract materials as in (mathematical symbols, numerals, as well as textbook content.
* varying the methodologies used in instruction (using implicit, explicit, guided practice, learning by discovery, authentic learning, and demonstrations).

The human voice is a powerful means of expressing facts, concepts, and generalizations in mathematics. It can be modulated to engage students in learning. Words may be pitched higher or lower, as well as varied pauses between words and sentences might well be used for effective teaching. Stress of words may also be varied for improved communication. Thus, stressing a word more than others might help students to realize what is salient in a given learning experience.

Mediated action provides a learner with relevant tools of instruction. Thus, the teacher assists students to use cultural tools such as a compass, protractor, ruler, number line, and technology, among others, to find solutions to problems. Interactive means of learning, here, are important (Wertsch, 1998). Students grow more proficient in learning as they use what has been initially acquired. Adult assistance is needed in mediation between the learner and the cultural tool.

Vygotsky (1934/78), believed strongly that ideas are mediated within a group. As subject matter is discussed and analyzed, it is synthesized and becomes more meaningful through interaction with others. There are diverse procedures involved in arranging a discussion as in understanding a new process in mathematics. Dyads, committees, small groups, and the class as a whole, for example, might then discuss finding the volume of a cylinder by using what has been learned previously. The background information acquired previously will then be used to ascertain volume in a purposeful activity. With interaction between and among learners occurs, modification of ideas occurs with critical and creative thinking in a problem solving situation. Mediation is a salient concept in these interactions.

Quality oral communication skills assist in presenting ideas clearly. They are developed sequentially in group settings. In an atmosphere of respect, students feel free to present needed ideas. Communication skills in securing ideas may also come from abstract, written materials in print. Thus, reading of mathematical content becomes important. In a specific reading experience from the basal textbook, the teacher may determine the purpose, after readiness has been established, in saying "Lets read to find out how to determine the area of a right triangle." Or, "Lets read to determine the meaning of a rhombus." It is good if students raise a question and then reading is done to secure an answer. The purpose then is student centered. The latter approach increases student perceived purpose (Ediger and Rao, 2007).

REFERENCES

Ediger, Marlow (2005), "Teaching Mathematics in the High Setting", *College Student Journal*, 39 (4), 711-715.

Ediger, Marlow (2006), "Writing in the Mathematics Curriculum", *Journal of Instructional Psychology*, 33 (1), 120-123.

Ediger, Marlow, and D. Bhaskara Rao (2007), *Reading Curriculum and Instruction*. New Delhi, India: Discovery Publishing House, Chapter Six.

Vygotsky, L.S. (1934/1978). *Mind in Society: The Development of Psychological Processes*. Cambridge, Massachusetts: Harvard University Press.

Wertch, J.V. (1998), *Mind as Action*. New York: Oxford University Press.

23

Guidelines to Follow in Teaching Mathematics

There are selected guidelines which mathematics teachers need to follow in the instructional arena. When implementing each guideline, students should be able to optimize achievement. Teaching the learner should be the focal point of instruction and learning situations. Mathematics teachers need to survey recent literature and research studies to determine how pupils can be assisted to attain as well as possible with the use of a variety of rich experiences in the curriculum. Experiences should assist in providing for individual differences in the curriculum among students (Ediger and Rao, 2000).

TEACHING MATHEMATICS IN THE SCHOOL SETTING

A variety of learning opportunities need to be available to pupils in the school setting. Variety is needed in order to develop and maintain student interest in mathematics. Students differ from each other in a plethora of ways. Some learn more from concrete objects while others prefer pictorial forms of learning while still other prefer the abstract. Generally, most students learn sequentially from the concrete to the semi-concrete, and then the abstract. What is salient is that all attain as much in mathematics as they can. Among others, students then need to make ordered progress in understanding:

* numbers and numeration
* addition and subtraction
* multiplication and division
* informal and formal geometry
* fractional numbers such as in common fractions, as well as fractional numbers expressed as decimals and per cents
* measurement concepts
* basic learnings in statistics such as in adequate emphasis placed on tables, graphs, and measures of central tendency (See Kennedy and Tipps. 1999).

Mathematics teachers need to understand diverse philosophies to be used in teaching. One philosophy emphasizes identifying and stressing the basics in mathematics. A carefully chosen textbook might well emphasize the basics in the curriculum. The scope and sequence of subject matter to be learned indicates essentials which students should attain. A related Manual accompanies the mathematics textbook. The involved committee in textbook selection should be comprised of highly knowledgeable instructors who are competent in identifying basic subject matter. Generally, reputable companies send to textbook committee members examination copies to evaluate as well as appraise their individual scope and sequence charts. Adequate, scheduled time needs to be given for committee members to make a selection on which text best stresses students learning basic mathematical subject matter.

A second philosophy emphasizes mandated objectives for student attainment. These objectives developed on the state level of instruction might also be viewed as the basics, however decisions made here are on the state rather than the local level.

With carefully followed mandated objectives, mathematics teachers align learning opportunities with the stated objectives. Here, states need to have clearly written objectives which teachers may use in choosing aligned experiences and activities for students. Then too, mandated assessments measure if the objectives have/have not been attained.

A third plan of instruction emphasizes a learning stations approach, in part or whole. For example, there may be six to seven stations set up in a classroom with five tasks at each station. Tasks, listed on a card, to be selected by students may stress individual or small group experiences. They need to be challenging, but achievable.

The above listed philosophies might well be integrated. Thus, to achieve mandated objectives, a basics approach may be used together with a learning stations procedure to achieve vital objectives of instruction. Philosophies do interact and may not be completely separate entities (Ediger, 2005).

The psychology of learning stresses how each philosophical school of thought is to be implemented. Thus, learning activities need to be implemented by using the following criteria in teaching and learning situations:

* learning experiences need to be engaging. Students then ideally are wholeheartedly involved in ongoing mathematical learning activities. Actively engaged learners, not passive recipients of knowledge, is to be encouraged.
* interesting activities which are goal centered need to be in the offing. Routine activities need to be changed to a variety of experiences which motivate achievement.
* learning should possess purpose. Thus, there are reasons for achieving which are acceptable to the learner.
* problem solving, rather than rote learning must be emphasized, in the mathematics curriculum. Problems solving is useful and stresses higher levels of cognition including critical and creative thinking.

* meaning in achieving must be in the offing. With meaning, students understand what is taught and what is taught possesses value to the learner.

* assisting the student to connect himself/herself to the subject matter being studied as well as connecting the self to the environment and to others is indeed salient! Too frequently, the student feels separated from different categories in the school/community setting. Thus, school and society should be integrated, not isolated entities (See Zimmerman, 1989).

By following the above named standards, the mathematics teacher might well optimize learner progress. The sequence being followed in mathematics should include continued progress in increasingly complex fields of mathematical learnings. Students need to attach meaning and understanding in what is being learned. Interest in achieving is always to be emphasized. Also, to optimize achievement, the mathematic teacher needs to group students whereby they achieve objectives of instruction. Diverse methods of grouping might then be stressed. Heterogeneous group may be the best at times. At other times, homogeneous grouping should be used. Students, too, should have opportunities to select what to learn when choosing ordered tasks from a mathematics learning center. There are definite purposes involved in grouping for instruction. Among others, the following are salient:

* to assist pupils to interact with each other in solving problems in mathematics

* to emphasize social development in being able to work harmoniously with peers

* to develop improved attitudes toward mathematics through peer interaction

* to cut down on behavioural problems which hinder growth and progress

* to develop achievement in learning the fundamentals in mathematics while studying cooperatively.

EVALUATION OF ACHIEVEMENT

There are common methods of assessing learner achievement and progress in mathematics. These include mandated tests, district wide and teacher written tests, teacher observation of student daily work in mathematics, anecdotal records, diary and log entries. In using diverse evaluation techniques, the mathematics teacher obtains a broad range of feedback from students in guiding each to achieve as well as possible. Guskey, et. al (2006) in writing about literacy assessment in New Zealand stress the importance of seeing literacy comprising skills in reading, speaking, writing, listening, viewing, and presenting with the following objectives, useful, too, in guiding/assessing achievement in mathematics (according to the writer):

* One-to-one interviews, in which students work with the teacher and students responses are recorded on video tape.
* Stations where four students work independently, rotating among a set of tasks, some of which are computer based.
* Teams, in which four groups of students work collaboratively on tasks supervised by the teacher, with their interactions video taped.
* Independently, in which students work individually, completing paper and pencil tasks, creating works of art or performing physical tasks, with their performance video taped.

REFERENCES

Ediger, Marlow (2005), "Present Day Philosophies of Education", *Journal of Instructional Psychology*, 33 (3), 179-182.

Ediger, Marlow, and D. Bhaskara Rao (2000), *Teaching Mathematics Successfully*. New Delhi, India: Discovery Publishing House, Chapters One and Two.

Guskey, Thomas R. *et al*. (2006), "Literacy Assessment New Zealand Style", *Educational Leadership* 64 (2), 76.

Kennedy, Leonard M., and Steve Tipps (1999), *Guiding Children's Learning of Mathematics*. Belmont, CA: Wadsworth Publishing Company, 3-20.

Zimmerman, B.J. (1989), "A Social Cognitive View of Self Regulated Academic Learning", *Journal of Educational Psychology*, 81, 329-339.

24

Attitudinal Development in Mathematics

Having proper attitudes toward mathematics is important in achieving objectives of instruction. The attitudinal dimension needs strong emphasis in ongoing lessons and units of study. Generally, cognitive objectives receive the most attention by mathematics teachers. This is salient; however, having good attitudes, also, help to increase achievement in securing relevant facts, concepts, and generalizations in mathematics. What might the teacher do to assist pupils to do well in attitudes?

THE PUPIL, QUALITY ATTITUDES, AND MATHEMATICS

Learners need to develop an adequate self-concept. The feeling needs to be that cach one can do well in mathematics. How the pupil feels about his/her self in regards to achieving objectives is important. The pupil needs to feel positively about himself/herself engaged in daily work in mathematics learning activities. Being able to lean upon the self and ask for assistance when needed are necessary ingredients for success in mathematics. Confidence in one's thinking and doing helps to insure for success. The teacher can help here by providing a developmentally appropriate curriculum.

The mathematics teacher must ascertain the preset achievement level of each pupil. Teacher observation with the use of quality criteria may assist in ascertain the starting point of instruction. The pupils then needs to be successful in doing in these initial experiences, but must feel challenge, also. There should be reasonable expectations for a challenging mathematics curriculum. If an objective appears to be too difficult, then the teacher must guide the learner to fill the gap between where the pupil is presently in achievement and the objective to be acquired. This needs to be done with sequential learning activities.

Careful teacher observation of learner progress is needed so that learning activities selected assist pupils to make continuous progress. Observations made from pupil feedback will provide the teacher with information on which are developmentally appropriate experiences for pupils. Good teacher written test items, too, may appraise the present sequential progress of learners. These tests need to be valid in that what has been taught is tested. They should not test other areas of knowledge which have not be taught. Reliability is salient in testing in that a test should measure consistently for pupils. Split half reliability may be used by all teachers to notice if a test measures consistently. What good is a test if a pupil's results vary much in split half reliability? The latter notices within a pupil's test results if the even numbered versus the odd numbered test items measure consistently and correlate well. The reader needs to consult a testing and measurement university textbook to notice standards in writing quality teacher written test items as well as how to determine reliability as well as validity in test writing. It is also appropriate to diagnose pupil difficulties in ensuing lessons to detect errors made by pupils so that corrections may be made. Practicing what is incorrect confounds the routine behaviour of making mistakes in every day mathematical work. Reteaching may be necessary after diagnosis of errors made. Good evaluation techniques used in assessing pupil achievement should result in procedures available to assist pupils in developing a good self-concept. Thus, the teacher needs to provide developmentally appropriate lessons so that the learner makes continuous progress in mathematics. With success in learning, the pupil has opportunities in developing a positive self-concept (Ediger and Rao, 2000).

Motivation in mathematical learning must be fostered. Through teacher observation, he/she may notice which types of activities engage learners. Selected pupils require experiences which emphasize the concrete phase of learning, such as objects and items used in teaching. Others prefer, the semi-concrete such as the use of pictures, computer programs, illustrations, study prints, drawings, diagrams, graphs, and charts. Still others may prefer the abstract phase of instruction as in reading, writing, listening, and speaking experiences. Generally, instruction should follow the concrete, semi-concrete, and abstract phases in sequence. However, pupils do possess different styles of learning and provisions need to be made to accommodate learners as much as possible (Ediger, 2005).

Methods used in teaching may provide for additional motivation needs of pupils. Interesting procedures include brainstorming. This is an inductive method. Here, pupils may pool information on how to solve a new problem, listed on the chalkboard. Procedures emphasized by pupils should not duplicate those already given. Learners should not interrupt each other when responding. Politeness and acceptance of each other should be in evidence. With ideas circulating among pupils, there should be an end result in understanding inherent subject matter when arriving at a solution. Ideas are presented in a group setting with each pupil's contributions building upon the thinking of others. Attitudinal development is positive when pupils are energized in suggesting possible solutions. It also is developed when pupils are learning from each other in a high quality learning environment. Answers given are not ridiculed or minimized, but accepted as having worth from each participant (See Searson and Dunn, 2001).

Anxiety toward mathematics comes about when the following are in evidence:

* an extremely difficult and complex curriculum

* peers and teachers are critical of answers given by a student

* a lack of acceptance by other pupils as well as of the teacher.

There needs to be a healthy level of anxiety in order to do well in life, but the tendency is for pupils to be overly anxious to avoid failure. Anxiety can be reduced by emphasizing a positive school climate for learning. Stressing competition excessively in a "dog eat dog" environment leaves too many learners out of the mainstream in which they cannot compete against the more gifted and talented. Each pupil generally has talents to contribute, but they may not be equal to the competition involved. Regardless of ability levels, pupils, individually, must achieve as much as possible and in an optimal manner. Individual differences might be provided for through using developmentally appropriate materials of instruction (Savithiri, (2006).

Negative attitudes restrict learner achievement and progress, whereas positive attitudes assist in pupils liking mathematics and being enthused in achieving ensuing objectives. Mathematics teachers tend to find teaching more enjoyable when pupils attend to the task at hand and are fully immersed in achieving. Further results of pupils having good attitudes toward learning include:

* fewer distractions in learning

* reduction in discipline problems

* lower rate of pupil failures in mathematics and other curriculum areas

* life being more enjoyable and adequate pupil progress provides for increased teacher satisfaction as a professional.

Pupils understanding what is taught is important in attitudinal development. Negative attitudes accrue as a result of meaningless learnings. Pupils then do not attach meaning to the subject matter being stressed within an ensuing objective. Moving on to more complex learnings at a time when a lack of understanding the current objectives being stressed is defeating to the learner. Mastering the mathematical subject matter presently being taught is necessary in order to understand the new content.

Definite provisions need to be made for those learners who excel in mathematics. To do otherwise is not providing for individual differences among pupils. Multiple intelligences theory (Gardner, 1993) emphasizes mathematics as being one of ten theories of intelligence. Then too, on state mandated tests, mathematics is one of three required areas of testing. The later indicates the need for all pupils to be able to solve mathematical problems. The best way to do this is to begin pupils at their present starting entry level of achievement and then assist each to experience continuous progress. Mediated learning experiences are necessary for selected pupils in order to achieve objectives of instruction. The mediation tools include using tools to experience success. These tools include place value and fraction charts, number lines, compasses, protractors, objects for counting and used in performing the four basic operations on number, hand held calculators, graphic materials, audio-visual aids, as well as software computer access (Sivakumar and Ponraj, 2007). They provide learnings and activities which assist in goal attainment. Mediation tools help pupils then to understand learnings involving problem solving, abstract thinking, mathematical computation, as well as reading comprehension of word problems. Meaningful experiences must be in the offing. Meaningful learning and quality attitudes are definitely related.

REFLECTIVE THINKING

Reflective thinking stresses such items as pupils rehearsing what has been achieved and how the achievement took place. Pupils then are assisted in evaluating their own progress in mathematics. They are guided in understanding and overcoming the kinds and types of errors made, such as in computation. Perhaps, the basics are not understood in performing four basic operations on number. It might be that pupils do not understand the reasons for reducing fractions to their lowest terms. It might not make sense to the learner why the length times the width is multiplied to ascertain the area of a rectangle. Here, the teacher needs to provide meaning and understanding as to why formulas are followed.

Reflecting upon how a word problem was solved and thinking of improved and refined methods of processes used provides the learner with a structure to do better in subject matter achievement and in methods of doing things. If reading is a problem here, the pupil needs to monitor why comprehension is a problem. Assistance then is easier to provide such as in the following kinds of difficulties in reading:

* use of phonics, particularly in initial consonants, to identify words
* use of context clues whereby words supplied by the learner for those not known must make sense with other surrounding words within the sentence/ paragraph
* use of syllabication clues. Sometimes by knowing a few commonly used prefixes and suffixes, the pupil may identify what otherwise appears to be a completely new word (Ediger, 2007).

Then too, with word/story problems, pupils may have difficulties in reasoning as well as in critical thinking. Rehearsing the steps involved in this engagement helps pupils to realize what went wrong in solving a previous word problem. Pupils then may reflect upon which techniques and approaches worked. Reflection is a wise procedure to use when pupils relate previous with new learnings. Perceiving relationships means that pupils do not perceive things in isolation, but as being connected. Pupil attitudes improve when reflective thinking helps in retention of learning as well as providing readiness for achieving ensuing objectives of instruction.

Pupils also are helped in planning and managing to complete school work satisfactorily on a daily basis. Self-monitoring should be the goal to attain. Too frequently when a pupil fails to complete assignments, he/she does not get to work on time or wastes time when the assignment is given. The writer's grandson felt he had too much homework, until it was reported by his teacher that he wasted much time in school. Following the parent/teacher conference, the grandson completed all his assignments during the school day, and he was much happier in his school work and at home. Parents and teachers need to work together for the good of the child. The grandson learned to plan effective time on task habits and his attitudes improved in academic learnings. Polite settings in parent-teacher conferences must be the order of the day (See Kennedy, 2006) .

SETTING CHALLENGING, REALISTIC GOALS IS SALIENT FOR EACH PERSON

These positive goals provide motivation for their achievement. Pupils need to develop trust in their own thinking for attainment. The mathematics teacher steps in, as needed, to offer assistance and guidance. Intrinsically, pupils ultimately become more proficient in doing mathematics. It is best if intrinsic, rather than extrinsic motivation, is being stressed; however extrinsic motivation cannot be ruled out, especially if the rewards are non-physical. Thus, the following may be used as verbal non-physical extrinsic motivators, for work done well in mathematics: That's fine; that's dandy work; I like they way you put forth effort; keep it up; and I know you can do that problem. Rewards should be given:

* judiciously and not overdone
* for quality effort and work done, not as lavish flattery
* to assist pupils to achieve well, and not for the sake of doing so
* to encourage learning and to make sequential progress
* for rewarding good behaviour (See Simpllico, 2002).

When should physical prizes be given to motivate learners to achieve? When supervising a university student teacher in a small rural school, which was a part of a larger administrative unit, the policy was to use extrinsic motivation practices to encourage learning. Here, the student teacher and the cooperating teacher frequently used a rubber stamp of different images to imprint upon pupil school work. Thus, for example, for each item done correctly in a work book exercise, a rubber stamp was used, and in the involved month, the image of Santa Clause was imprinted. The imprint was visible and clear. Generally, the page was filled with "Santa Clauses". Pupils were truly engaged and doing accurate computations. How could thirteen pupils in the classroom be rewarded that frequently? There were two teachers, the student teacher and the cooperating teacher, ready to stamp a Santa Claus for each correct response. Will this work as a long-term method of extrinsic motivation? Probably not, but methods of teaching need to be changed regardless if intrinsic or extrinsic motivation is used to encourage mathematical achievement. The writer prefers to stress the use of intrinsic motivation to encourage pupil learning. However, it is up to the judgement of the teacher as to which is a positive procedure in guiding optimal pupil mathematical attainment. Pupils must come to realize that not all of life's endeavours will stress positive reinforcement.

CONCLUSION

When developing quality attitudes within pupils and within the teacher, the concept "self efficacy" is important. Self efficacy is based upon having acquired important subject matter knowledge as well as necessary skills. The knowledge and skills are used situationally as in teaching and learning mathematics in the classroom setting. Confidence is then developed within the individual of being able to do well in the instructional arena of mathematics. Self-efficacy then emphasizes how well one's thinking is in performing appropriately in different situations. How individuals think, feel, motivate themselves, and behave, stresses self-efficacy (See Swars, 2005).

REFERENCES

Ediger, Marlow (2005), "Teaching Mathematics in the School Setting", *College Student Journal*, 39 (4), 711-715.

Ediger, Marlow (2007), "The Substitute Teacher in Reading Instruction", *Sub-Journal, for Personnel Responsible for Substitute Teaching*, 8(2), 67-73.

Ediger, Marlow, and D. Bhaskara Rao (2000), *Teaching Mathematics Successfully*. New Delhi, India: Discovery Publishing House.

Gardner, Howard (1993), *Multiple Intelligences; Theory Into Practice*. New York: Basic Books.

Kennedy, Mary (2006), "From Teacher Quality to Quality Teaching", *Educational Leadership*, 63(6), 14-19.

Searson, Robert, and Rita Dunn (2001), "The Learning Styles Teaching Model", *Science and Children*, 38(5), 22-36.

Savithiri, V. (2006), "Impact of Metacognitve Strategies in Enhancing Perceptual Skills Among High School Students on Learning Geometry". Ph.D. theses from Alagappa University, India, evaluated by the writer.

Sivakumar and Ponraj (2007), "Information Technology in Education", *Edutracks*, 7(4), 17-19.

Simpllico, Joseph (2002), "Miscommunication in the Classroom, What Teachers Say and What Students Really Hear", *Education*, 122(3), 599-601, 478.

Swars, Susan Lee (2005), "Examining Perceptions of Mathematics Teaching Effectiveness Among Preservice Teachers with Different Levels of Mathematics Teacher Efficacy", *Journal of Instructional Psychology*, 32 (2), 139-147.

25

Student Interest in Mathematics Achievement

Interest is a powerful factor in teaching and learning situations. With an interesting environment, learning seems to propel its very own development. Students then do more work/study in an academic area due to intrinsic motivation. Interest increases energy levels for achieving. It sets higher levels for achieving objectives in ongoing lessons/units of study as well as in society. Teachers have long struggled with how to interest pupils in the curriculum. This purpose in this writing emphasizes securing learner interest in mathematics.

STUDENT INTEREST IN MATHEMATICS

Young children appear to have a plethora of interests in the pre-school years. They see many scenes and sights which propel learning in its diverse forms. Thus, a puddle of water has its fascination for wading and splashing. Intrinsically, interest is there to explore and to marvel. Then too, preschoolers like to hold up the number of fingers they believe make for their present age level, even though the number of fingers shown may be incorrect. How might these kinds of interests be motivated to academic learnings, particularly mathematics.

Whatever is taught in mathematics, the teacher needs to attempt to secure learner interests. Otherwise, achievement may be at a minimal level. Sometimes, the objectives may seem trivial to the student. Relevant objectives then need to be carefully selected. These salient objectives need to be challenging, but achievable. The mathematics teacher may assist students to achieve, what initially appears to be too complex, with the use of scaffolding. Here, the teacher senses the gap between where a student is presently in achievement with some ideal to be attained. The ideal might then be accomplished by scaffolding, that is assisting the learner in small steps to reach the terminal objective. Through careful sequencing, the student may then achieve more complex objectives. Scaffolding might wisely be used to close gaps from where the student is now to a challenging goal. The gap should not be too great, but reasonable enough to make for a challenging closure (See Kennedy, 2006).

Readiness for learning is a very important factor in assisting learner progress in mathematics. Interest in learning may go downhill due to struggling with the unknown. Background information then needs to be in the offing for a student to achieve an ensuing objective. Frequently, students experience failure in goal attainment due to lacking necessary facts, concepts, and generalizations to be successful in achievement. A variety of learning activities should be provided so that adequate related knowledge exists in the student's repertoire to understand the new learnings. The readiness concept is very valuable in teaching mathematics since a lack of prerequisite subject matter may hinder student achievement. In the history of education, Johann Friedrich Herbart (1776-1841) stressed student interest as being a major outcome of education and advocated the following ordered steps in teaching:

* preparation (getting pupils ready for learning)
* presentation (teaching the new subject matter)
* association (relating the new ideas taught to those previously presented)

* generalization (drawing a conclusion of ideas gained)

* use of what had been taught (Ediger and Rao 2002).

The very first step of teaching, according to Herbart, was preparation or readiness. This is as important presently as it ever has been. The concept "preparation" has changed to other terms which indicate providing background information in order for students to benefit from the new learnings to be introduced, which Herbart termed "presentation". New subject matter to be acquired needs to be related directly to previous learnings. This involves quality order. David Ausubel (1963), American educational psychologist, used the term "sequence" when teachers assist students to hurdle this gap. He stated that good teaching always stressed for teachers to ascertain where students are presently in achievement and then with good sequence they can take care of this gap in reasonable manner. This makes for success in student learning. Interest in mathematics flourishes when success in learning is experienced. The sequencing here is in larger steps than when scaffolding is used as an instructional technique.

Meaning accrues when students understand the ensuing facts, concepts, and generalizations in mathematics. Students tend to like high expectations desired by the teacher. However, the new ideas gleaned must be understood and meaning attached. Students who do not understand the new learnings tend to lose out more and more in ensuing lessons and units in mathematics. From the very beginning in kindergarden, pupils need to understand counting objects, addition of sets, among other mathematical concepts, so they can build on the known to attach meaning to what becomes new learnings. Interest comes about through meaningful experiences (Ediger and Rao, 2003).

A variety of experiences to achieve objectives need to be in the offing to assist student learning. These need to be engaging and interesting. The student who lacks interest in mathematics is bound to underachieve. The mathematics teacher must observe learners carefully to notice those who attend as compared to those who are not concentrating on the task at hand. Three categories of learning activities are the concrete, the semi-concrete, and the abstract. With the concrete, actual objects are used such as in counting, addition, subtraction, multiplication, and division. Semi-concrete include such items as ordered illustrations indicating a certain number of members in a set; place value charts to show regrouping and renaming in addition and subtraction; number lines; as well as line, bar, picture, and circle graphs; tables, figures, and charts. The abstract consists of word/story problems, practice with number pairs to compute the four basic operations, and basal textbook content, among others (See, Halawah, 2006).

A variety of methods should be used with the three categories of learning activities listed above. These include:

* induction with rather heavy emphasis placed upon learners responding indepth to questions from the mathematics teacher as well as from peers.

* deduction with stress placed upon demonstrations, given by the teacher, followed by questions with responses from students pertaining to what was learned.

* problem solving including stating the problem, gathering information, developing an hypothesis, followed by evaluation of the hypothesis.

* project methods involving the individual student, committees, peer teaching/demonstrations, and learning center experiences (See Smith *et al.*, 2006).

* integrated mathematical experiences involving art (using and naming geometrical figures to develop a picture), science (using numerals in developmentally appropriate formulas in chemistry), and social studies (as in showing population figures of a nation being studied or elevation features on a student drawn map).

As a student centered method of teaching which encourages interests of pupils in learning is a constructivist philosophy of education. Constructivism emphasizes the following tenets in the curriculum:

* absolute knowledge, in many cases, is not possible; however pupils come closer and closer to reality with problem solving.
* knowledge is tentative and subject to change.
* knowledge becomes valuable if it is subject to evaluation in ongoing learning activities.
* knowledge is not learned for its own sake, but must be used in contextual situations.
* knowledge is sequenced by the student, not by others.
* knowledge and skills are interrelated, not learned separately; they are useful in school and in society (Ediger, 2006).

REFERENCES

Ausubel, David (1963), "The Psychology of Meaningful Learning," New York: Grune and Stratton.

Ediger, Marlow (2006), "Testing Versus Portfolios to Assess Achievement," *OASCD Journal*, 13 (1) 31-32.

Ediger, Marlow, and D. Bhaskara Rao (2003), *Psychology and Curriculum*. New Delhi, India: Discovery Publishing House.

Ediger, Marlow, and D. Bhaskara Rao (2002), *Philosophy and Curriculum*. New Delhi, India: Discovery Publishing House.

Halawah, Ibtesam (2006), "The Effect of Motivation, Family Environment, and Student Characteristics on Student Achievement," *Journal of Instructional Psychology*, 33 (2), 91-99.

Kennedy, Mary M. (2006), "From Teacher Quality to Quality Teaching," *Educational Leadership*, 63 (6), 14-19.

Smith, Lorraine A., *et al*., "Activities that Really Measure Up," *Science and Children,* 44 (2), 30-33.

26

Teacher Observation to Evaluate Mathematics Achievement

There are a plethora of assessment techniques to use in the evaluation of student achievement in mathematics. Each has its pros and cons; however, selected methods of assessment do a more comprehensive job than do others. Too frequently, mandated tests provide most of the emphasis on evaluation in educational literature. And yet, the most frequently used procedure needs to be teacher observation. Teacher observation may be used continuously in the classroom. Immediately, the teacher may diagnose and remedy a difficulty faced in mathematics by one or more students at their desks. Mandated tests are given once a year and then in selected grade levels. Also, feedback from these tests are not adequate to provide information on specific errors made by learners to be used for remedial purposes. How might teacher observation of students help in teaching and learning situations?

ASSESSING MATHEMATICAL PROGRESS

Each teacher of mathematics must have a good knowledge of subject matter as well as of teaching methodology to do quality work in observing learner progress. They need to be upper most in the teacher's mind when observing. Alert minds are necessary in the observation process. Which characteristics of student behaviour need to be noticed by the teacher in the observational process?

* is the student on task and engaged in learning?
* does the learner show interest, not boredom, in mathematics?
* what specifically does the student not understand in an ongoing activity?
* how might this student best understand how to remedy the deficiency?
* what do individual learners need as background information in order to attach meaning to the ensuing learning experience?
* does the learning style of the student favour individual or cooperative endeavours?
* do students reflect upon past mathematical experiences?

Assignments in mathematics need to make provision for individual differences. Students are of different ability and interest levels and need to make sequential progress. The mathematics teacher may notice if a sequence is not working when students fail to make continuous progress in the curriculum. The assignments need to be clear and relevant. Adequate prerequisite information must precede each new process being emphasized. There is a zone of proximal development (Vygotsky, 1986) for each student; thus, the student has a present achievement level, for example in adding negative numbers and the ensuing learnings require their multiplication. The gap is reasonable in being ameliorated. In small steps with meaningful experiences, the teacher can assist the learner to realize what was intended. Vygotsky (1986) also stressed the importance of students mediating experiences through language such as discussions in large and small group sessions. This might, too, involve peer mediated discussion groups.

Teacher observation of student participation in discussions should include the following:

* meaningful mathematical learnings are being developed
* observing that all participate, but no one dominates the activity
* ideas circulate among the participants
* enthusiasm for learning is in evidence
* ideas are being expressed with clarity
* indepth discussions are being stressed
* optimal achievement is a focal point for each student (Ediger and Rao, 2001).

What might a mathematics teacher observe specifically about "meaningful mathematical learnings are being developed," listed at the top of the enumerated items? What is accomplished must make sense to the student. Thus, if a student is unable to come up with the correct answer to a set of three two place numerals with carrying, what might be some possibilities for error? The teacher needs to evaluate if the learner understands the concept of addition. The student may even need to use markers to show the sum of two addends. A place value chart with ones and tens columns might well assist the learner to attach meaning to adding two and then three digit numerals. If meaning is lacking, then it is very difficult to proceed to more complex learnings, such as regrouping from the ones to the tens column. Understanding place value is very important here. Problems might even arise in terms of writing numerals legibly for ease of comprehension. Once student understanding is in evidence, the use of technology, such as hand held calculators/computers, can truly make subject matter learnings interesting and challenging (Ediger, 2006).

ANECDOTAL RECORDS AND STUDENT PORTFOLIOS

Teacher observations may and should be recorded. Observations may be forgotten or modified unless a careful system of record keeping is involved. Each recording needs to contain vital data with clarity in writing. The observer might then review as well as notice patterns of student behaviour in mathematics. What needs to be recorded? If a student has problems with reducing fractions to lowest terms, he/she may not understand factoring. Or in division of fractions, the learner may not attach meaning as to why the divisor is inverted and then the operation of multiplication is emphasized. By recording specific errors, the teacher may diagnose and remediate student sequence for the next lesson in mathematics.

Portfolios can be an excellent way for students showing progress, in time, in ongoing lessons and units of study. The contents chosen by the student with teacher guidance need to stress a representative sampling of the learner's completed work in mathematics. The duration of time emphasized within the portfolio might be a semester or entire school year. The contents of a student's portfolio may consist of the following entries, among others:

* mathematical work completed on paper from textbook use
* relevant worksheets showing important work of the learner
* drawings made of geometrical figures
* graphs, charts, and tables of data from ongoing lessons and units of study
* printouts of the involved student's test results in mathematics
* self evaluation by the student, using agreed upon teacher/learner criteria, of his/her progress in mathematics (Ediger, 2006).

Portfolio results should be viewed/discussed by the parents in parenti teacher conferences. Agreed upon ways of assisting the student in achievement should be an end result of the conference. The home and school need to work together for the good of the learner. Independent evaluators may also assess the portfolio contents for purposes of noting student progress and teacher accountability. The focus is upon the child in improving mathematics achievement. Teacher observation is needed, here, to diagnose and remedy problems of the student in mathematics achievement. As a result of assessing the portfolio, the following questions need consideration:

* how might the teacher guide the learner in attaining as optimally as possible?
* which objectives need to be stressed specifically?
* what kinds of learning opportunities will assist the student to achieve these objectives?
* what should be done to help the student to reflect upon his/her progress and monitor the self adequately?
* how can the student be motivated more thoroughly in developing an inward desire to learn?
* how might the student become more conscientious in careful proof reading?

Portfolios provide feedback to the teacher on how to assist students in overcoming selected problems as well as make for continuous progress in mathematics. Decisions may then be made on large group, small group, and individual student endeavours. The teacher needs to use the feedback wisely in providing for individual differences among learners (See National Council Teachers of Mathematics, 1989).

IMPROVING THE CLASSROOM ENVIRONMENT

Classroom environments are highly significant in improving mathematical achievement. The teacher must observe what hinders achievement due to environmental factors. Criteria need to be posted and rules enforced to optimize learner achievement and progress in mathematics. What are selected behaviours which hinder students attending to ongoing lessons and units of study? Student distraction from attending to a lesson disrupts sequential learnings. Learners then loose out on specific and major ideas. On task behaviour is very important.

Sometimes, students are rude to ideas presented in a discussion. This hinders the free flow of ideas discussed in mathematics. Rules need to be set up for discussions such as all participating but no one dominating, interrupting others should be avoided if at all possible, respect for the thinking of others must be adhered to, and active participation is important. Steen (2007) wrote the following:

> "Experience shows that many students fail to master important mathematical topics. What's missing from traditional instruction is sufficient emphasis on three important ingredients: communication, connections, and contexts. Colleges expect students to communicate effectively with people from different backgrounds and with different expertise and to synthesize skills from multiple areas. Employers expect the same things. They emphasize that formal knowledge is not, by itself, sufficient to deal with today's challenges. Instead of looking primarily for technical skills, today's business leaders talk more about teamwork and adaptability. Interviewers examine candidates' ability to synthesize information, make sound assumptions, capitalize on ambiguity, and explain their reasoning. They seek graduates who can interpret data as well as calculate with it and who can communicate effectively about quantitative topics."

To meet these demands of college and work, k-12 students need extensive practice expressing verbally the quantitative meanings of both problems and solutions. They need to be able to write fluently in complete sentences and coherent paragraphs; to explain the meaning of data, tables, graphs, and formulas; and to express the relationships among the different representations.

CONCLUSION

Mathematics teachers need to assist each student to achieve as optimally as possible. Strategies must be developed to guide learner progress. The demands of the work place require increased proficiency in mathematics. The elementary, middle school, and high school years are essential for students to attain as well as possible. The basics need to be taught in problem solving experiences. However, for selected students, essential content may be taught more systematically. The psychology of learning must be stressed in teaching and learning situations. This includes making learnings interesting, meaningful, as well as purposeful. The learning style of the individual student needs adequate consideration in the curriculum. Thus, students should learn in cooperative settings as well as individually. Connections must be made by the student to relate what is acquired in the school setting with that in society. What is learned needs to be used in school and in society. Relevancy is then in evidence. A rich mathematics vocabulary needs to be in the offing. Remedial assistance must be provided as necessary.

REFERENCES

Ediger, Marlow (2006), "Writing in the Mathematics Curriculum," *The Journal of Instructional Psychology*, 33 (1),120-123.

Ediger, Marlow (2006), "Testing Versus Portfolios to Assess Achievement," *OASCD Journal*, 1391),31, 31-32.

Ediger, Marlow, and D. Bhaskara Rao (2001), *Teaching Mathematics Successfully*. New Delhi, India; Discovery Publishing House.

National Council Teachers of Mathematics (1989), *Curriculum and Evaluation Standards for School Mathematics*. Reston, Va: NCTM.

Steen, Lynn Arthur, (2007), "How Mathematics Counts," *Educational Leadership*, 65 (3), 9-14.

Vygotsky, L.S. (1986), *Thought and Language*. Cambridge. Massachusetts, the MIT Press.

27

Assisting Student Achievement in Mathematics

There are a plethora of things which teachers may provide to aid students in mathematics achievement. The total learning environment needs to be assessed to provide an atmosphere of achievement and progress. Each learner needs to feel that he/she is provided an environment conducive to success in achieving objectives of mathematics instruction. A relaxed environment, free of worry and tension, generally facilitates progress of students in the mathematics curriculum (Ediger and Rao, 2001).

MATHEMATICS AND THE STUDENT

What kind of environment for learning should be in the offing? There are students who prefer a quiet atmosphere for ongoing task completion whereas others prefer a business like environment with committees at work who do make constructive noise in making deliberations. Perhaps, this may be harmonized with individual activities as well as committee endeavours in pursuing ongoing objectives in mathematics. Students do need to achieve well personally as well as in groups. Both are salient in school as well as in society.

Second, the mathematics teacher needs to consider attitudes and feelings possessed by students. Attitudinal development in a positive direction is important. If students feel negatively toward mathematics, the chances are achievement will go downhill. The mathematics teacher then needs to ascertain which learning opportunities will best suffice here. Activities may be changed from the concrete to the semi-concrete or from a hands on approach to the abstract mode. Meeting the needs of students is very important for optimal achievement to take place and for proper attitudinal growth to occur. A polite, helping learning environment must be in the offing. Reasonable time needs to be given to assist learners to complete projects and assignments.

Third, boredom and frustration need to be avoided. Too frequently, the routine has been stressed in teaching and learning mathematics. It is much better to have challenging experiences whereby students feel successful in ongoing lessons and units of study. Excessive leaning upon the basal text must be avoided to prevent boredom. Rather, a variety of interesting learning opportunities in mathematics need to be in the offing.

Fourth, praise for done well in mathematics should and can be experienced by all students in class. This needs to be given judiciously and fairly. Never should mathematics assignments be used as punishment. If it is used as punishment, the chances are negative affect will accrue. An atmosphere of acceptance needs to be provided for all students.

Fifth, students need to experience encouragement in learning. Ridiculing and minimizing student worth should never be done. Instead, a positive environment of encouragement needs to be experienced. A feeling of, "You can do it if you try", should prevail along with needed assistance to the learner. Students need encouragement, not discouragement in learning.

Sixth, proper sequence in learning needs to be in the offing. Too frequently, students fail because quality sequence in mathematical learnings are missing. With quality sequence,

There is adequate background knowledge and skill to achieve the new objective of instruction. The background knowledge relates directly to the new learnings and moves forward in increasingly optimal levels of complexity, but success is still involved. When jumping too far ahead of teaching learners with excessively difficult facts, concepts, and generalizations, students lose out on sequential ideas, essential for understanding the new subject matter. With prior learnings, new achievable objectives are stressed.

Seventh, students need to understand and attach meaning to each new process and product in mathematics. Failure to understand will definitely hinder when more complex objectives in mathematics are being achieved. The order of learnings in mathematics indicates a need for in-depth understanding. Survey learnings too frequently hinder in ordered progress in mathematics. It takes a thorough understanding of mathematics for the learner to understand that subtraction is the inverse operation of addition or division is inverse to multiplication. Students who face problems in understanding a new process might well not understood necessary background information.

Eighth, adequate attention must be given in having students apply what was learned. With application, use is made of acquired subject mater and skill. Thus, students need to apply learnings achieved with use in both school and society. Practical application should be made which indicates values of mathematics to the learner. This does not preclude learning mathematics for its own sake. Mathematics might well have intrinsic worth to many students. The writer learned the following indepth, some of it for its own sake: the volume of a sphere, area of a circle, as well as volumes of pyramids and cones. He finds it fascinating, for example, to reason why the formula for finding the volume of a sphere works. There are hardly any practical learnings inherent here. As a retired professor, he reads mathematics content for its own sake.

Ninth, different kinds of thinking need emphasis in ongoing lessons and units of study. Facts are important to secure; however, mathematics learnings should include higher levels of cognition. Thus, critical thinking must be stressed to separate the necessary from unnecessary information necessary in problem solving. Creative thought is needed to devise new, novel solutions to problematic situations. Logical thinking is needed to emphasize relationships among numerical values. Thinking about mathematics involves reflecting upon what has been learned.

Tenth, positive attitudes and a desire to learn more mathematics truly stresses a cap stone in the mathematics curriculum.

Inservice education of mathematics teachers should be ongoing. A professional library for mathematics teachers in the school setting should be in the offing. There are a plethora of available plans to follow in teaching students. Each plan needs to be appraised in terms of definite standards. These criteria need to follow what is beneficial to the learner. Newton (2007), after much study of Chinese schools and education, offers the following:

* The K-5 institutional design must free elementary teachers from being generalists. They need to become experts in specific subjects and will need opportunities to practice teaching single-subject curriculum and continue to develop their content knowledge.

* The K-12 institutional design must free both elementary and secondary teachers from spending every second of their time in teaching. The system must build in time for other equally important activities, such as lesson planning, collaborating with colleagues, grading student work, and providing high quality feedback to students. The allocation of time to teaching and to other activities must reflect the complex demands of teaching.

* The K-12 math curriculum must be designed to respect both the disciplinary structure of mathematics and the cognitive development of children. For example, the

Singapore math curriculum—much praised and much maligned by contending factions in US math education reform—is an excellent example of a curriculum in which the structure and hierarchy of different mathematical topics are maintained. And it is written in English.

* The accountability system must reflect the purpose of education and be reasonable. For example, elementary schools are accountable for adequately preparing students for middle schools, while middle schools are accountable for preparing students for high school, and high school students are accountable for graduating students who possess adequate literacy and quantitative skills to enable them to pursue different educational and career paths and to be productive citizens (Newton, 2007).

REFERENCES

Ediger, Marlow, and D. Bhaskara Rao (2001), *Teaching Mathematics Successfully*, New Delhi, India: Discovery Publishing House.

Newton, Xiaoxia (2007), "Reflections on Math Reforms in the U.S.," *Phi Delta Kappan*, 88 (9), 676-680.

28

Evaluation of Student Mathematics Achievement

There are a variety of techniques to use in the evaluation of student mathematics achievement. The teacher needs to appraise rather continuously how well students are doing as well as ascertain the kinds of errors made by learners. Students then reveal progress and diagnosis results. The results must be used to assist students to achieve more optimally.

Different approaches in evaluation will indicate diverse areas of achievement such as in subject matter, in skills, and in attitudes.

METHODS OF EVALUATION

Standardized tests are frequently used in mandated situations. They are published by a leading testing company or corporation. Standardized tests are accompanied by a Manual which gives precise directions for test-taking for each grade level or age level of students. The directions state the length of test-taking for all students, as well as directions for students pursuing the test items. Generally, there are practice test items for the student to take prior to taking the regular test items whose results are counted in providing each student with a percentile ranking or grade level equivalent. The same directions, time limits, and test items per grade or age level make for standardization or a standardized test.

The percentile ranking or grade equivalent for a student who took the standardized test comes from a set of norms contained in the Manual. A comparison of the student's test scores with that of students in a pilot study provides information for percentile readings or grade equivalents. Students in the pilot study are representative of a general defined population. The Manual provides information on the general population used in the pilot study and tested in providing norm information (Ediger and Rao, 2000).

Standardized tests, also called norm referenced, spread students out in test results, from high to low. How is this done? Pilot studies are done several times on the same representative group of learners. From the first pilot study, evaluators look at how many in the top group got each answer correct. They also notice how many of the bottom achievers responded correctly to a test item. In item analysis, a test item discriminated positively if the top achievers answered a test item correctly. A test item discriminated negatively if a correct answer was given by the bottom achievers. Only those test items in item analysis were used for the standardized test if there were positive discriminations. Test items are generally multiple choice with four possible responses, one of which is correct. There is a statistical procedure used which eliminates a certain per cent of the top and of the lowest achievers in the pilot studies.

Validity and reliability are two important concepts to remember in testing students. Validity emphasizes that the test measures what it purports to measure. Thus, a mathematics test measures achievement in mathematics and not in something else. Reliability as a concept states that consistency of test results is salient. For example, if a student rates on the seventieth percentile the first time the test is given and, approximately on the seventieth percentile, approximately the seconded time the same test is taken, the test seemingly measures in a reliable manner. However, if the second item the student took the same test, he/she ranked on the thirtieth percentile, the test did not measure in a reliable manner the second time for that student. If this happens for a large number of students, then the test does a poor job of measuring reliably. The Manual of a standardized test should indicate the reliability figures, consistency of measurement of the test. Also, the validity figures are given in the Manual and how these were obtained (Ediger and Rao, 2007).

Second, criterion referenced testing has become increasingly popular for selected educators. With criterion referenced testing, there are statements of specific objectives available to teachers. These objectives are generally precise and provide guidance to the teacher as to what to teach. The mathematics curriculum in the local school may then be aligned with the precise objectives. Testing should also be quite reliable if the test results are consistent for students. Thus, with the first administration of the test, the student would receive approximately the same results as for the second testing. This should also be true for a larger set of students. Again, the test is valid if it measures what has been taught in ongoing and units of study. Thus, the test items are aligned with the stated specific objectives of instruction.

Criterion referenced tests may be customized for mandated tested in a given state. They become standardized if all students of a specific grade level receive the same test items, the same directions for test-taking, and the same scoring key is used. Criterion referenced tests do not have the same purpose as standardized tests, discussed above. Thus, from test rests, the spread of student scores from criterion scores will not be nearly as great as is in .the case of standardized tests. Why? With criterion referenced testing, teachers have related objectives available to guide instruction. More students will then achieve the specific objectives, available to teachers prior to instruction. Learning opportunities are aligned with the objectives and evaluation of student achievement is strictly guided by the objectives of instruction. In fact, the goal for criterion referenced testing is to assist students to achieve the precise objectives. This increases student probability for success in goal attainment (See also, National Council Teachers of Mathematics, 1989).

Third, teacher written tests may be an excellent way to assess learner achievement. Why? The mathematics teacher establishes/writes the objectives which may be based on mandated objectives of instruction. He/she selects learning opportunities for students to achieve the objectives. The instruction needs to be sequenced and paced according to learner needs and abilities. Students should always be challenged to achieve optimally. Success is important in achievement, providing that student motivation is high and reasonable. Appraisal in terms of the written objectives needs to be in the offing. Valid and reliable tests need to be written to measure achievement and progress.

To optimize achievement, regardless of the kind of test used, the mathematics teacher needs to assist learners in focusing upon each activity being provided. Each activity then needs to be of interest to students. It also needs to be purposeful in that there are reasons for achieving. Understanding and meaning are also important concepts to stress in teaching and learning situations. Individual differences among learners must be provided for such as possessed talents and abilities (Maslow, 1954).

Fourth, teacher observation of student's daily work in mathematics is highly salient to monitor. He/she needs to use quality criteria in observing the specifics involved in ascertaining learner progress. The following suggested criteria might well be used in student observation:

* time on task
* understanding the underlying principles of each operation or process
* self evaluation to diagnose and remediate errors
* communicating ideas clearly in mathematics
* reading word problems in an understandable, fluent manner

* assisting others when necessary
* being polite and considerate.

Teacher observation can be continuous and provide immediate feedback to the teacher. He/she may then provide students individually with necessary assistance (Ediger, 1989),

ANECDOTAL RECORDS

Anecdotal records are based on teacher observation. The teacher dates and records observations made for each learner. Each entry made needs to be clear on assistance provided to a student. If observations, alone, are used, they may be forgotten unless recorded. Items which might be recorded for students individually, for example, might well include the following:

* fails to understand the commutative property of multiplication
* memorizes basic addition facts without understanding their meanings
* does not attach meaning to the concept of regrouping and renaming
* equivalent fractions cause misunderstanding
* additional problems pertain to changing mixed numbers to improper fractions understanding place value in decimal numbers, understanding per cent, as well as multiplication and division of fractions.

Whatever the problem is of an identified student, diagnosis and remediation should then occur. A check mark may be placed where a student has corrected and now understands the previously identified problem area.

INTERVIEWING STUDENTS

There are a plethora of times when a teacher may interview a student pertaining to mathematical learnings.

When a transfer student enters a receiving school, the mathematics teacher must determine where the student is presently in achievement and progress. With information from the receiving school and an interview with the teacher, placement data assists in ascertaining which specific group best meets the needs of the transfer student. Questions such as the following need to be answered:

* at which specific point in an ongoing lesson and unit is the student achieving?
* are there prerequisites which the student will need to master?
* how might the student best be introduced to others in a class?
* might a buddy plan work to induct the new student satisfactorily?
* which is the best way to instill good human relations among learners?

Transfer students need careful consideration in becoming highly motivated and optimal achievers in mathematics. They must be made to feel at home in the new school. Feelings of belonging are important for all students. Their needs must be identified and fulfilled. Esteem needs must be met. They can be met for all students with a developmentally appropriate mathematics curriculum. What has been said for transfer students is also true for any learner. Most of the above criteria with asterisks might well be used equally effectively with all students in the school and classroom setting. Even a buddy system may work well with students who have known each other for a definite period of time. They may assist each other as needed in ongoing lessons and units of study.

PARENT/TEACHER CONFERENCES

Parent/teacher conferences have considerable potential in assisting learner achievement in mathematics. An atmosphere must prevail which is conducive to a set of wholesome interactions. A two way street of conversation needs to be in the offing. Both parent and teacher then needs to ask questions and receive information to help the learner do well. A developmentally appropriate curriculum should result.

Portfolios provide a good opportunity to discuss student achievement. The portfolio consists of a representative collection of student products and work in mathematics, covering a designated period of time. The parent may then notice progress from one time to the next within the sequential items contained in the portfolio. The portfolio needs to have a title and a table of contents. Student errors and remediation are revealed in a portfolio. Questions such as the following might well be discussed:

* how well the learner is progressing
* which areas does the student need to make more progress
* what hindrances, if any, keep the child from achieving more optimally
* what kind of assistance may be provided by parents
* might specific kinds of homework help the student to attain objectives more effectively
* does the child achieve mathematical learnings in depth?
* how might computers and technology, in general, assist a student's achievement in mathematics?

The parent/teacher conference should work in the direction of solving identified problems. Later parent/teacher conferences may focus on what was accomplished in the interim and which new goals need to be solved cooperatively between parent and teacher. There are conferences, in part or whole, in which the student is also invited. This has advantages in that the student may provide worthwhile information during the conference (See Peressini, 1997).

Change is a key concept in any curriculum area, mathematics being no exception. In evaluating student achievement, there are many things which need to be considered in aiding learner progress.

The instructional technology community needs to actively encourage teachers to reflect on technology and engage them in discussions about technology's role in fostering learning. Teachers should reflect on the following questions:

* What kinds of software should I use in the classroom and why?
* When should my students use computers in class? When should they not use them?
* Does the current technology use in my classroom support the curriculum and deepen content? How?
* Do certain uses of technology match certain learning outcomes?
* Does my current technology use improve my student's learning?

More specific questions, among others, might deal with how teachers use spreadsheets to help students better understand linear algebra. (Burns, 2005-2006).

REFERENCES

Burns, Mary (2006), "Tools for the Mind," *Educational Leadership* (December 2005/January, 63 (4), 48-53.

Ediger, Marlow (1989), "Psychology in Teaching Mathematics," Delta K, 27 (4), 20-23.

Ediger, Marlow, and D. Bhaskara Rao (2000), *Teaching Mathematics Successfully*. New Delhi, India: Discovery Publishing House.

Ediger, Marlow, and D. Bhaskara Rao (2007), *Curriculum of School Subjects*. New Delhi, India: Discovery Publishing House, 28-34.

Maslow, A.H. (1954), *Motivation and Personality*. New York: Harper and Row.

National Council Teachers of Mathematics (1989), *Curriculum and Evaluation Standards for School Mathematics*. Reston, Virginia: NCTM.

Peressini, Dominic (1997), "Parental Reform of Mathematics Education," *The Mathematics Teacher*, 90 (6), 423-427.

29

Trends in Teaching Science

There are selected trends in science which have important implications for teachers of science in the public schools. These need to be studied, analyzed, and implemented, if feasible. Trends in science instruction, carefully assessed, represent quality ideas, considered to be among the best in teaching and learning situations. Students need to achieve viable science objectives in the school and classroom setting. Which trends might then be considered by teachers and supervisors in he science curriculum?

NEEDED CRITERIA IN TEACHING SCIENCE

The heart of science instruction should be experimentation. The experiments need to be performed by students with teacher guidance. They must be developmentally appropriate and clearly visible for all learners to see in the classroom. Both commercial and local items brought from home may be used in science experiments. It is good, too, for students to make science equipment for an ongoing unit of study. Each experiment should stress a problem solving approach with a clearly stated problem. An hypothesis is developed by learners in answer to doing the experiment. A procedure to evaluate the hypothesis results in its testing. In gathering data to evaluate the hypothesis, a variety of rich learning opportunities should be in the offing. These include doing the experiment itself, reading from basal textbooks, science encyclopedias, information based library books, as well as viewing video tapes to locate relevant information. Internet sources, excursions where applicable, and resource personnel are further reference sources in securing information to evaluate the hypothesis. With a variety of information sources used, the hypothesis might well be evaluated thoroughly. Students may then brainstorm hypothesis acceptance, modification, and/or rejection (Ediger and Rao, 2003).

Objectives to be achieved by students include knowledge, skills, and attitudes. Knowledge objectives should result from experimentation and related information gathered from various reference sources to solve identified problems. Knowledge ends should incorporate salient facts, concepts, and generalizations. Relevant knowledge may be used in ensuing science units of study as well as in society. Obtained knowledge may include the following concepts and generalizations in a unit on "The Changing Surface of the Earth":

* wind and water erosion
* earthquakes, volcanic eruptions, floods, and mudslides
* tornados, cyclones, and hurricanes

Vital facts acquired should support important major concepts and generalizations achieved. Skills objectives to be achieved by students need to include the following:

* critical thinking to separate the important from the lesser important ideas as well as accurate from inaccurate content
* creative thinking to come up with novel, unique ideas such as in brain storming in problem solving
* predicting as in thinking about the possible outcomes of an experiment or demonstration
* inferring when "reading between the lines" as in reading information from a graph containing scientific data (Ediger and Rao, 2005).

The National Science Teachers Association (NSTA) Board of Directors (March, 2007) has come up with a developmentally appropriate sequence in conducting science experiments in that they:

* have a definite purpose that is clearly stated to students
* focus on the processes of science as a way to convey information
* incorporate ongoing student reflection and discussion; and
* enable students to develop safe and conscientious lab habits and procedures.

Skills objectives also need to incorporate reading/writing experiences within the framework of problem solving. Students need to become proficient in word recognition in reading content. Readiness needs to be in evidence for using phonics, syllabication, as well as context clues in comprehension of subject matter. What has been read, in many cases, involves writing activities. Thus, the following science writing experiences are salient:

* write-ups of science experimentation
* outlines for book reports to be given in class
* summaries of information read
* information in charts, graphs, bulletin boards, and tables
* essays written such as on global warming (See Horejsi, 2003).

Attitudinal objectives are developed as outcomes from diverse kinds of learning experiences. Quality attitudes assist in achieving knowledge and skills ends of instruction. An inward desire to learn becomes a by-product of achieving knowledge and skills objectives. More specifically, attitudes to be achieved in ongoing science units include the following:

* developing ideas indepth pertaining to science subject matter

* being curious about science phenomena in school and in society
* wanting to learn more content and skills in a daily lesson or unit in science
* desiring to use the internet and modern technology in the science curriculum.

EVALUATION OF ACHIEVEMENT

A variety of evaluation techniques must be used to assess learner achievement. Formative and summative evaluation techniques might well include valid and reliable:

* teacher written tests
* mandated district and state developed tests
* teacher observation, rating scales, and check lists.

Evaluative results should be studied to ascertain what must be done to improve the science curriculum. The best science curriculum possible needs to be experienced by students.

REFERENCES

Ediger, Marlow, and D. Bhaskara Rao (2003), *Teaching Science in Elementary Schools*. New Delhi, India: Discovery Publishing House.

Ediger, Marlow, and D. Bhaskara Rao (2005), *Quality School Education*. New Delhi, India: Discovery Publishing House.

Horejsi, Martin (2003), "Making Technology Inclusive," *Science and Children*, 41 (3), 20-24.

NSTA Reports (March 2007), "NSTA Board Revises Statement on Lab Investigation," Arlington, Virginia: National Science Teachers Association.

30

Developing Student Interest in Technical Education

There will always be a need for quality individuals in technical education. Skilled carpenters, bricklayers, carpet layers, electricians, plumbers, mechanics, heating and air conditioning personnel, medical/dental technicians, among many others, are very important people in society. Post-secondary education is needed to improve skills for technical education workers in the 21st century. A shortage of critical workers in technical education has been documented.

Skills need to be updated to make for competent people at the work-place. More is demanded of workers than ever before. Trained, educated workers are needed in diverse fields of technical education. Schools involved in post-secondary technical education need to study the objectives, learning opportunities to achieve objectives, and assessment procedures, to make ongoing modifications in making for improved competency at the work-place (See Ediger and Rao, 2006).

SECURING TECHNICAL EDUCATION STUDENTS

Not every student, by any means, benefits from an academic curriculum on the secondary and post-secondary level of instruction. Multiple intelligences theory (See Gardner, 1993) indicates that there are nine unique intelligences possessed by individuals. One of these has to do with the predominate use of physical prowess and eye/hand coordination. Technical education needs to possess the same status as do the academic fields. These workers are very much needed in society. How can people work effectively in society when the heating or air conditioning system does not work properly? Or, the water system and plumbing fail to function properly? The list goes on and on as to what technicians do to make efficient surroundings for others to make the work-place conducive to achievement and productivity.

Technical education must be perceived as a need for upgrading skills and knowledge. The importance of technical education needs to be communicated clearly and in a variety of ways. Leadership must come from community colleges, and technical schools, among others, in presenting technical education as being very important. A leader from each institution must visit and meet with high school seniors to present the cause for technical education. A polite, well planned speech for seniors to convey a mission must be in the offing. Conference time also needs to be available for high school seniors who have questions and problems. Diverse needs for technical education workers in the work-place must be stressed. Inexpensive, attractive brochures may be printed by thc computer to hand out to participants. E-mail addresses and telephone numbers should be listed for correspondence purposes. What are selected questions which high school students might have?:

* specific areas of training desired which was not discussed in the allotted time
* locations of nearby places where employment opportunities exist
* salaries being paid for particular technical education positions
* duration of training needed for work-place job
* financial aid available (See Holland, 1984).

High school teachers and guidance counselors must inform students of the worth and values of entering technical education. Students should appraise the self to ascertain that which is of personal interest, purpose, and worth at the work-place. No person should be stuck at a dead end job where personal goals are hazy or non-existent. Individuals like to posses feelings of belonging in a group. Technicians might well develop feelings of camaraderie. They may feel as being members of a special group. Recognition for work well done can come about as quality work is performed at the work-place. Meeting esteem needs is salient! Each person desires to be paid adequately for services performed and maintain a wholesome life style. For many, it will mean supporting a family as time goes on (See Penick and Jepson, 1992).

Above all, the importance of technical education in society needs to be emphasized. Societal progress cannot occur without success in technical work. For too long, there has been bias against technical education and this cannot be justified when one looks at the many necessities performed by workers in the field.

Information also must reach the federal/state legislatures pertaining to the necessity of funding technical education adequately. Definite needs must be discussed and shown here, reaching to the highest level of government possible. Networking is necessary. There needs to be much cooperation among schools offering technical education in showing the need for adequate funding for high quality technical education. These needs must be clearly spelled out. Reinforcement in presenting these ideas is salient. Thus, follow up approaches to inform of technical education positions and needs must be in the offing.

The business world and industry can provide valuable assistance in getting the word out for updated technicians at the work-place. They might well offer assistance in helping high school seniors view the local work-place as well as provide assistance in ascertaining which skills are necessary to achieve objectives at the work-place such as:

* being punctual, neatly dressed, and polite
* being persistent in work habits and skills
* being able to communicate well in oral communication and in writing
* being able to read needed materials such as manuals for doing repair work
* being able to work collaboratively with others
* being able to listen carefully (See Super, 1957).

The above named skills and habits are needed by all at the work-place. There are then selected abilities and amenities which workers must possess to secure and maintain a job at the work-place.

Schools involved in post-secondary education must post available positions for jobs at the work-place. They need to be posted also in public libraries and other acceptable public buildings. Future workers need to be informed and matched with available jobs. It is best to use the skills of workers in positive environments where feelings of satisfaction occurs. Recruitment of instructors for positions in technical education also need to be listed. Stereotypes need to be eliminated and openings must be written and listed with a positive attitude. Newspaper articles need to be written for daily and weekly newspapers on the contributions made by skilled workers. In smaller cities and in all weekly small town papers, the chances are generally good in having good articles published. Accuracy of content, quality grammar, and careful editing help to indicate the worthiness of a news item.

Technical education must emphasize the latest in technological equipment and its effective use. Outdated equipment and methods of instruction must be shunned. Objectives need to be carefully selected for students to attain. Learning opportunities need to be engaging. The attention of students needs to be secured to achieve objectives assessment of student progress needs to be systematic and ongoing. Diagnosis and remediation needs to be in the evaluation repertoire.

Feedback from students in a quality questionnaire to the instructor must be in the offing. In this way, the technician has necessary data to use in appraising the self as well as work for continuous improvement of instruction (Ediger and Rao, 2003).

ADDITIONAL NEEDS OF TECHNICIANS

The technical trainer/teacher needs to stay abreast of the latest trends and innovations in his/her field. Talking to peers about technical education should stimulate discussions on teaching and learning situations. Professional literature such as the ATEA Journal must be available for reading and study. It is good to analyze the latest in technical education literature in small study groups. Articles need to be appraised in terms of connections to the self, others, the class of students being taught, as well as society. Questions need to be identified and analyzed. Problem solving is an excellent method to use in discussion situations where each participates actively in offering solutions. Video-tapes and power point presentations need to be available for viewing. This brings in ideas pertaining to technical education beyond that of the printed word. One of the better ways of inservice education is to attend state and national technical education conventions. Here, excellent opportunities exist to share relevant information in improving the curriculum. Technical education is of vital importance in highlighting its significance to the lay public and, particularly, to those wishing to pursue specialized work.

The importance of technical education, beyond the secondary school level, needs to be communicated to salient publics. Its relevance makes for the following:

* improved goods and services
* better paying jobs
* work-place efficiency and harmony
* trained technicians and trouble shooting
* quality competition to upgrade skills, knowledge, and ıttitudes

* continuing education in the field
* proficiency in computer use in technologically related fields.

REFERENCES

Ediger, M., and D.B. Rao (2006), *Community College*. New Delhi, India: Discovery Publishing House.

Ediger, M., and D.B. Rao (2003), *Psychology and Curriculum*. New Delhi, India: Discovery Publishing House.

Gardner, H. (1993), *Multiple Intelligences*. New York: Basic Books.

Holland, J.L. (1984), *Making Vocational Decisions: A Theory of Vocational Personalities and Work Environments* (Second Edition). Englewood Cliffs, New Jersey: Prentice Hall, Inc.

Penick, N. and D. Jepson (1992), "Family Functioning and Adolescent Career Development." Career Development Quarterly, 40 (4), 208-222.

Super, D. (1957), *The Psychology of Careers: An Introduction to Vocational Development*. New York: Harper and Row Company.

31

Technical Education, Work-place and Student

Which skills should students acquire to prepare for work-place competency? There are skills needed which cover all areas of employment as well as those related to a specific job at the work-place. Technical education instructors in high school need to work together with those in post-secondary education to develop an agreed upon set of necessary skills. These skills need to be developed indepth sequentially. Additions, modifications, and deletions may be made as needed. Upgrading knowledge and skills must be ongoing. Positive student attitudes should be an end result. Quality attitudes do affect the development of knowledge and skills ends of instruction.

MEANINGFUL OBJECTIVES IN TECHNICAL EDUCATION

What skills do workers need to improve work-place achievement? This is a key question when identifying major objectives for students to achieve. Relevant ends need to be available to technicians in assisting students to improve work out put. What skills do employers desire of future workers at the work-place? Problem solving is vital. Thus, the worker must be able to identify problems and know how to solve them.

Trouble shooting is involved and the worker needs to lean on others for assistance, as needed. As much as possible, the worker needs to lean upon the self for solutions to problems. Resources are there, human and material, to provide assistance in problem solving situations. These reference sources need to be used wisely in dilemma situations (See Ediger and Rao, 2006).

Critical thinking skills are very valuable at any work-place. To be able to analyze and synthesize information are necessary. When difficulties are faced, workers need to separate significant from the lesser important ideas. Relevant from the irrelevant need to be considered in problem solving situations. Critical thinking is important in all of life's endeavours. In selecting a career, the individual starts sorting out those which he/she is interested in as well as possesses needed abilities to do well at the work-place. There are a plethora of factors involved in career selection and these need analyzation and attention to arrive at an informed decision (Juneau, 2006).

Not always, by any means are answers to problems ready made, but they need a unique solution. The creative mind seeks solutions in diverse ways and is not easily frustrated. Creativity looks for newness, novelty, and originality, as concepts to solve problems. The creative mind perceives gaps in knowledge and skills and looks for closure. By trying out new ways of doing things, the technician discovers a possible solution. Creativity and critical thinking are desired and encouraged at the work-place. These two types of thinking are different from each other. Creativity emphasizes originality and uniqueness of ideas whereas critical thinking advocates separation of an idea in terms of accuracy from inaccuracy of each part or that part which is logical from the illogical.

Pertaining to problem solving, McDonald (2006) wrote the following:

> Problem based learning is a powerful pedagogy of engagement that reaches beyond traditional methods of

teaching and learning, recognizing that students need to be actively engaged if they are to retain and apply important course content when they reach the work force. Problem based learning has the potential to be a bridge for both professors and students to a more engaged student/teacher relationship. A classroom that is engaging for both the student and the instructor in the process of learning orients the central mission of the university from a place where knowledge is simply transmitted to a place where students can begin to see the value of newly constructed knowledge. Pedagogy is transformed to that of engaged teaching, connecting student activities to real world problems in the field of study.

Problem solving stresses a motivated environment for technical education students to raise questions and identify problems in ongoing training sessions. These questions/problems emphasize deliberation, not factual responses. They require indepth thinking. Time is necessary in problem based learning. A variety of reference sources may be used here. Individual and group sessions devoted to problem solving may be stressed. An hypothesis should be attained from information gathering. The hypothesis is tested in a life like situation. If the consequences indicate the problem was solved, then the hypothesis is accepted as is. If not, then new approaches need to be used. Problems need to be relevant and challenging. Active student involvement is wanted, not passive learners. Problems may come form students, but vital problems coming from instructors are also necessary. Open ended questions encourage learner curiosity.

Ideas must be presented accurately in oral communication. Clarity with voice inflection is significant in orally attracting the attention of others. No one enjoys listening to a monotone. With written communication the writer must be able to communicate effectively with printed symbols. In both oral and written communication, each sentence must have a skeleton (subject and predicate), and modifiers placed in the proper position. This can be explained further with different kinds of sentences such as simple, compound, complex, and compound/

complex. Assistance in this area may be obtained by the reader from a textbook in grammar. Quality oral and written communication are salient at the work-place when interacting with others as well as in society.

Interpersonal skills must be honed to make for more harmonious relationships at the work-place. Individuals have lost jobs due to bursts of anger, extreme rudeness, and hatred of others. Workers need to govern their very own behaviour so that it meets standards of getting along well with others. Cooperation is important in getting work done well and efficiently. Many interactions transpire daily at most places of work. In fact, technical skills and knowledge cannot be separated from good human relations at the daily schedule of work experiences. Then too, good human relations are equally important away from the work-place.

An increased number of immigrants from different nationalities must be accommodated. Multi-culturism is important to emphasize in technical education. Cultural differences in languages spoken, foods eaten, customs, holidays celebrated, among others need to be accepted. In fact, they may enrich any environment by noticing how cultural traits differ and yet integrated places of training can function very effectively and efficiently. Watts (2003) suggested the following guidelines in teaching native people at any level: these are applicable in teaching minority and regular technical education students:

* practice a personal warmth plus high expectations
* respect cultural differences
* learn the cultural resources of your students
* develop multiple instructional approaches
* be aware of the ways you ask questions
* remember some of your students do not like to be spot lighted in front of a group.

Such suggestions are common sense. There are many excellent resources for educating children about stereotypes. Learning about, other cultures, their histories and their beliefs, gives students a basis for judgement that goes beyond generalizations.

Feeling well physically certainly helps when attending technical education classes and in doing a good job at the work-place as well as when enjoying leisure time activities. Proper nutrition, cleanliness, oral hygiene, sleep and rest, as well as appropriate, comfortable attire are needed for all future workers. Precaution needs to be taken to monitor proper blood pressure, as well as having periodical check-ups and physicals. Sanitary conditions need to abound. The late A.H. Maslow (1954) listed the following sequential needs of individuals to function well:

* proper diet, exercise, sleep and rest, sanitation facilities, clothing
* safety in being free from danger and harm
* belonging to a group, not feeling isolated
* esteem needs, feelings of being rewarded for things well done
* becoming the kind of person desired.

Striving to meet the above named needs stresses a theory of motivation. The motivated person attempts to reach higher levels of achievement, sequentially.

Safety, as indicated above, is an important factor in doing work well. Unsafe, faulty equipment makes for concerns, worry, and strain. A safe environment, conducive to optimal technical education achievement needs thorough consideration and implementation. Suggestion boxes need to be available to voice concerns. The suggestions offered have assisted in improving environmental conditions for all concerned in technical education. Oversight is necessary to develop and maintain safe and effective places of training and employment.

REFERENCES

Ediger, Marlow, and D.B. Rao (2006), *Community College*. New Delhi, India: Discovery Publishing House.

Juneau, Karen (2006), "Teaching Critical Thinking," *ATEA Journal*, 34 (1), 18-20.

Maslow, A. H. (1954), *Motivation and Personality*. New York: Harper and Row.

Mc Donald, James T. (2006), "Problem Based Learning in the Science Classroom,", *MSTA Journal*, 51(2), 6-9.

Watts, John (2003) "Native American Students," Teaching Learning Committee, Montana State University, Bozeman. Quoted in *Phi Delta Kappan* , 88(3), 216.

32

Reading Across the Curriculum

There is a great need for teachers in different subject matter fields to emphasize reading instruction on each level of achievement. Why? Reading knowledge and skills acquired transfer across the curriculum. Pupils need to have guidance and direction in reading in different curriculum areas. This is needed so that a quality, sequential program of reading instruction assists each pupil to read in as optimal manner as possible. Principals and supervisors must accept leadership roles to foster the concept of excellence in teaching reading across the curriculum.

STAFF DEVELOPMENT IN THE TEACHING OF READING

There are specific areas in the teaching of reading which need to be emphasized within inservice education programs. As a university professor, having supervised student teachers in the public schools for thirty years, I have noticed which areas of expertise tend to need strengthening among teachers. The following are necessary to stress for teachers in teaching reading across the curriculum:

* word recognition skills, including phonetic analysis, syllabication, and using context clues to help pupils in unlocking unknown words

* comprehension of ideas be it in narrative or expository reading, including critical and creative thinking
* structural analysis to assist pupils in understanding the significance of word order when reading
* syntax, including vocabulary development, in guiding pupils to attach meaning to what is being read
* problem solving and gathering information in offering solutions (Ediger, 2007).

Developing a love for reading is a very important objective for all pupils to achieve. Thus, individualized reading might well be stressed. Here, a pupil chooses which sequential library books to read. The books are selected based on interest factors as well as readability. After completing reading a book, the pupil has a conference with the teacher to check comprehension and word recognition growth. The teacher together with the pupil discuss what changes/and improvements, if any, need to be made to make for optimal learner growth in reading progress. He/she writes brief comments, and dated, to use in future conferences with the same pupil. Generally, individualized reading then replaces of supplements the basal reader approach.

A more open ended procedure is to use Sustained Silent Reading (SSR). From a selection of appropriate library books, the pupil chooses which to read sequentially. There is no conference with the teacher after completing the reading of a library book. In either case, reading across the curriculum is emphasized in that the pupil may choose social studies, science, mathematics, and or literature content. Also, stories pertaining to physical education, music, and art, might be selected for reading. Enjoyment and motivation for reading is salient. Through teacher observation, the teacher may notice if pupils are connected to reading (Ediger and Rao, 2007).

The use of basal readers in the reading curriculum makes for a more formal program of instruction, but interest in and reading content dealing with different subject mater areas may still be stressed. For example, the following sequence may be followed:

* developing background information for reading the ensuing selection. This can be done with interesting questions, raised by the teacher and pupils, dealing with the embedded illustrations within in the print discourse.
* new words contained in the printed text may be printed on the chalkboard, relating to the illustrations discussed. Sentences, given by the teacher and pupils, containing these new words, should relate to those in the printed text. Thus, pupils have a good chance of identifying the new words correctly when reading (See Gunning, 2000).

Following the reading activity, pupils with teacher guidance need to discuss the contents which lead learners to higher levels of cognition with challenging questions and comments. An appreciation for people of different cultures and from different academic perspectives should make for more optimal pupil growth in understanding others. This should be an objective for reading stories across the curriculum.

LEADERSHIP TO ENCOURAGE READING ACROSS THE CURRICULUM

The principal needs to provide strong leadership in having teachers stress reading across the curriculum. By doing much reading, attending professional meetings, studying, and talking to teachers about innovative approaches in teaching including computer and technology use, faculty members can move forward toward a changing program of reading instruction. In addition to faculty and staff, parents also need to perceive values in pupils reading across the curriculum. Being sold on the new philosophy of instruction and uniting in efforts for its implementation, moving from the old to the new is definitely possible. Securing an increased number of library books on different reading levels, as well as on different genres, as well as demonstrating their possible classroom uses at faculty meetings and workshops assists in implementing the concept of reading across the curriculum. Stressing reading across the curriculum from basal science, social studies, mathematics, and literature textbooks on different grade levels helps teachers to understand how important it is to be excellent reading instructors. The trouble has been in the past that teachers and parents have not perceived the need for the new approach. Pupils should definitely become proficient readers with a concerted effort. One must remember that quality methods of instruction are very necessary here. Teachers need to try out ideas expressed at faculty meetings and workshops and notice how they work in classroom teaching. Reporting the results back to participants can make for productive discussions on innovative methods of reading instruction. Teachers need to pinpoint how they assisted pupils in reading comprehension across the subject matter areas of science, social studies, mathematics, and literature, among other academic disciplines (See Cochran-Smith, 2006).

REFERENCES

Cochran-Smith, Marilyn (2006), "Ten Promising Trends (and Three Big Worries," *Educational Leadership* (2006), 20-25.

Ediger, Marlow (2007), "The Substitute Teacher in Reading Instruction," *The Subjournal*, 8 (2), 67-73.

Ediger, Marlow, and D. Bhaskara Rao (2007), *Reading Curriculum and Instruction*. New Delhi, India: Discovery Publishing House, Chapter Two.

Gunning, T. (2000), *Creating Literacy for All Children*. Needham Heights, Massachusetts, Massachusetts.

33

Substitute Teacher and Reading Instruction

The substitute teacher has a plethora of responsibilities in reading instruction. He/she needs to ascertain what was taught the previous day before beginning the actual teaching of students. Connections must be made between the two periods of instructional time. If students are assisted in perceiving relationships, retention of knowledge will be more certain as compared to seeing things in isolation. Thus, the substitute teacher needs too have access to the previous day's lesson plans as guidelines for planning today's lessons. In this manuscript, the writer will zero in on what the substitute teacher needs to know in order to plan well in the teaching of reading.

PLANNING FOR TEACHING

The substitute teacher needs to be well prepared for each day of teaching. He/she needs to become acquainted with each pupil in the classroom as soon as possible. Calling each pupil by name is highly salient to the learner. Politeness and consideration for each pupil as well as for the substitute teacher must be in the offing. Proper standards of conduct need to be in the offing. Negative forms of behaviour such as any form of bullying or belittling is forbidden. Achievement is hindered if a negative environment is inherent in the classroom. Cooperatively, a quality learning environment needs to be developed. This leads to the curriculum. Which areas of reading instruction should the substitute teacher plan for?

First, the substitute teacher needs to evaluate when a pupil needs assistance in phonics instruction. Readiness to benefit from phonics instruction needs to be in the offing. There are words which are spelled consistently between symbol and sound. Also, there are diphthongs which vary somewhat in vowel sounds from those with short/long vowel sound. A study of consonant and vowel digraphs might well benefit selected pupils in becoming better readers. Consonant blends as well as consonant/vowel/consonant/silent "e" ending words may also become a part of the needs of a pupil in studying word analysis. Perceiving compound words and seeing their respective separate parts do benefit selected pupils in independent word recognition. Those words which lack many consistencies (through, cough, bough, thought, though, among others), need to be taught as sight words. Syllabication skills also need to be taught as needed. A word then might be identified by taking away an initial or final consonant. The above are a few phonic generalizations which may be taught as needed, but should not be taught for the sake of doing so. The substitute teacher needs to notice which phonic learnings are already possessed by individual pupils and should not be duplicated in teaching and learning situations. Proper sequence in learning is salient (See Fiene and McMahon, 2007).

The use of context clues should be taught when a pupil cannot identify an unknown word. Any word filled in for the unknown should at least make sense. Meaning theory is involved here. After that, the pupil should be guided to view the initial consonant in order to decode correctly.

Phonics, syllabication, and context clues should be taught only as needed. Independent readers are wanted as a result of instruction.

COMPREHENSION OF SUBJECT MATTER READ

What is important in reading is that pupils understand printed ideas being read. The lowest level of comprehension is for the pupil to secure the author's literal meaning. This is important; however, more complex comprehension skills are to be developed after obtaining the author's meaning. Beyond that, the pupil should be guided to determine the accuracy or lack thereof from expository reading. With expository reading, pupils learn to separate fantasy from reality, fact from fiction, as well as choice of words made in the actual writing. Critical reading is then involved. Creative interpretation also needs to be in the offing. Originality and novel ways of looking at printed materials is then in evidence. This enriches the learner's thinking. Relating the subject matter being read to the self, to the environment/society, and toward others expands the pupil's way of reasoning and thought. Reading between the lines should also be stressed, for example, when numerals are contained in chart form. Meaning, then, needs to be attached to numerals contained in population data, compared sizes of nations given in making comparisons in land area, as well as gross national product (GNP) information given. Otherwise a hodge podge of numbers might be presented with no meaning attached unless the reader does some interpreting with inferential reading or reading between the lines.

Narrative reading usually contains novel ideas and is appraised differently such as the pupil's enjoyment of reading, comprehension of ideas, and the number of library books read. In structuring a novel/short story, the substitute teacher must provide guidance in assisting pupils to understand the concepts of setting, characterization, theme, plot, satire, and/or point of view. Pupils do need to do much reading in order to hone and practice necessary thinking skills (See Feldman, 2003).

In addition to expository and narrative reading, pupils, when ready, should also learn to appreciate creative forms of writing such as poetry. Key ingredients in poetry involve novel ways of using words in the writing of poems. Thus, writers use the following, among others, in writing such as:

* imagery with its metaphors and similes
* onomatopoeia with its echoic sounding words
* rhymed verse to include couplets, triplets, quatrains, and limericks
* syllabic poems including haiku and tanka
* acrostic verse and free verse
* originality of expression (See Tiedt, 1983).

From the above discussion, it is quite obvious that the substitute teacher has a plethora of responsibilities and needs to be ready to teach what is relevant with, perhaps, little time alloted for preparation. The writer believes that he/she needs to secure structural ideas, as listed above, pertaining:

* phonetic analysis and syllabication
* comprehension skills involving higher levels of cognition
* key ideas in reading short stories and novels
* appreciation for unique ideas gleaned through reading.

INTEGRATING TEACHING SKILLS WITH HUMAN RELATIONS FACTORS

The substitute teacher must provide a role model for good behaviour in the classroom. He/she needs to be able to get along well with children. Being positive and showing continual evidence of quality human relations are musts! The substitute teacher needs to do a good job of asking quality questions of pupils. A child should never be ridiculed for answering incorrectly or for the responses given, Rather, the substitute teacher accepts learners where they are individually in present achievement. From that point on, the teacher assists pupils to make optimal continuous progress. Learning activities in reading are presented in respect toward all learners. No child is to be minimized, but rather helped to achieve and make progress. The substitute teacher may wish to model using a word attack skill as in context clues. He/she then thinks aloud as if one is attempting to ascertain an unknown word.

Children may not achieve well due to health and dental problems. Also appropriate attire needs to be in possession of all children. Ways need to be found to remedy these problems. Then too, pupils can be hostile toward each other such as being rude. Correct manners need to be practiced at all times. Bullying is a continual problem in the school setting. It is a practice which needs to be continually monitored and eliminated. Many of the violent situations in schools have originated with causes of bullying. Columbine High School in Denver with its school related murders in 1997 had bullying as a source. The persons being bullied resorted to violence as a solution to the problem. These are unfortunate situations for the ones being bullied as well as for the perpetrators. Fear abounds when no one is there to stop the bullying. Name calling and egging individuals on in a fight can indeed make for disasters. Rather, efforts should be made for peaceful solutions to problems. Pupils should achieve worthwhile objectives in the school curriculum.

The psychology of learning needs to be used in teaching situations including the following:

* interest in learning needs to be motivated. With increased energy for learning, the pupil puts forth adequate effort for achieving. Learners need to be actively engaged in ongoing experiences. Active, not passive, learners do better in teaching and learning situations.
* meaningful experiences must be in the offing. With attached meaning, pupils understand what is being taught and learned. Rote learning and memorization are definitely not recommended, but rather that which makes sense needs to be in the offing.

* purpose in learning needs to be emphasized in that pupils perceive reasons for achieving goals of instruction. The goals become clear and attainable when purpose is inherent in the learning process.

* relevancy in learning must be stressed. With relevancy, the pupil perceives the subject matter to be acquired as being salient. Importance is attached to what is being acquired.

* scaffolding is needed when there is a gap between where the pupil is and a desired reasonable goal. The substitute teacher may then fill the gap with sequential activities for goal attainment (Ediger, 2006).

EVALUATION OF ACHIEVEMENT

Substitute teachers need to possess a broad repertoire of testing and evaluation methods. The philosophy of testing to ascertain student achievement stresses precision in determining how much has been learned. The use of tests which measures learner progress emphasizes specificity with the use of numerical indicators. A student's achievement may then be on the fortieth percentile, for example. Thus, there are 60 being above and 40 below for every 100 students tested. Each test has a standard error of measurement since none measures achievement perfectly. Thus, if from pilot studies, a test has a standard error of measurement of two percentiles, the student's results on the 40th percentile can vary from the 38th to the 42nd percentile. The standard error of measurement, for example, is computed from the test/retest situation in the pilot study. Perfect reliability is not possible since no test measures perfectly.

Standardized testing emphasizes that all variables are controlled, except the test-taker. Thus, the following are held constant:

* test items for a particular age or grade level

* directions for test-taking

* time limits for taking the test
* test scoring with the same key in computerized scoring used for each age level of test-takers
* mass numbers of tests scored with modern technology
* the same objectives being available for each grade/age level of achievement.

Constructivism is somewhat opposite in philosophy as compared to standardized testing. What is important to learn is not always measurable such as having quality values, caring for others, and having positive feelings toward learning. With constructivism, students are more in control of the curriculum in choosing what to learn. The substitute teacher is a guide and encourages continuous pupil progress. The objectives are rather open ended in terms of what to learn. Pupils tend to sequence their own learnings. Knowledge is tentative and subject to change. To evaluate learner achievement, additional approaches than testing must be used to assess achievement such as using teacher observation of pupil progress. Pupil self-evaluation is also used. Portfolios, a carefully chosen selection of pupil daily work, are used by teachers, parents, and school administrators to assess in noticing learner achievement and progress (Ediger, 2006).

By asking questions, the substitute teacher notices if pupils understand and are able to make sense of subject matter studied. In closing, the substitute teacher needs to be a good classroom manager of instruction. He/she needs to be aware of acceptable noise levels in the classroom, if pupils prefer formal versus informal seating arrangements, as well as the degree of conformity as compared to nonconformity in learning experiences preferred. Then too, the substitute teacher must consider if pupils like to study by themselves as compared to working in committee endeavours. Pupils also differ from each other in terms of preferring auditory, tactual, and kinesthetic ways of learning (Searson and Dunn, 2001).

The substitute teacher is a decision maker and determines objectives, learning activities, and appraisal procedures. He/

she needs to be flexible in arriving at curricular choices made and ways of doing things since the regular teacher will also make decisions prior to and after the professional services rendered by the substitute teacher. However, the substitute teacher also needs to be a change agent and bring innovations to any classroom (See, Kent, 2005).

REFERENCES

Ediger, Marlow (2006), "Scaffolding and the Reading Curriculum," *Iowa Educational Leadership*, 8(4), 24-26.

Ediger, Marlow (2006), "Testing vs. Portfolios to Assess Achievement," *Journal of Instructional Psychology*, 13(1), 31-32.

Feldman, S. (2003), "The Right Line of Questioning," *Teaching Pre K-8*, 33(4), 8.

Fiene, Judy, and Susan Mc Mahan (2007), "Assessing Comprehension: A Classroom Based Process," *The Reading Teacher*, 60(5), 406-419.

Kent, Andrea Moore (2005), Acknowledging the Need Facing Teacher Education Programs: Responding to Make A Difference," *Education*, 125(3), 343-348.

Searson, Robert, and Rita Dunn (2001), "The Learning Styles Teaching Model", *Science and Children*, 38 (5), 22-36.

Tiedt, Iris M. (1983), *The Language Arts Handbook*. Englewood Cliffs, New Jersey: Prentice-Hall, Inc.

34

Meaning in Reading Instruction

Students are challenged to pass mandated tests in grades three through eight and the exit test on the secondary school level in order to be promoted to the next higher grade level or to receive a high school diploma. Failure is certainly a negative experience. It behooves reading teachers to assist learners to attach meaning to what is being learned in each lesson and unit of study. Meaningful learnings provide building blocks for the ensuing achievable objectives of instruction. Understandings then need to be developed for the learner to benefit sequentially from ongoing experiences. What might the teacher do to facilitate meaning in the reading curriculum?

MEANING IN READING

The reading curriculum needs to be designed so that objectives are achieved sequentially. Each achieved objective provides readiness for the ensuing end to be attained by learners. Thus, the objectives are closely ordered in complexity, making it possible for meaning to be achieved in each step along the way.

Ideas gleaned from reading need to make sense. For example, in using the Big Book in teaching reading, all children in a small group should see the illustrations and the large print clearly, as well as make sense of the subject matter on each page. Holism is involved in learning to read ideas.

First of all in teaching from the Big Book, the teacher points to the illustrations for discussion purposes so that learners might possess the background knowledge to attach meaning to the ensuing content. He/she then reads the first page and points briefly to each printed word pronounced. The content is read holistically so that learners understand what is being read. Next, students read along aloud with the teacher pointing to each word briefly as it is being read. The procedure may be repeated as often as desired. Here, students learn to identify each word while still focusing upon ideas being read. The teacher might play games with children after the selection has been read such as students

* locate a word or words which begin like the one the teacher pronounced
* find a word which ends like a given word
* find a word which has medial letters as the given word (Ediger and Rao, 2001).

The above three activities bring phonics to bear in game form, but not as drill. The attention span of children must be maintained and not minimized.

During story time, the teacher has a plethora of opportunities to have children enjoy literature. Library books chosen to be read aloud to children should be engaging so that meaningful ideas are secured. To engage children further, the teacher may ask a few questions pertaining to content read. Thus, children have opportunities to expand ideas and whet desires to read more literature.

Learners should have ample chances to select library books of personal interest to read silently. A peer may assist when help is necessary to identify unknown words in print. The student needs to read library book content holistically so that understanding of ideas is in evidence. Meaningful learnings are salient. With success in reading, increased effort in mastering the printed words should be forthcoming. Once students have a basic sight vocabulary and enjoy hearing ideas read, then progress in reading will increase. Teacher observation may be used to notice learner achievement and progress in reading. Thus, the student will reveal ability to concentrate, read an increased number of books, and talk about what has been read within ongoing lessons and units of study (See, Short *et al.*, 2002).

Individualized reading is also an approach which might be used to secure and maintain learner interest in a desire to read meaningful content. Here, the student selects, from among others, sequential library books to read. A wide variety of library books, consisting of different genres should be in the offing. After completion of reading a book, the student has a conference with the teacher to appraise learner appreciation of the book read as well as comprehension of content. The student may read aloud a section of the book to reveal reading fluency. The teacher dates and records comprehension of ideas as well as developed reading skills. The information is referred to for the next sequential conference of the same student. Holism and meaning are salient to stress in individualized reading. Independence in reading is being emphasized when the student makes choices of sequential books to read. Assistance in word recognition may be provided as needed (Tiedt, 1983).

With the use of basal readers, there are numerous opportunities for learners to attach meaning to each activity. Prior to reading a selection, students individually may hypothesize what the selection will pertain to by viewing the related contextual illustrations. After the completion of the reading experience, students may check their individual hypothesis. When studying the illustrations and listening to student hypotheses, learners glean much background information which is beneficial to attach meaning to subject matter being read. Then too, as students hypothesize, new words in the ensuing reading selection may be printed on the chalkboard. The new words being introduced help students to view and become familiar with the words so they are recognized in print. Contextual meaning of the new words should be discussed as they will appear in the reading selection. Meaningful vocabulary development is very important in becoming a good reader.

Students might then read the selection. A followup experience involves discussing questions pertaining to subject matter read. Understanding of the contents is highly salient in a meaningful reading curriculum. Attached meaning assists a student to become an increasingly fluent reader. A branching out of ideas might well accrue when learners are encouraged to read library books or stories written by the same author, of the same genera, or of similar content.

The experience chart for young readers, in particular, has assisted many children to enjoy reading experiences. The teacher then needs to have children experience something of interest, such as objects at a learning center. After viewing and discussing these objects among themselves and with the teacher, students may then present ideas as to what has been observed. The ideas need to be presented slowly so they can be recorded in neat manuscript letters on the chalkboard by the teacher. Learners see talk written down. The presented ideas are encoded. Later, the ideas may be decoded when the teacher points to each printed word in sequence as it is read aloud. The entire experience chart may be reread as often as desired to assist students in developing a basic sight vocabulary as well as comprehending content. With rereading, students can become fluent readers without the props such as the teacher pointing to each printed word being read. Meaningful learnings are being developed when learners associate the concrete objects on the learning center with the encoded words, resulting in fluent reading.

Experience charts may be filed and bound for future use. This procedure may also be used in remedial reading for older students.

FRAMEWORKS FOR READING INSTRUCTION

Liang and Dole (2006) asks, "What are comprehension instructional frameworks?" A framework is commonly defined as a set of ideas or principles that provides the basis or outline that is more fully developed at a later stage. When teachers use frameworks—a set of ideas or principles—to organize their instruction, we can say they are using an instructional framework. The set of ideas or principles serves as an outline for later developing more complete lessons for their instruction.

As one framework, Palincsar and Brown (1984) developed reciprocal teaching which contained four strategies: predicting what a story will entail; summarizing the predictions; asking questions about the ensuing story to be read; and clarifying what has been read. These four strategies when emphasized stress comprehension or meaning in reading instruction.

A framework may also be built around principles of learning when developing a sound reading curriculum such as

* providing interesting goal centered experiences
* assisting learners to be actively engaged in achieving
* helping pupils perceive meaning in the reading curriculum
* motivating learners to achieve in ongoing lessons and units of study
* guiding students to experience purposeful activities (Ediger and Rao, 2003).

By having the above principles of learning in mind when teaching reading, a quality reading lesson or unit should accrue.

CONCLUSION

A variety of procedures may be used in teaching reading. The reading teacher needs to be careful in assisting learners to attach meaning to what is being read. Thus, learnings make sense and it becomes useful in reading fluently. Technology can certainly make its contributions in assisting students in reading.

One of the greatest problems that poor readers face is deficit in background knowledge in many subject areas. We have all read text that made no sense even though we could read all the words. Typically in these cases, we don't have the knowledge needed to comprehend the text. READ 180 remedies this problem. Before reading a text passage, the learner watches a short anchor video that provides the background knowledge to make sense of the text. The anchor videos are clustered around three areas: people and culture, science and math, history and geography. After viewing the video, the student is shown a text passage about the video that is on his/her pre-tested reading level. READ 180 includes support much like that found in text-reader software, when needed, the student can prompt the computer to provide help in decoding words, phrases, or the entire passage (Hesselbring and Bausch, 2006).

Computer technology can assist students in many facets of reading instruction to develop increasingly fluent readers.

REFERENCES

Ediger, Marlow, and D. Bhaskara Rao (2003), *Psychology and the curriculum*. New Delhi, India: Discovery Publishing House.

Ediger, Marlow, and D. Bhaskara Rao (2001), *Teaching Reading Successfully*. New Delhi, India: Discovery Publishing House.

Hesselbring, Ted S., and Margaret E. Bausch (2006), "Assistive technologies for reading," *Educational Leadership*, 63(4), 72-75.

Liang, Lauren Aimonette, and Janice Dole (2006), "Help with teaching reading comprehension: comprehension instructional frameworks," *The Reading Teacher*, 59(8), 2006.

Palincsar, A.S., and A.L. Brown (1984), "Reciprocal Teaching of Comprehension Fostering and Comprehension Monitoring Activities", *Cognition and Instruction*, 1, 117-175.

Short, Kathy, et. al. (2002), "Thoughts from the editor," *Language Arts*, 80 (2), 91.

Tiedt, Iris M. (1983), *The Language arts Handbook*, Englewood Cliffs, New Jersey: Prentice-Hall, Inc.

35

Problems in Reading Instruction

There are numerous issues in the teaching of reading. These need to be resolved through discussion and debate. A familiar issue pertains to phonics versus whole language approach. Thus, how much of decoding should be taught such as in sound symbol relationships as compared to students learning to read content more holistically. The former approach provides keys to unlock unknown words. When this is done, students do tend to lose out on subject matter content. In holism, students may attach meaning to the story but might have difficulties in determining unknown words. Perhaps, a blend of the two can be stressed. The needs of the learner need primary consideration, be it in word recognition (phonics) or in comprehension of subject matter as in holism (Ediger and Rao, 2007).

FLUENCY IN READING

Fluency in reading has always been a major goal in teaching students. It has been a major objective in the teaching of reading. Fluency has always meant to read words sequentially, using proper voice inflection, without pauses or stops unless punctuation is involved. Then too, the reading is done at a reasonable rate of speed, involving appropriate comprehension. What is read must always be understood. Word recognition and comprehension are involved. This has eliminated repeating a word or phrase. Also, rereading a sentence is not desired. It would be good if a reader pronounced all words correctly and comprehension were at a 100 per cent level. However, a good reader may also retrack at times to notice if ideas were interpreted correctly and particular words were correctly identified (See McKenna, et.al. (Dec-Jan, 2007).

Meaning attached to subject matter read matter read is emphasized in reading. The following ingredients are then being stressed:

* grapheme and phoneme relationships are being emphasized,
* attention is given to words which are non-phonetic in spelling,
* silent letters are omitted in pronunciation,
* contextual meaning of words is in evidence,
* words form sentences and sentences form paragraphs,
* holism is taking shape when entire structures make sense.

Higher levels of comprehension are involved when the reader consciously

* analyzes and thinks critically pertaining to ideas read. Ideas are then separated in terms of being factual from those being opinions, or statements representing reality versus fantasy.
* thinks in an original manner and comes up with unique, novel, interpretations.
* reads between the lines to interpret content. Literal interpretation of what the author says is important; however, the reader also needs to determine if there are additional ideas inherent beyond what the author is stating.

* locates information to solve problems. Generally, a variety of reference sources are necessary in problem solving.

There certainly are a variety of ~inds of interpretation of content read as noted above. Diverse methods of interpretation are necessary in reading narrative, expository, and creative content. Thus, students need to use higher levels of cognition when engaged in the act of reading (Ediger, 2007).

The digital age is certainly upon us. Contributions from the digital age need careful attention and implemented where warranted. Prensky (2005-06) wrote the following:

> Educators have slid into the 21 st century—and into the digital age—still doing a great many things the old way. It's time for education leaders to raise their heads above the daily grind and observe the new landscape that's emerging. Recognizing and analyzing its characteristics will help define the education leadership with which we should be providing our students, both now and in the coming decades.

Times have changed. So, too, have the students, the tools and the requisite skills and knowledge. Let's take a look at some of the features of our 21st century landscape that will be of utmost to those entrusted with the stewardship of our children's 21st century education.

Computer technology has certainly changed the way teachers teach. Many consider digital tools as an extension of student brains. A major problem pertains to evaluating which types of programs are effective to assist students achieve objectives of instruction. Then too, are there methods of instruction which might help students to gain increased proficiency in selected facets of reading instruction other than the use of computers and technology? There have been challenges to students being engaged excessively with computers to the exclusion of interacting with other children in school and society (See Mattox and Zeeff, 2006).

Much attention is being paid to teaching diverse word recognition techniques to students. Each major approach has definite recommendations. Which word recognition techniques in teaching and learning, predominately, should students receive major attention?

Phonics instruction has had a long history in teaching reading. With phonics, students learn to associate phonemes (letters) with graphemes (related sounds). The learning activities here need to possess purpose and be engaging. Those words which show a direct relationship between symbol and sound should be taught. A lack of consistency indicates a need for sight methods of instruction.

Syllabication skills should also be taught as a word recognition technique. Thus, if a student does not recognize a word, dividing it into syllables may help in correct identification. There are common prefixes and suffixes which may assist students to correctly identify words. Thus, a student may know the root word, but fail to recognize it with the added prefix/suffix. Removing the prefix/suffix may then assists in its correct identification. A variety of learning activities should be used to teach word recognition skills, including games. Too frequently, word recognition techniques have been taught through the use of drill and more drill. And yet, there are a variety of interesting experiences to use to engage students in ongoing learning opportunities.

Word recognition lessons need to incorporate meaning theory: With meaning, students understand what has been read. They enjoy and appreciate the contents of subject matter.

HOLISM AND READING

There are recommendable holistic procedures in the teaching of reading. The Big Book approach has a plethora of followers in the teaching of reading. Here, a quality library book, with print large enough for a set of six to seven readers to see clearly is used in reading instruction. The teacher discusses the illustrations in the library book with children.

He/she then reads aloud the contents of the selection while students follow along to each pointed word. In the next activity, students read aloud with the teacher as the latter again points to each word. Rereading may be done as often as necessary for students to recognize each word in print. Phonics and syllabication skills are taught as needed. However, the emphasis is upon holism in gaining ideas from the reading selection. Students learn to identify words through group reading of the selection, repeated as necessary and desired.

A second approach, namely individualized reading, also stresses reading subject matter holistically. Thus, from a selection of library books, the student individually chooses a book to read. Generally, students choose books to read based on their individual developmental level. The selected book, hopefully, is then on the reading level of the chooser. Self selected books capture student interest more so than if the teacher makes choices for learners, according to advocates of individualized reading programs.

After having read the chosen library book, the student has a conference with the teacher to appraise comprehension and reading fluency through oral reading. The teacher appraises student achievement in reading and records/dates important information. Comparisons may then be made with later conferences for each individual student. Word recognition skills to be taught are left to the discretion of the teacher (See Harris and Sipay, 1985).

CONCLUSION

There are a plethora of issues in the teaching of reading. Teachers, supervisors, and administrators need to study and analyze each issue in depth, using a variety of high quality reference sources. Decision making requires a broad base of knowledge and skills. Each student needs adequate attention in teaching and learning situations in order to become proficient in reading. Carefully chosen objectives, learning opportunities, and evaluation procedures to be implemented are musts in doing a good job of teaching reading.

REFERENCES

Ediger, Marlow (2007), "Purposeful Reading and the Student," *Edutracks* , 6 (9), 11-12.

Ediger, Marlow, and D. Bhaskara Rao (2007), *Reading Curriculum and Instruction*. New Delhi, India: Discovery Publishing House.

Harris, Albert J., and Edward Sipay (1985), *How to Increase Reading Ability*. White Plains, New York:, Inc.

Mattox, Stephen, and Colleen Zeeff (2006), "'Teaching Through' Trade Books," *Science and Children*, 44 (2), 14-16.

Mc Kenna, et. al. (Dec.-Jan. 2006-2007), "Revisiting the Role of Miscue Analysis in Effective Teaching," *The Reading Teacher*, 60 (4), 378..381.

Prensky, Marc (Dec-Jan 2005-2006), "Listen to the Natives," *Educational Leadership*, 63 (4), 9-13.

36

Sequence in Reading Achievement

There are a plethora of issues in reading instruction. Each issue needs study, examination, and analysis. Synthesis is necessary to come up with an appropriate plan for teaching reading. The accepted plan must provide for the needs of each student. No student should fail, but be successful in a developmentally important plan of instruction. A major problem is to find that procedure of teaching and learning in reading.

ANALYSIS OF PLANS FOR READING INSTRUCTION

Selected specialists in reading instruction advocate heavy teaching of decoding skills in beginning instruction for young learners. Thus, phonemics should receive considerable attention in that students hear likenesses and differences in sounds. Students also need to receive much assistance in phonics to unlock words in associating symbol (graphemes) associated with sounds (phonemes). Automatic decoding is an ultimate goal here. Words which are consistent between symbol and sound provide the best basis in helping students associate graphemes and phonemes. Words which do not have this consistency, but follow a pattern may also be taught in sequence. Word families may not possess the sound symbol relationship but do patten provide students with aids to identify unknown words. Concept and vocabulary activities provide opportunities for word recognition involving young children. Eventually in sequence, students will do more reading of narrative and expository materials. However, phonics will still receive major emphasis in teaching reading. According to phonics advocates, decoding skills come first in helping students learn to read (Ediger, 2006).

In order to comprehend, readers must be able to read the words. Some level of automatic decoding must be present so that short-term memory can work on comprehending, not on decoding words. Teachers help students to get to the level of automatic decoding by phonemic awareness and phonics at all grade levels. If students put too much mental energy into sounding out the words, they will have less mental energy left to think about the meaning. While teachers on the primary grades work with phonemic awareness and phonics, teachers in the intermediate grades support students' continued development of automatic decoding through spelling, vocabulary, and high frequency word activities. (Pardo, 2006).

Somewhat opposite of the decoding process in reading instruction are approaches stressing holism. The big book approach is an example. Here, the teacher selects an interesting book for learners which is large in size so that all students in a small group can see the contents clearly. The teacher briefly discusses the illustrations contained adjacent to the script. This activity provides background information as well as readiness for reading. The teacher reads a short selection from the big book, pointing to individual words read aloud as students follow along. For the second read aloud, students read together with the teacher. As the reading act progresses, children begin to recognize more words for developing a basic sight vocabulary. The oral reading experience may be repeated as often as desired. The teacher may ask a few questions covering content read. He/she may also have learners notice words which begin alike and those which end alike, but these experiences occur after children establish meaning and understanding of story content.

Holism emphasized in big book use stresses students acquiring interesting content as they identify words in print. Repetition in the read aloud assists students to reinforce sight word recognition.

Poetry may also be read aloud with choric reading stressed. Alliteration, similes, and metaphors provide further interest as poetic forms.

The teacher may use selected phonic learnings to develop a basic sight vocabulary of words. Thus, students may notice:

* words patterning with the same initial letters and those with terminal letters.
* words having patterning with a long vowel sound.
* words with rhyme.

IMPORTANT CONSIDERATIONS IN TEACHING READING

The question often arises "What makes for quality instruction?" Perhaps, the question may be stated more specifically in terms of what makes for good teaching in reading. Guidelines for reading instruction may be stated to assist in understanding the answer:

* Students need to understand and attach meaning to what is being learned in reading. Rote learning and memorization will not suffice. Knowledge and skills must be developmentally appropriate, be it in phonics instruction or in comprehension of content. Learners tend to turn off if meaning is lacking in teaching and learning situation. Knowledge and skills must make sense to the learner. Indepth learning is recommended.
* learning opportunities need to be challenging, yet realistic to students. They may be too complex and demanding. The opposite extreme stresses learning opportunities being so easy that little effort needs to be put forth in learning to read. The teacher faces a problem in reading instruction in harmonizing the

excessively complex learnings with that of being too easy and lacking challenge. Each student needs to achieve as optimally as possible in reading instruction. Success is a motivator for students which provides readiness for the next sequential learning.

Students should have opportunities to select what to learn, from among alternatives. An ample supply of quality library books on the reading level of students should be in the offing. Choices may then be made in terms of which books to read sequentially. Energized learning occurs when each student has a voice in decision-making:

* scaffolding needs to be used in teaching reading when a learning activity becomes too difficult. Here, the teacher sequences experiences carefully so that the perceived goal is achieved. Poor sequencing in ordering learning opportunities makes for lower student achievement. Each student is important and should not fall through the slats.

* a positive learning environment needs to be in evidence whereby students and teachers respect and care for each other. Feelings of belonging must be met by school personnel and classmates. An extremely competitive learning environment makes for dissension and put downs. Rather, assistance should be provided where needed to learners in order that continual progress is in evidence.

* learners need to be recognized for achieving as well as possible. Then all can receive praise for work well done. Students have esteem needs and these must be recognized. Each desires to be recognized for dong as well as possible. Formative evaluation needs to be stressed so that learning activities are sequential within a unit of study. Learning activities can still be improved upon in the ongoing unit of study. Feedback from students will provide needed information on redoing what is left in the ongoing unit of study. Summative evaluation, too, needs to be emphasized in

that the completed unit now needs assessment to ascertain what needs to be changed and modified the next time the unit is taught.

* resources need to be organized to make for improved instruction in reading. The following then need to be available in a multimedia approach in teaching reading:

(1) basal readers, library books, encyclopedias, and other verbal materials for teaching

(2) audio visual aids such as video tapes, power print presentations, CDs, DVDs, and cassettes

(3) written work including the writing of reports, summaries, conclusions, outlines, plays, poems, and stories, among others

(4) oral communication activities such as oral reports, explanations, directions given, public speaking, experiences, dramatic activities, peer teaching, discussions, and debates (Ediger and Rao, 2005).

Student achievement needs to be carefully monitored and assistance given where needed. A variety of evaluation techniques must be used to assess learner progress.

Technology has made great inroads into todays' programs of reading instruction. Revisiting the literature from the 1990s on instructional technology is like journeying back to a more nostalgic and hopeful time when promises of computers—and their potential impact on student learning—appeared boundless. Used in concert with a learner centered instructional approach and a curriculum that focused on authentic learning, computers, it was thought, would serve as "mind tools (Jonassen, 1996) to build students' higher order thinking skills. In fact, the terms "computers" and higher order thinking" formed a sort of double helix in instructional technology parlance instructional supports in the United States—such as E-rate and federal funding for hardware, software, and teacher training initiatives—exemplified a commitment to the belief that computers could transform student learning...

The jury is still out on the impact of computers on student learning but before we dismiss computers as an expensive fad or boondoggle, schools must take measures to ensure that they are using computers to their fullest instructional potential. Only then can we reclaim the optimism that greeted technology's dawn in the classroom. Only then will we witness the good work that results when schools use good tools well (Burns, 2006).

Children's beliefs about their ability to learn also affect their learning. Children who develop perceptions of themselves as academically incompetent and expect to fail don't exert much effort on school tasks, and they give up as soon as they encounter difficulty. Engagement in academic tasks is also affected by students' sense of personal control. Children enjoy school work less and are less engaged when they feel they are working only because they have too

Luckily, much is known about practices that foster feelings of competence and expectations for success. These beliefs are not taught "directly". Rather they are influenced by the nature and difficulty level of the tasks children are asked to complete and by the kind of evaluation used and the nature of feedback they receive. Children's self confidence is maintained by working on tasks that require some effort (so that when they complete them they have a sense of satisfaction and achievement). However, the tasks must not be so difficult that children cannot complete them even if they try. The huge variability in children's skill is why rigidly paced instruction is inappropriate; if all children are asked do the same task, It will inevitably be too easy (and thus boring) for some students too difficult (and thus discouraging) for others (Stipek, 2006).

CONCLUSION

Quality sequence is needed to provide for student optimal achievement in reading. Objectives must be ordered properly so that students individually might tackle those which harmonize with their individual present level of achievement. Learning opportunities to achieve objectives need to be on the developmental level of students and sequenced so that continual progress may be made. Assessment procedures need to be ongoing to provide valid/reliable feedback to students as well as indicate sequential progress.

REFERENCES

Burns, Mary (2006), "Tools for the Mind," *Educational Leadership*, 63 (4), 48-53.

Ediger, Marlow (2006), "Present day Philosophies of Education", *Journal of Instructional Psychology*, 32(3), 179-182.

Ediger, Marlow, and D. Bhaskara Rao (2005), Quality School Education. New Delhi, India: Discovery Publishing House.

Jonassen, D.H., *et al*. "Computers as Mind Tools for Engaging Learners in Critical Thinking," *Tech trends*, 43 (2), 24-32.

Pardo, Laura S. (2006), "What every teacher needs to know about comprehension, *The Reading Teacher*, 58(3), 272-279.

Stipek, Deborah (2006), "Accountability comes to Preschool: Can We make it Work for Young Children?" *Phi delta kappan*, 87(10), 740-744.

37

Student Teacher and Reading Curriculum

Student teachers have completed undergraduate degree requirements and are now ready for the final phase of becoming fully certified and licensed in the profession of teaching. They now work together with a supervisor in the public schools, generally named the cooperating teacher. The cooperating teacher, during the allotted time, provides rich learning opportunities for the student teacher to experience sequentially that which a fully certified professional does in every day operations in the school setting.

Harmonious relationships between the student teacher and the cooperating teacher must be in evidence in order to plan objectives, learning activities to achieve the objectives, as well as evaluation procedures to ascertain if the chosen ends have been achieved. The writer will pursue this paper in terms of what the student teacher needs to develop proficiency in one major curriculum area and that is reading instruction. This will make selected assumptions that the cooperating teacher is involved in planning and supervision.

TEACHING READING AND THE PUPIL

Reading across the curriculum has been a slogan for some time. Reading is generally emphasized in most academic disciplines. One problem which has received scant attention pertains to what should be stated as objectives for pupils to achieve in reading across the curriculum. Which skills should student teachers possess in stressing reading across the curriculum?

Student teachers need to be prepared to select relevant objectives of instruction. These ends need to stress meaningful learnings which pupils understand. Purpose or reasons for learning must be emphasized. The learnings need to be useful and practical in learning to read as well as reading to learn. The following skills have utilitarian values for student teachers:

* teaching phonics to a pupil as needed and not for the sake of doing so. Phonic knowledge for its own sake has little value for the child. Rather, these skills need to be applied in practical situations.

* context clues can be useful when a word is not identified. The pupil then tries a word for the unknown to see if it fits in meaningfully. Phonics may also be applied to assist in correct selection of the originally unknown word.

* pictures in context might well help in the identification of an unknown word. Thus, if a pupil cannot identify a word, he/she may view the same page illustration in securing clues. The picture then may give away what the "unknown word" is.

* reading words, alone, is not meaningful unless the pupil understands what is being read. Each pupil needs to consciously attach meaning to words, sentences, and paragraphs read. Reading is done to obtain ideas, not merely pronounce words. Comprehension of ideas read by pupils must be stressed by the teacher. Critical and creative thinking, as well as problem solving needs to be emphasized (Ediger and Rao, 2007).

READING FOR ENJOYMENT

There are a plethora of approaches which might well assist pupils to enjoy reading. Intrinsically, learners then reach out to view and choose library books to read. Individualized reading is one procedure. Here, the classroom needs to have an ample number of books on different genres. This makes it possible for a pupil to choose what is of interest. Also, the books available need to be on diverse reading levels so that a developmentally appropriate book may be selected. Once these two criteria have been met, the child is ready to settle down to read. A good reader needs to be available to pronounce unknown words to the pupil. Reading experiences tend to be enjoyable if the learner:

* is able to choose his/her own reading materials
* likes the topic being pursued
* reads independently the contents of the library book
* uses his/her own abilities to unlock unknown words
* applies learnings to new situations (See Gardner, 1995).

Appreciating subject matter learned through reading is vital in gaining increased proficiency in reading. Then too, knowledge that is used is retained longer. Knowledge not used tends to be forgotten sooner.

Second, what is read should relate to concrete situations if it is to be used in practical situations, and this can be emphasized in a language experience approach. The concrete phase of learning for children is always easier than the abstract standing by itself. The concrete pertains to lifelike situations, things, and reality. In small group work then children may view selected objects on a learning center. The objects are of interest and stimulate curiosity. Pupils may examine each object and discuss ideas pertaining thereto with other committee members. Pupils might then say aloud what was observed with the student teacher recording each idea on the chalkboard or using a computer and large screen to project content clearly. One pupil at a time should present ideas so that the student teacher may readily record each. Learners need to listen carefully to each idea presented to avoid duplication of ideas. After the student teacher has recorded content in neat manuscript letters or via computer and screen, he/she needs to read aloud each sentence, pointing to each recorded word. Next, pupils together read aloud the sentences with the teacher, followed by the pupils solely reading on their own. The rereading might be done again as often as desired. Here, pupils are developing a basic sight vocabulary of words read. The sentences given relate to the observed concrete objects, making the ideas meaningful to pupils. Then too, pupils are learning to read not only meaningful words, but also sentences and short paragraphs. They have noted that talk can be written down. What has been written may also be read. Ideas read should be meaningful since pupils presented the content from personal concrete experiences pertaining to objects at the learning center.

Without the ability to read and write, students are placed at a disadvantage in almost every educational and real world setting. In order to better understand how to meet individual needs of young learners, it is important to identify what constitutes an effective teacher of reading. Effective teachers of reading will not only enhance student's reading development, but they will also lead learners to a lifelong love of literacy.

Reading is an interactive process, which consists of multiple interactions between variables such as the reader's background, the classroom context, reading materials, developmental levels, teacher's instructional style, and learning goals. Teachers must use a variety of classroom teaching strategies, because no single method can reach all readers successfully (Mohr and Mohr, 2007).

Third holism in reading instruction may be stressed by the student teacher with the Big Book approach. Here, a large book with interesting illustrations and related content is placed on a stand for all to see clearly within a small group of four to six pupils. Background information is developed within pupils by discussing the large illustrations. The student teacher reads a loud the content as pupils follow along to the pointed abstract words in the Big Book. This is followed by pupils joining in the oral reading and looking carefully at each word being read. Next, pupils need to read the text together. Rereading might be stressed as often as desired. Pupils learn to recognize words in a contextual situation. Vocabulary development is also emphasized contextually.

With the Big Book approach, pupils are reading without interruptions; not being able to identify words correctly is not a problem. A basic sight word vocabulary is being developed in reading and rereading the Big Book content. The student teacher may teach phonics after the oral reading has been completed with interesting experiences such as asking pupils to find words in context which begin or end as a specific word such as "cat". Additional phonic leanings may be stressed as desired.

Although it is laudatory to raise academic standards and demand proficiency from all students, schools should stand for more than academic success. Schools should also be protected places where students can develop the character and capacities that make us human...(Farbman, 2007).

Holism in reading might well be expanded to educating the whole child. An individual consists of more than the academic facet, but involves, among others, the emotions, physical development, as well social competence. It is the whole child who is involved in learning. Too frequently, only one facet has been emphasized/mandated and that being the academic. Measurement philosophy of education tends to stress that which can be measured after instruction has been completed. Precise objectives are then determined. Learning activities are aligned with the objectives. Too assess learner achievement, teachers need to measure such as in standardized testing. Test results are provided in numerical terms including percentiles, and grade equivalents. Humanism stresses holism in the curriculum such as integration of subject matter, reading and literature, as well as the fine arts. Creativity and critical thinking receive high priority (Ediger, 2005).

Fourth, the basal reading approach has been important traditionally. It still has considerable merit in reading instruction. The accompanying manual of a basal offers objectives for pupils to achieve, learning activities, and evaluation procedures. Creative teachers might use the best of these learning experiences and choose others from their very own experiences which have worked well in the past to motivate pupils progress. The basal reader and its accompanying manual may be considered as a complete reading program. A brief summary might well be given here to indicate a model for basal reader use:

* the illustrations for each story may be used to provide readiness experiences for the ensuing reading opportunity
* questions need to be encouraged from learners when activating pupil background information, and these should be recorded to assist pupils in locating answers from the actual reading activity
* it is good to have pupils predict what will happen in the contents, prior to its reading. They can then check their predictions from the actual reading
* new words from the story to be encountered should be printed on the chalkboard. The manual will provide suggested words in addition to what the teacher believes pupils will need to identify in context. By pronouncing orally each of these words clearly ahead of time, the pupil has a better chance of their recognition while reading.
* decoding skills may be taught as needed, such as short and long vowel sounds, among others.

Following the reading activity, pupils might be guided by the student teacher to evaluate their individual predictions as well as discuss in-depth the story contents. Higher levels of cognition should be stressed such as critical thinking when analyzing facts from opinions, fantasy from reality, as well as accurate from inaccurate subject matter. Creative thinking, too, should be emphasized in that pupils are encouraged to come up with novel, unique ideas, as well as originality in thinking. Then too, problems may be identified, and information gathered to reach a possible solution to a problem. The resulting information must be evaluated to ascertain if it truly solves the problem. Generally, tentative solutions are in the offing. New problems might well arrive due to the problem solving activity which invites identifying additional problems.

In addition, activities engaged in may assist pupils to better understand the subject matter. These activities used to clarify and comprehend ideas gleaned from reading include

* doing a drawing to indicate a summary of content attained
* dramatizing a selection from the story
* writing a conclusion
* making one or more models
* completing a collage

The student teacher needs to continually appraise pupil progress. Weaknesses must be diagnosed and remedied. With readiness developed from the pre-service program and from personal experiences, the student teacher may develop a repertoire of ideas used in the instructional arena.

EVALUATION OF ACHIEVEMENT

A variety of procedures need to be used to assess learner achievement which include student teacher observations and prepared tests, rating scales, check lists, standardized tests to measure learner achievement in reading as well as those which diagnose and remedy errors. Creative ways of assessing pupil progress also need development. The following questions need to be answered by the student teacher:

* did I help the pupil begin where he/she is presently achieving and then stress sequential progress for the involved learner?
* did I provide adequate readiness experiences for the ensuing reading lesson for pupils?
* were pupils challenged to achieve proficiency in reading?
* was scaffolding used to assist pupils to attain more optimally?
* were pupils engaged in higher levels of cognition such as critical and creative thinking as well as problem solving in ongoing lessons?
* did pupils use word attack skills successfully to unlock unknown words?
* were individual differences in reading levels among pupils adequately provided for?
* in discussion groups, did pupils show respect for each other?

A variety of methods need to be used to assess learner achievement in the curriculum (See Stiggins, 2007).

SELF SUSTAINED READING

The student teacher needs to experience pupils reading to themselves. Time should be set aside for pupils to read for enjoyment and practice. A goodly selection of library books on different genera and reading levels need to be available for pupil selection at a learning center. Pupils individually might then browse through and choose sequential library books to read. The classroom atmosphere needs to be one which is conducive to silent reading. The student teacher needs to be available to pronounce words which pupils cannot identify. Pupils need to secure ideas from reading and not spend unnecessary time in attempting to decode words. Reading self selected library books emphasizes interest in choosing materials which are motivating.

A time for sharing ideas gleaned in sustained silent reading should be in the offing. Here, the learner may take turns in presenting ideas clearly and succinctly. Quality standards for sharing include each presenting ideas, but no dominating during sharing time. Interrupting others needs to be avoided. Pupils learn from each other in making choices of what to read by listening to interesting ideas presented during sharing time.

The student teacher needs to supervise well during silent reading time so that each pupil engages actively in the ongoing experience. Assistance needs to be available to make for orderly progress in reading (See Duke, 2006).

CONCLUSION

With increasing availability of computers and technology, the student teacher needs to be highly knowledgeable in innovative methods of reading instruction. A new paradigm is needed to stay abreast of trends and problems in teaching reading. The student teacher of today must be very versatile of modern means of assisting pupils to achieve as optimally as possible in reading. The old has passed away and behold the new is with us. Relevancy and richness in the reading curriculum are essential elements to implement.

REFERENCES

Duke, David L. (2006), "What We Know and Don't Know About Improving Low Performing Schools," *Phi Delta Kappan*, 87 (10),729-724.

Ediger, Marlow (2005), "Present Day Philosophies of Education," *Journal of Instructional Psychology*, 33 (3),179-182.

Ediger, Marlow, and D. Bhaskara Rao (207), *Reading Curriculum and Instruction*. New Delhi, India: Discovery Publishing House.

Farbman, David (2007), "A New Day for Kids," *Educational Leadership*, 64 (8), 62-65.

Gardner, Howard (1995), *Multiple Intelligences: Theory into Practice*. New York: Basic Books.

Mohr, Kathleen A.J., and Eric S. Mohr (2007, "The Effective Teacher of Reading: Considering the what and how of Instruction," *The Reading Teacher*, 60 (5), 437.

Stiggins, Rick (2007), "Assessment Through the Student's Eyes," *Educational Leadership*, 64 (8), 22-26.

38

Motivation in Reading

It is important to motivate students in reading so that more optimal achievement is possible. Motivation increases energy levels for reading. Each student needs to become proficient in reading to do well in school and in society. Later, at the work-place, most need to do a considerable amount of reading to perform and do well. Much of university course work consists of reading. It is important for the young child, entering school, to achieve as well as possible so that delayed progress, for anyone student, might be minimized. Which are selected means to use in teaching to motivate learners in reading instruction?

STRATEGIES TO USE

Learners need to do well in narrative, expository, and creative types of reading materials. Students need to become excited about reading. There are a plethora of interesting ideas to read. Interest makes for effort and motivation. When children individually choose library books to read, interest is a first personal factor in making a book selection. Curiosity as to what will be between the covers of the book stimulates the reading activity. The child wants to know and the desire has to be satisfied. The teacher needs to take time to whet student appetites for reading by telling a little bit of fascination about selected books. Children, in return will want to consume the contents, voluntarily (Ediger and Rao, 2006).

A good bulletin board display of new library book jackets further motivates reading. Calling attention to attractive, new library books are motivators for reading. Telling students a few interesting ideas about each book promotes a desire to read these library books. The teacher's voice needs to be encouraging with inflection to stimulate reading. If students see others read library books, they will sense there is something important in these acts.

During story time, the teacher needs to choose and read aloud library books which motivate student reading. With a good knowledge of children's literature, the teacher might well know which books would be of interest to read orally. Appropriate stress, pitch, and juncture must be involved in the read aloud (See Duke, 2006).

Special time needs to be set aside for students to select and read library books silently in sustained, silent reading (SSR). During this time, teacher observation should be used to ascertain the degree of success of SSR, such as time on task. There should be a time for sharing of ideas read. Sharing ideas assists in students learning content about other library books which might be of interest to read.

Easy access to library books is a must. The student needs to have accessibility to choose and read library books. Browsing in the central library and exploring library book content whets appetites for enjoyment of reading. The librarian should be a helpful person who desires to assist students in the selection of library books. He/she knows the contents of a plethora of library books and enjoys assisting others in securing reading materials.

Reading clubs are beneficial in motivating selected students to read. The club may meet once a week. Officers might be elected for the club. Most of the time in the reading club should be devoted to silent reading and discussion of chosen library books. Indepth discussions need to be stressed.

Oral reading may be emphasized for young children as well as for those who do not read well. Peers may volunteer to do the reading. It is good for peers to assist each other in understanding library book content. Quality attitudes may well be forthcoming when students assist each other. A major goal here is to get students to read and enjoy reading. Purpose for reading may be emphasized when learners secure information from expository book content in answer to a question or to solve a problem. Thus, the student needs to identify a question/problem with teacher guidance in an ongoing unit of study. Deliberation and thought are involved. Critical and creative thinking are necessary to appraise the gathered information, resulting in an hypothesis. The hypothesis is subject to evaluation, analytically and synthetically, before its acceptance (See Goldstein and Noguera, 2006).

Having a rich speaking vocabulary is very helpful in learning to read as well as reading proficiently. Interesting and meaningful ways should be established to guide students in vocabulary development. New words in print discourse should be clearly visible. They may be dramatized, pantomimed, defined orally, used in context, among other procedures, to ascertain understanding. Students then need to recognize the new words in print.

The following should not be done in motivating good reading behaviour:

* criticizing reading behaviour of students who read poorly. Rather, encouragement needs to be given.
* letting students stumble on unidentified words. Rather, the teacher needs to provide assistance when necessary in aiding learners to become independent, successful readers.
* failure to help students to become fluent readers. The teacher needs to model fluency in reading and eliminate deficiencies in students becoming fluent readers.

Edmunds and Bauserman (2006) wrote the following involving student motivation to read library books:

> Based on findings in this study, we have made five recommendations for motivating students in the classroom: Self selection, attention to characteristics of the book, personal interests, access to books, and active involvement of others. We think these suggestions will help increase children motivation to read. We would much rather hear positive comments about reading such as the following ones from students in our study: "Books are interesting and cool," and "I love to read a good story."

REFERENCES

Duke, Daniel L. Duke (2006), "What We Know and Don't Know About Improving Low Performing Schools." *Phi Delta Kappan*, 87 (10), 729-734.

Ediger, Marlow, and D. Bhaskara Rao (2006), *Issues in School Curriculum*. New Delhi, India: Discovery Publishing House.

Edmunds, Kathryn M., and Kathryn L. Bauserman (2006), "What Teachers Can Learn About Reading Motivation Through", *Conversations with Children*, 59(5),414- 424.

Goldstein, Jennifer, and Pedro Noguera (2006), "A Thoughtful Approach to Teacher Evaluation," *Educational Leadership*, 63(6), 31-37.

39

Motivating Student Learning in Reading

Motivating learning is a key element in student success. The teacher needs to possess a wide repertoire of techniques to encourage student learning. Intrinsic motivation comes from within the learner and is considered to be better than extrinsic motivation in which the motivator comes from outside the student. With intrinsic motivation, the learner internally achieves, grows, and develops. Having motivation coming from within the student, he/she sets goals intrinsically. With extrinsic motivation, the teacher announces the award prior to instruction in terms of what the student must do to attain and be successful in goal achievement. Securing the award is continent upon the student achieving the stated goal.

Inservice education is important in order to stress pupil intrinsic motivation in reading. Inservice programs need to stress what is:

* relevant in the teaching of reading
* meaningful to participants
* purposeful in implementation of ideas in the classroom
* useful and practical in assisting pupils with problems in reading

* interesting so that the attention of learners is secured (Ediqer and Rao, 2007a).

INTRINSIC MOTIVATION AND THE STUDENT

Models for intrinsic motivation in reading might well be stressed when the teacher reads aloud to children during story time. The teacher is aware of what interests pupils and selects a library book to read aloud which engages learners in careful listening. With appropriate voice inflection, proper stress, and pitch while reading aloud, the teacher is able to capture the attention of pupils. It is good, too, if the teacher shows the illustrations to pupils as the read aloud progresses. Pupils' appetites for reading may well be motivated though story time read alouds. Teacher enthusiasm for good literature is salient!

To emphasize intrinsic motivation in pupil reading, the teacher may select a set of library books on different genres and reading levels, to be placed at an interest center. The teacher needs to present brief overviews on selected library books. By looking at the illustrations presented by the teacher in a stimulating manner, the pupil will feel motivated to read a self selected book. Hopefully, this will stimulate all to choose a book for reading. For individualized reading, it is best if the child chooses the library book to read; however if the learner cannot settle down to read a book, the teacher may do the selecting based on the learner's personal interests. Intrinsic interests emphasize pupils' intrinsic desires to read (See Vardell, *et al.*, 2006).

Following the reading of a book, the pupil has a conference with the teacher. During the conference, the contents of the book are discussed. The discussion should motivate increased interest in reading. The learner may choose a brief section of the book to read aloud. In this way, the teacher may notice what kind of assistance is necessary for the child to improve reading skills, including comprehension. Motivation to read should come from within the child.

As a university supervisor of student teachers, the author noticed an interesting class whereby a science teacher taught a unit on "The Changing Surface of the Earth". Instead of using the basal textbook as a common source, pupils read a self selected library book based on the unit title. Each pupil volunteered information read from these expository books which answered questions being discussed. The discussion was lively and enthusiastic, as well as focused. Thus, as questions pertaining to the causes of volcanic eruptions was pursued, learners responded with related information from their personal reading. This was a chance in reading from a single source of information. The pupils then had read information pertaining to the unit title using a reference source of personal choice and interest.

One university Student Teacher (ST) listed topics on an overhead for pupil choice in obtaining information pertaining to a social studies unit of study. A few comments were made by the ST on each topic to provide specific background information to motivate interest in learning. Sources to use included the internet as well as more traditional references. Choices included knighthood, noblemen, the guild, castles, peasants, the manor, and serts/slaves. Pupils might choose to work individually or in small groups. This was a very open ended project. The ST and the cooperating teacher worked as resource personnel. They supervised and encouraged pupils in locating sources of information as well as in reading subject matter content. Through teacher observation, the project was considered a success with high learner interest and purpose. Self selection of topics within limitations worked well here.

Another university student teacher, supervised by the author, placed items of interest on a learning center. The items consisted of articles pertaining to a unit on Mexico. Pupils viewed and handled each item carefully and discussed it with peers. Next, the ST asked for comments of what the learners had viewed. These were written down for overhead use. Pupils could then see talk written down. Rules were developed so only one child spoke at time. Politeness and respect were emphasized. Following the writing, pupils with teacher guidance read aloud the content as the latter pointed to each word.

In this activity, pupil interest was involved in looking at each object, chosen to motivate learners, at the interest center. They presented information for the teacher to record. Talk written down was observed. This was followed by pupils reading their very own ideas as the teacher pointed to individual words being read.

To bring a science unit to a satisfactory conclusion, a student teacher listed topics covered in the unit on the chalkboard. Pupils might then choose one of the following and give a few summary statements pertaining: mudslides, floods, hurricanes and tornados, hail, lightening, earthquakes, volcanic eruptions, soil erosion, and avalanches. Here, pupils revealed learnings acquired and, also what was left to learn. Each pupil wrote down summary statements for each concept. He/she was encouraged to develop a related drawing for each concept by viewing a model from a science encyclopedia or textbook. Voluntarily, fifty per cent of pupils in the classroom did the drawings for each concept. Neatness and accuracy were two standards stressed.

Sustained Silent Reading (SSR) reveals the genres of library books chosen by pupils, individually, for reading from the classroom library. The complexity level of library books selected assists in providing for individual differences in reading levels among learners. Then too, the teacher may observe the following:

* time on task for each pupil
* attitudes towards reading
* using reading time wisely
* enjoyment of silent reading time
* sharing ideas read in related ongoing units of study
* enthusiasm toward reading.

Ediger and Rao (2007b) wrote the following:

A rather popular approach in reading silently is sustained silent reading (SSR). Here, each student chooses his/her very own library book to read at a designated time. The learner generally selects a book which is of high interest in inherent content. The SSR activity may be flexible in length, depending upon student interest. Ideally, all in the room read a library book to provide a model for enjoyable reading. There are advocates who say that all in the school should read silently to themselves, including the school custodians, cafeteria workers, and support personnel. This might be difficult to implement, but it is important for each to motivate others to read to the self-model.

Individualized reading is a different program of instruction which emphasizes that each pupil in the class chooses a library book of personal interest to read silently. The student tends to select sequential library books which he/she can read independently with few errors in word recognition. Those words unidentified may become clear as the student continues to read and make sense of ensuing content in the library book. Content is being used to identify original unknown words. Being interested in reading a book has tremendous motivational factors in reading and in learning to read. The excitement of reading its content stimulates a reader to pursue story book contents. After reading the library book, the student generally has a conference with the teacher to check comprehension. The student also reads orally a short selection for the teacher to appraise decoding skills. The teacher records key ideas from the conference to use in assessing the next sequential conference held after the student has again completed reading a library book (See Franzen and Allington, 2006).

CONCLUSION

The teachers and school administrators need to study and implement diverse approaches to motivate students intrinsically. An inward desire to learn is important students then develop feelings of wanting to read in school and in the home setting. Doing much reading assists the learner to improve in reading skins. During the summer months, pupils can lose reading abilities unless intrinsically they are motivated to read interesting books on their own

REFERENCES

Ediger, Marlow, and D. Bhaskara Rao (2007a), *Reading Curriculum and Instruction*. New Delhi, India: Discovery Publishing House.

Ediger, Marlow, and D. Bhaskara Rao (2007b), *Curriculum of School Subjects*. New Delhi, India: Discovery Publishing House, 251.

Franzen, Anne McGill, and Richard Allington (2006), "Contamination of Current Accountability Systems," *Phi Delta Kappan*, 87 (10), 762-766.

Vardell, Sylvia, et. at. (2006), "Matching books and Readers: Selecting Literature for English Learners," *The Reading Teacher*, 59 (8), 734-741.

40

Philosophy of Spelling Instruction

When the writer was in the elementary school during the 1934-1942 school years, he experienced a spelling program whereby twenty words per week were to be mastered. This was for the fourth grade level. The list was adjusted in number for lower as well as higher grade levels. These words were listed in a spelling textbook for each week of study. Learning activities consisted of writing each word five times after the new weekly list was introduced on Monday. The introduction consisted of correct pronunciation of the new words and attaching meaning to each in context or by definition. On Tuesdays, each spelling word was written in a sentence or contained in a paragraph. A mid week test was given on Wednesday and each mis-spelled word was written ten times. On Thursday, students reviewed the correct spelling of words, using a self-chosen method. The final test for the week was on Friday with grades given on the results for each student. A separate category for spelling grades appeared on the monthly report card.

Much emphasis was placed upon correct spelling of words listed in the text book. Spelling received about twenty minutes of time per day. An annual spelling contest was held county wide in McPherson County, Kansas. The writer still has two red ribbons for winning second place in 1937/1939 school years. From each school in the county wide contest, words were pronounced orally and also spelled aloud as in a spelling bee. It was thrilling and exciting to be chosen to represent my school as well as to travel to McPherson, a distance of nine miles, at time when cars travelled 35-40 miles per hour on rather narrow paved roads. Trips made to town were somewhat limited when living in a rural area.

What a change from writing with paper and pencil in the 1930s to computer use with spell checkers in 2006!

MODERN PHILOSOPHIES OF SPELLING INSTRUCTION

It is much more likely, presently, that a philosophy of holism is involved in teaching spelling. Within a writing activity, students learn to spell words correctly; holism is then involved in student learning to spell words. Misspelled words are identified and each, perhaps, written a few times. Rather than writing each word several times, the incorrectly spelled words may be written in a functional writing situation. If a word processor is used, spell checkers will be used in making corrections. Misspelled words might be written several times each in long hand. Drill in learning to spell words lacks appeal and may minimize interest in learning. Thus, when the computer is used, it might be good to depend upon spell check alone. However, a word needs to be spelled close enough to the correct spelling for the computer to list on the monitor, possible correct spellings of a mis-spelled word. To build readiness for written work, using the computer, the student will need to have an adequate number of sight words in his/her spelling vocabulary. These may be learned through traditional methods of spelling instruction, using a reputable textbook, and rich teacher developed materials. Key boarding skills need to become increasingly sophisticated and refined as the student progresses through the public school years so that the focus is upon writing ideas. With the rapid increase of computer sophistication, it might not be necessary for anyone to use paper and pencil in future writing, including the making of shopping lists with a very small hand held device (Ediger and Rao, 2003).

Many writing situations in school and in society which are functional:

* do not stress predetermined objectives, but a need arises to communicate which indicates necessary formal/informal communication. Spelling errors are corrected within a situational activity.
* do not emphasize the use of measurably stated ends but the stress is upon responding in written form when responses need to be made such as in letter writing and includes paying attention to appropriate standards in spelling. Correct spelling becomes a means of communication.
* do not align with objectives stated prior to instruction but the writing is purposeful at a given time. Correct spelling of words become important in functional writing outside the framework of predetermined ends. Incorrectly spelled words may be diagnosed and written correctly.
* are not evaluated precisely in measurable terms, but in general, effective communication occurs using broadly developed standards and objectives. A well designed rubric may be used to assess the written product (See Ediger, 2006).

Toward the other end of the continuum, behaviorists stress measurability as a key factor in teaching. Thus, objectives must be stated with precision so that students know what is expected of them in terms of definite criteria for written work, including the correct spelling of words. No leeway, ideally exists for interpretation of what is desired in written products.

Prior to instruction, specific objectives indicate to students that which is necessary to achieve. In a formal list of spelling words for student mastery, the acceptable level of achievement must be indicated. Students either do/do not attain the stated objectives. A variety of learning opportunities may be used to help students achieve the precise objectives, the focal point being the correct spelling of each word. The following criteria are salient to use in stating objectives behaviorally:

* objectives are stated in measurable terms.
* learning activities in spelling are directly related to the objectives.
* students achieve the measurably stated objectives as a result of instruction.
* accurate measurement is possible to ascertain student achievement.
* record keeping is available to monitor student progress over a period of time to notice if progress is being made sequentially.
* student achievement in spelling might well be diagnosed to ascertain the type(s) of errors made. Remediation is then possible (See Stipek, 2006).

PSYCHOLOGY OF LEARNING

There are selected tenets of educational psychology which are applicable to the teaching of spelling. This would be true for holistic approaches as well as behaviourism. First, students need to attach meaning to any word to be learned in spelling. The understanding here may involve defining the word, using it in a sentence, or describing its use in society. Contextual use is important in that the learner can use the word meaningfully in a sentence.

Second, the student needs to be able to pronounce the word correctly and listen to the ensuing phonetic sounds. Being able to sound out the letters in a word, if consistent between symbol and sound, may assist in its correct spelling. Being able to write the word correctly the first time, after its introduction, and then practicing its correct spelling several times, will aid in retention of being able to spell the word correctly.

Third, the student needs to develop a method of learning to spell a word correctly, such as:

* looking at the word and inherent parts carefully
* pronouncing the word accurately and hearing individual sounds made
* practice writing the word once and checking its correctness
* then practice writing the word several times until mastery (See Hawkins, 2006).

Students individually need to find a method of learning to spell words correctly which work. A variety of approaches must be used to teach spelling to avoid boredom. These include the use of the following materials of instruction: technology, spelling text books, workbooks, writing for diverse purposes, as well as working in committees to practice correct spelling of words. Purposeful writing may include writing with correct spelling of words in each:

* business and friendly letters,
* announcements, invitations, and notices,
* poems, narrative and expository content, plays, and handbooks,
* taking notes, making an outline, and preparing a report,
* making the following kinds of charts: experience, organizational, time lines, vocabulary, and narrative,
* labeling and making line, bar, and picture graphs.

There are a plethora of writing activities which might well provide practice for students in spelling words correctly. These activities must provide for diverse achievement levels of students. They must be developmentally appropriate and provide for sequential progress.

REFERENCES

Ediger, Marlow, and D. Bhaskara Rao (2003), *Teaching Language Arts Successfully*. New Delhi, India: Discovery Publishing House.

Ediger, Marlow (2006), "Assisting pupils in learning in the classroom," *Georgia Journal of Reading*, 29(2), 10-13.

Hawkins, Joanna (2006), "Think before you write," *Educational Leadership*, 64(2), 63-67.

Stipek, Deborah (2006), "Accountability comes to preschool: can we make it work for young children?" *Phi delta Kappan*, 87(10), 740-744).

41

Trends in Teaching Social Studies

Teachers, supervisors, and school administrators need to study indepth, analyze, and implement desired trends of teaching the social studies. The social studies needs to be updated to harmonize with recommendations in subject matter and pedagogy which will assist students to achieve as optimally as possible. Individual differences need adequate provision to provide for each student in terms of interests, abilities, and purposes. A well prepared teacher chooses salient objectives, learning opportunities to achieve these objectives, and appraisal techniques to diagnose as well as assess student progress.

SOCIAL STUDIES INSTRUCTION

The social studies teacher needs to choose relevant objectives consisting of three categories. As one category, knowledge ends need to emphasize salient subject matter. Trivia and the irrelevant must be omitted. Rather, major generalizations and main ideas need to be considered by students. Subordinate ideas are acquired by students to assist in understanding/support the broader ideas. Knowledge is useful in the solving of problems in school and in society. It also is to be valued for its own sake.

A separate category of objectives for students to acquire is skills ends. With skills, the student makes application of knowledge in diverse situations. Use of knowledge makes it retainable as well as functional (Ediger and Rao, 2003).

Quality attitudes are also necessary for student attainment. Good attitudes are needed for optimal achievement of objectives. An increased number of knowledge and skills ends may be acquired due to possessing quality attitudes. Each category of objectives should be attained indepth rather than through survey approaches. With indepth approaches knowledge, skills, and attitudes are emphasized frequently in diverse units but at a more complex level.

A second trend in the teaching of social studies is to use a variety of methods of instruction. Concrete (actual objects and sights), semi-concrete (pictorial in nature), and abstract materials (printed sources) should be in the offing to provide for individual differences among students. Students learn in different ways in with the use of diverse media. Multimedia approaches help students to attain as optimally as possible (Parker, 2001).

Third, proper sequence in learning is necessary for students. Background experiences are needed to achieve a new objective. Social studies teachers must assess the readiness of students to learn from an ensuing activity. Being ready for the new learnings assists in sequential success of the learner. The teacher needs to assess continually if students are experiencing quality sequence in the social studies. Students do not do well if the new learnings are too complex to understand. Boredom might set in if the subject matter/skills to be achieved are too elementary.

Fourth, purpose in learning needs to be stressed. The teacher may state the purpose and/or students may identify viable questions to answer and problems to solve in ongoing units of study. Having a purpose helps students to perceive value in learning. What is not salient to the student might well make for little effort in achieving. Each student needs to prize learning to the fullest degree. Challenging questions and problems stimulate student learning. The challenge comes to bear in locating necessary information as answers to questions and solutions to problems. Developmentally appropriate learning activities might well then be in evidence (See Jayanthi, 2006).

Fifth, learners need to be actively engaged in ongoing learning experiences. Thus in discussions, students are motivated to contribute optimally. Discussion groups need to be small enough so that each may contribute as frequently as possible and yet provide adequate opportunities for all to be involved. Quality manners need to be emphasized in that respect for the thinking of others is involved. Rudeness and interruptions should definitely not be a part of any discussion.

Sixth, learning styles of students need to receive much attention. The following are examples of how students may differ in styles of learning: preferring a teacher determined versus a student centered curriculum; working by the self as compared to working collectively with others: using project methods of instruction versus subject matter approaches; and having a very quiet learning environment as compared to a busy learning situation involving movement and motion. Higher levels of thinking should receive much attention. Thus, students need to engaged in critical thought in separating fact from opinion, fantasy from reality: and as well as accurate from inaccurate ideas. They should also participate in creative thought whereby unique, novel ideas accrue in ongoing social studies units of study (See Searson and Dunn, 2001).

Seventh, integration of subject matter from the different areas of the social sciences should be stressed. There are times, too, in which separate academic disciplines are emphasized in the social studies. A well prepared teacher in knowledge/skills needs to do much planning of the curriculum to provide students with the best in objectives, learning experiences, and appraisal techniques in the social studies.

Eighth, multiple intelligences theory must be stressed in order to use the talents of learners. These intelligences include the following which students individually possess:

* thinking logically as in mathematics. Logical thinking may certainly be stressed in the social studies.
* verbal intelligence, involving abstract symbols, as in reading subject matter and in writing experiences.
* musical/rhythmical as in singing activities which relate to a social studies unit or folk dances learned pertaining to another culture/nation being studied.
* intrapersonal skills whereby a student achieves most optimally in working by the self.
* interpersonal abilities which stress small group and committee endeavours.
* kinesthetic in which the learner prefers activities involving manual dexterity. There are a variety of projects and art work experiences, correlated with the social studies, which might be inherent in ongoing units of study.
* objective thinking as stressed by science. Objective thought is involved in an analyzing subject matter read in the social studies when separating the important from the mundane. Then too, science content may be integrated into social studies units where applicable such as in units of study on the environment and ecology (See Nolen 2003).

Ninth, a quality program of assessment should be in emphasis. Assessment procedures need to be valid and reliable. They need to provide feedback to the teacher in terms of diagnostic/remedial information and how well the student is doing in general in the social studies. Information on student growth in critical and creative thinking as well as problem solving need to be in the offing (Barton, 2006).

Tenth, reflective thinking must be stressed. The learner then thinks critically about what has been learned and analyzes how the ideas were gleaned. Reflection assists students to review, synthesize, and evaluate salient ideas achieved.

The writers have presented ten means of assisting students in the social studies to experience a quality curriculum. Each guideline needs to be assessed throughly by teachers individually and in committees with the intent of reviewing what is done presently in the social studies and making plans for needed modifications and change. The best curriculum possible needs to be developed for students in the social studies.

REFERENCES

Barton, Paul (2006), "Needed: Higher Standards of Accountability," *Educational Leadership* 64(3), 28-31.

Ediger, Marlow, and D. Bhaskara Rao (2003), *Elementary Curriculum Improvement*. New Delhi, India: Discovery Publishing House.

Dr. Jayanthi and Reena Agarwal (2006), "Enhancing Creativity of Teachers for Building Positive Socio-Emotional Clasroom Climate," *Edutracks*, 6(3), 21-23. Published in India.

Nolen, Jennifer (2003), "Multiple Intelligences in the Classroom," *Education*, 124 (1), 115-119.

Parker, Walter C. (2001), Social Studies in Elementary Education. Upper Saddle River, New Jersey: Merrill, Prentice-Hall.

Searson, Robert, and Rita Dunn (2001), "The Learning Styles Teaching Model," *Science and Children*, 38(5), 22-38.

Bibliography

Amala, P.A. and Anupama, P., authors and Digumarti Bhaskara Rao, editor (2004). *History of Education*. New Delhi: Discovery Publishing House. ISBN 81-7141-860-0.

Appala Naidu, P.Ch., author and Digumarti Bhaskara Rao, editor (2007). *Student Feedback Methods*. New Delhi: Discovery Publishing House.

Babu, P.C., author and Digumarti Bhaskara Rao, editor (2004). *Flowers of Wisdom*. New Delhi: Discovery Publishing House. ISBN 81-7141-695-0.

Babu, P.C., author and Digumarti Bhaskara Rao, editor (2007). *Words of Wisdom*. New Delhi: Discovery Publishing House.

Babu, author and Digumarti Bhaskara Rao, editor (2007). *Teaching Aptitude of Primary School Teachers*. New Delhi: Discovery Publishing House.

Bhagya Lakshmi, L., author and Digumarti Bhaskara Rao, editor (2000). *Reading and Comprehension*. New Delhi: Discovery Publishing House. ISBN 81-7141-543-1.

Bhaskara Rao, Digumarti (1994). *Scientific Aptitude*. New Delhi: Ashish Publishing House. ISBN 81-7024-658-X.

Bhaskara Rao, Digumarti (1995). *Animal Kingdom*. New Delhi: Discovery Publishing House. ISBN 81-7141-274-2.

Bhaskara Rao, Digumarti (1995). *Batracology*. New Delhi: Discovery Publishing House. ISBN 81-7141-279-3.

Bhaskara Rao, Digumarti (1997). *Scientific Attitude*. New Delhi: Discovery Publishing House. ISBN 81-7141-381-1.

Bhaskara Rao, Digumarti (1996). *Scientific Attitude vis-à-vis Scientific Aptitude.* New Delhi: Discovery Publishing House. ISBN 81-7141-308-0.

Bhaskara Rao, Digumarti (2004). *Scientific Attitude, Scientific Aptitude and Achievement.* New Delhi: Discovery Publishing House. ISBN 81-7141-781-7.

Bhaskara Rao, Digumarti (2004). *Educational Administration.* New Delhi: Discovery Publishing House. ISBN 81-7141-842-2.

Bhaskara Rao, Digumarti (2004). *Issues in School Eduation.* New Delhi: Discovery Publishing House. ISBN 81-8356-025-3.

Bhaskara Rao, Digumarti, editor (1996). *Encyclopaedia of Education For All*, 5 volumes. New Delhi: APH Publishing Corporation. ISBN 81-7024-759-4 (set).

Vol. I *Education For All: The World Conference.* ISBN 81-7024-760-8.

Vol. II *Education For All: The EPA-9 Summit.* ISBN 81-7024-761-6

Vol. III *Education For All: Quality Education For All.* ISBN 81-7024-762-6.

Vol. IV *Education For All: Planning and Monitoring.* ISBN 81-7024-763-4.

Vol. V *Education For All: The Indian Scenario.* ISBN-81-7024-764-0.

Bhaskara Rao, Digumarti, editor (1996). *National Policy on Education,* 2 volumes. New Delhi: Anmol Publications Pvt. Ltd. ISBN 81-7488-323-1.

Bhaskara Rao, Digumarti, editor (1996). *Global Perceptions on Peace Education,* 3 volumes. New Delhi: Discovery Publishing House. ISBN81-7141-319-6.

Bhaskara Rao, Digumarti, editor (1997). *Education for the 21st Century.* New Delhi: Discovery Publishing House. ISBN 81-7141-389-7.

Bhaskara Rao, Digumarti, editor (1997). *Reflections on Scientific Attitude.* New Delhi: Discovery Publishing House. ISBN 81-7141-319-6.

Bhaskara Rao, Digumarti, editor (1997). *Success Story of a Primary Eduation Project.* New Delhi: APH Publishing Corporation. ISBN 81-7024-850-7.

Bhaskara Rao, Digumarti, editor (1997). *World Food Summit.* New Delhi: Discovery Publishing House. ISBN 81-7141-386-2.

Bhaskara Rao, Digumarti, editor (1997). *Care and Child,* 2 volumes. New Delhi: Discovery Publishing House. ISBN 81-7141-394-3.

Bhaskara Rao, Digumarti, editor (1998). *Earth Summit,* 2 volumes. New Delhi: Discovery Publishing House. ISBN 81-7141-435-4.

Bhaskara Rao, Digumarti, editor (1998). *Adolescence Education.* New Delhi: Discovery Publishing House. ISBN 81-7141-432-X.

Bhaskara Rao, Digumarti, editor (1998). *Community and School Nutrition Education.* New Delhi: Discovery Publishing House. ISBN 81-7141-435-4.

Bhaskara Rao, Digumarti, editor (1998). *District Primary Education Programme.* New Delhi: Discovery Publishing House. ISBN 81-7141-396-X.

Bhaskara Rao, Digumarti, editor (1998). *National Policy on Education: Towards an Enlightened and Humane Society.* New Delhi: Discovery Publishing House. ISBN 81-7141-426-5.

Bhaskara Rao, Digumarti, editor (1998). *Reforming School Education.* New Delhi: Discovery Publishing House. ISBN 81-7141-403-6.

Bhaskara Rao, Digumarti, editor (1998). *Teacher Education in India:* New Delhi: Discovery Publishing House. ISBN 81-7141-406-0.

Bhaskara Rao, Digumarti, editor (1998). *World Summit for Social Development.* New Delhi: Discovery Publishing House. ISBN 81-7141-420-6.

Bhaskara Rao, Digumarti, editor (1999). *International Encyclopaedia of AIDS,* 11 volumes. New Delhi: Discovery House. ISBN 81-7141-522-6 (set).

Vol. 1 *Introduction to HIV/AIDS.* ISBN 81-7141-523-7.

Vol. 2 *HIV/AIDS-Issues and Challenges,* 2 parts. ISBN 81-7141-524-5.

Vol. 3 *HIV/AIDS-Socio Economic Realities.* ISBN 81-7141-524-3.

Vol. 4 *HIV/AIDS-Law Ethics and Human Rights,* 2 parts. ISBN 81-7141-526-1.

Vol. 5 *AIDS and NGOs.* ISBN 81-7141-527-X.

Vol. 6 *AIDS and Home Care.* ISBN 81-7141-528-8.

Vol. 7 *STD Case Management.* ISBN 81-7141-529-6.

Vol. 8 *HIV/AIDS Prevention and Care-Teaching Modules for Nurses and Midwives.* ISBN 81-7141-530-X.

Vol. 9 *HIV Prevention Education for Educational Institutions.* ISBN 81-7141-531-8.

Vol. 10 *Instructional Modules for AIDS Education.* ISBN 81-7141-532-6.

Vol. 11 *School Health Education to prevent AIDS and STD—A Package for Curriculum Planners.* ISBN 81-7141-533-4.

Bhaskara Rao, Digumarti, editor (2000). *International Encyclopaedia of Human Rights,* 7 volumes in 13 parts. New Delhi: Discovery Publishing House. ISBN 81-7141-567-9 (set).

Vol. 1 *International Instruments of Human Rights,* 2 parts. ISBN 81-7141-569-4.

Vol. 2 *Regional Instruments of Human Rights.* ISBN 81-7141-604-7.

Vol. 3 *Human Rights and the United Nations,* 2 parts. ISBN 81-7141-605-5.

Vol. 4 *Fact Files of Human Rights,* 3 parts. ISBN 81-7141-606-3.

Vol. 5 *Study Stories of Human Rights,* 3 parts. ISBN 81-7141-607-3.

Vol. 6 *International Meetings on Human Rights,* 2 parts. ISBN 81-7141-608-X.

Vol. 7 *Professional Training in Human Rights.* ISBN 81-7141-609-8.

Bhaskara Rao, Digumarti, editor (2000). *International Encyclopaedia of Science and Technology Education,* 11 volumes, New Delhi: Discovery Publishing House. ISBN 81-7141-548-2 (set).

Vol. 1 *Science and Technology Education.* ISBN 81-7141-568-7.

Vol. 2 *Science Education in Developing Countries.* ISBN 81-7141-569-9.

Vol. 3 *Organizational Structure of Science.* ISBN 81-7141-570-9.

Vol. 4 *Science Education in Asia and the Pacific.* ISBN 81-7141-571-7.

Vol. 5 *Science and Technology Education for All.* ISBN 81-7141-572-5.

Vol. 6 *Values, Ethics, Talent and Girls in Science and Technology Education.* ISBN 81-7141-573-3.

Vol. 7 *Popularization of Science and Technology Education.* ISBN 81-7141574-1.

Vol. 8 *Science, Power and Society.* ISBN 81-7141-575-X.

Vol. 9 *Information Technology.* ISBN 81-7141-576-8.

Vol. 10 *Teacher Training in Science and Technology Education.* ISBN 81-7142-577-6.

Vol. 11 *Teacher Training in Science and Technology: A Curriculum Framework.* ISBN 81-7141-578-4.

Bhaskara Rao, Digumarti, editor (2000). *Education For All: Achieving the Goal,* 3 volumes. New Delhi: APH Publishing Corporation. ISBN 81-7648-151-1 (set).

Vol. I *The Global Consensus.* ISBN 81-7648-155-6.

Vol. II *Mid-Decade Review Reports of Regional Seminars.* ISBN 81-7648-154-8.

Vol. III *Issues and Trends.* ISBN 81-7648-155-6.

Bhaskara Rao, Digumarti, editor (2001). *Nuclear Materials: Issues and Concerns,* 2 volumes, New Delhi: Discovery Publishing House. ISBN 81-7141-611-X.

Bhaskara Rao, Digumarti, editor (2001). *Distance Education in Different Countries.* New Delhi: APH Publishing Corporation. ISBN 81-648-229-3.

Bhaskara Rao, Digumarti, editor (2001). *Decentralised Management of Education: Management of Education in Panchayati Raj and Municipal Bodies.* New Delhi: Discovery Publishing House. ISBN 81-7141-617-9.

Bhaskara Rao, Digumarti, editor (2001). *Electrochemistry for Environmental Protection.* New Delhi: Discovery Publishing House. ISBN 81-7141-619-5.

Bhaskara Rao, Digumarti, editor (2001). *Global Educational Studies.* New Delhi: Discovery Publishing House. ISBN 81-7141-616-0.

Bhaskara Rao, Digumarti, editor (2001). *Global Synthesis of Educational Assessment.* New Delhi: Discovery Publishing House. ISBN 81-7141-613-6.

Bhaskara Rao, Digumarti, editor (2001). *Jomtein Decade of Education.* New Delhi: Discovery Publishing House. ISBN 81-7141-618-7.

Bhaskara Rao, Digumarti, editor (2001). *World Conference on Education for All.* New Delhi: APH Publishing Corporation. ISBN 81-7141-274-9.

Bhaskara Rao, Digumarti, editor (2001). *World Conference on Higher Education.* New Delhi: Discovery Publishing House. ISBN 81-7141-610-1.

Bhaskara Rao, Digumarti, editor (2001). *World Conference on Science.* New Delhi: Discovery Publishing House. ISBN 81-7141-612-8.

Bhaskara Rao, Digumarti, editor (2003). *Inspiring Experiences in Teacher Education.* New Delhi: Discovery Publishing House. ISBN 81-7141-656-X.

Bhaskara Rao, Digumarti, editor (2003). *International Studies in Education,* 3 volumes. New Delhi: Discovery Publishing House. ISBN 81-7141-647-0.

Bhaskara Rao, Digumarti, editor (2003). *Military Conversion: Impact on Science and Technology.* New Delhi: Discovery Publishing House. ISBN 81-7141-578-4.

Bhaskara Rao, Digumarti, editor (2003). *United Nations Millennium Summit.* New Delhi: Discovery Publishing House. ISBN 81-7141-632-2.

Bhaskara Rao, Digumarti, editor (2003). *World Assembly on Aging.* New Delhi: Discovery Publishing House. ISBN 81-7141-637-3.

Bhaskara Rao, Digumarti, editor (2003). *World Conference on Human Rights.* New Delhi: Discovery Publishing House. ISBN 81-7141-661-6.

Bhaskara Rao, Digumarti, editor (2003). *World Education Forum.* New Delhi: Discovery Publishing House. ISBN 81-7141-639-X.

Bhaskara Rao, Digumarti, editor (2003). *Education, Employment and Human Resource Development.* New Delhi: Discovery Publishing House. ISBN 81-7141-681-0.

Bhaskara Rao, Digumarti, editor (2003). *Successful Schooling.* New Delhi: Discovery Publishing House. ISBN 81-7141-677-2.

Bhaskara Rao, Digumarti, editor (2003). *European Education and Teachers.* New Delhi: Discovery Publishing House. ISBN 81-7141-702-7.

Bhaskara Rao, Digumarti, editor (2003). *Teachers in a Changing World.* New Delhi: Discovery Publishing House. ISBN 81-7141-694-2.

Bhaskara Rao, Digumarti, editor (2004). *International Guidelines on Open and Distance Teacher Education.* New Delhi: Discovery Publishing House. ISBN 81-7141-777-9.

Bhaskara Rao, Digumarti, editor (2004). *Adult Learning in the 21st Century.* New Delhi: Discovery Publishing House. ISBN 81-7141-797-3.

Bhaskara Rao, Digumarti, editor (2004). *Educational Practices: Research and Recommendations.* New Delhi: Discovery Publishing House. ISBN 81-7141-835-X.

Bhaskara Rao, Digumarti, editor (2004). *General Secondary Education in the 21st Century.* New Delhi: Discovery Publishing House.

Bhaskara Rao, Digumarti, editor (2004). *International Encyclopaedia of Learning to Live Together,* 4 volumes. New Delhi: Discovery Publishing House. ISBN 81-7141-848-1.

Vol. 1 *International Conference on Learning to Live Together.*

Vol. 2 *Globalization and Living Together.*

Vol. 3 *Curriculum for Learning to Live Together.*

Vol. 4 *Science Education for the Contemporary Society.*

Bhaskara Rao, Digumarti, editor (2004). *Reforming Secondary Education.* New Delhi: Discovery Publishing House. ISBN 81-7141-843-0.

Bhaskara Rao, Digumarti, editor (2004). *Human Rights Education.* New Delhi: Discovery Publishing House. ISBN 81-7141-882-1.

Bhaskara Rao, Digumarti, editor (2004). *United Nations Decade for Human Rights Education.* New Delhi: Discovery Publishing House. ISBN 81-7141-887-2.

Bhaskara Rao, Digumarti, editor (2004). *Technical and Vocational Education and Training in the 21st Century.* New Delhi: Discovery Publishing House. ISBN 81-7141-984-4.

Bhaskara Rao, Digumarti, editor (2005). *Encyclopaedia of Education For All,* 5 volumes. New Delhi: Discovery Publishing House.

Bhaskara Rao, Digumarti and B.S.V. Dutt, editor (2003). *Eduation: Programmes adn Policies.* New Delhi: APH Publishing Corporation. ISBN 81-7648-470-9.

Bhaskara Rao, Digumarti, C.A.P. Swamy and B.S.V. Dutt (1997). *Self-Evaluation in Student Teaching.* New Delhi: Discovery Publishing House. ISBN 81-7141-374-9.

Bhaskara Rao, Digumarti and D. Naresh Kumar (2004). *School Teacher Effectiveness.* New Delhi: Discovery Publishing House.

Bhaskara Rao, Digumarti and D. Sridhar (2002). *Job Satisfaction of School Teachers.* New Delhi: Discovery Publishing House. ISBN 81-7141-652-7.

Bhaskara Rao, Digumarti, C. Sridevi and K. Vijaya (1995). *Achievement in Social Studies.* New Delhi: Discovery Publishing House. ISBN 81-7141-281-5.

Bhaskara Rao, Digumarti and Digumarti Pushpa Latha (1994). *Achievement in Biology.* New Delhi: Discovery Publishing House. ISBN 81-7141-254-5.

Bhaskara Rao, Digumarti and Digumarti Pushpa Latha (1995). *Achievement in English.* New Delhi: Discovery Publishing House. ISBN 81-7141-283-1.

Bhaskara Rao, Digumarti and Digumarti Pushpa Latha (1994). *Achievement in Sciecne.* New Delhi: Discovery Publishing House. ISBN 81-7141-280-70.

Bhaskara Rao, Digumarti and Digumarti Pushpa Latha (1995). *Achieveent in Mathematics.* New Delhi: Discovery Publishing House. ISBN 81-7141-278-5.

Bhaskara Rao, Digumarti and Digumarti Pushpa Latha (2004). *Education for Women.* New Delhi: Discovery Publishing House. ISBN 81-7141-873-2.

Bhaskara Rao, Digumarti, Digumarti Pushpa Latha and Digumarthi Harshitha, editors (2001). *Biological Warfare.* New Delhi: Discovery Publishing House. *ISBN* 81-7141-597-0.

Bhaskara Rao, Digumarti, Digumarti Pushpa Latha and Digumarthi Harshitha, editors (2001). *Women as Educators.* New Delhi: Discovery Publishing House. ISBN 81-7141-602-0.

Bhaskara Rao, Digumarti and Digumarthi Harshitha (2004). *Adjustment of Adolescents.* New Delhi: APH Publishing House. ISBN 81-7648-207-2.

Bhaskara Rao, Digumarti and Digumarti Pushpa Latha, editors (1998). *International Encyclopaedia of Women,* 5 volumes. New Delhi: Discovery Publishing House. ISBN 81-7141-410-9 (set).

Vol. 1 *Status of World's Women.* ISBN 81-7141-494-X.

Vol. 2 *Women, Education and Empowerment.* ISBN 81-7141-498-1.

Vol. 3 *Women Challenges and Advancement.* ISBN 81-7141-497-4.

Vol. 4 *Women and Family Health.* ISBN 81-7141-497-4.

Vol. 5 *Women and International Action.* ISBN 81-7141-498-2.

Bhaskara Rao, Digumarti, Digumarti Pushpa Latha and Digumarthi Harshitha, editors (2001). *Assessing Learning Achievement.* New Delhi: Discovery Publishing House. ISBN 81-7141-601-2.

Bhaskara Rao, Digumarti, Digumarti Pushpa Latha and Digumarthi Harshitha, editors (2001). *Energy Security.* New Delhi: Discovery Publishing House. ISBN 81-7141-598-9.

Bhaskara Rao, Digumarti, Digumarthi Harshitha and K.R.S. Sambasiva Rao, editors (1999). *Advanced Biotechnology.* New Delhi: Discovery Publishing House. ISBN 81-7141-516-4.

Bhaskara Rao, Digumarti and K.R.S. Sambasiva Rao, editors (1996). *Current Trends in Indian Education.* New Delhi: Discovery Publishing House. ISBN 81-7141-311-0.

Bhaskara Rao, Digumarti and D. Naresh Kumar (2004). *School Teacher Effectiveness.* New Delhi: Discovery Publishing House. ISBN 81-7141-782-5.

Bhaskara Rao, Digumarti and E. Sreekanth Babu (2004). *Educational Interests of School Students.* New Delhi: Discovery Publishing House. ISBN 81-7141-837-6.

Bhaskara Rao, Digumarti and K. Vijaya (1995). *A Text Book Evaluation.* Ambala Cantt: The Associated Publishers.

Bhaskara Rao, Digumarti and M.A. Fayaz (2004). *Problems of Primary School Drop-outs.* New Delhi: Discovery Publishing House. ISBN 81-7141-834-1.

Bhaskara Rao, Digumarti and N.V.M. Mohana Rao (2002). *Problems of Mentally Handicapped Children.* New Delhi: Discovery Publishing House. ISBN 81-7141-645-4.

Bhaskara Rao, Digumarti and S. Chandra Mohan (2002). *Sports Management.* New Delhi: APH Publishing House. ISBN 81-7648-467-9.

Bhaskara Rao, Digumarti and S.A. Khader (2004). *Problems of Private School Teachers.* New Delhi: Discovery Publishing Corporation. ISBN 81-7141-838-4.

Bhaskara Rao, Digumarti and S.A. Khader (2004). *School Education in India.* New Delhi: Discovery Publishing Corporation. ISBN 81-7141-849-X.

Bhaskara Rao, Digumarti and Sk. Johni Basha (2004). *Teachers' Population Education Awareness.* New Delhi: Discovery Publishing House. ISBN 81-7141-832-5.

Bhaskara Rao, Digumarti, V.V. Rao, V.V. Lakshmi and V.V. Krishna, editors (1999). Status and Advancement of

Women. New Delhi: APH Publishing Corporation. ISBN 81-7648-169-6.

Bhasha, S.A., author and Digumarti Bhaskara Rao, editor (2004). *Methods of Teaching Geography*. New Delhi: Discovery Publishing House. ISBN 81-7141-807-4.

Bhuvaneswara Lakshmi, Gadde, author and Digumarti Bhaskara Rao, editor (2000). *Attitude Towards Science*. New Delhi: Discovery Publishing House. ISBN 81-7141-541-6.

Bhuvanesara Lakshmi, G., author and Digumarti Bhaskara Rao, editor (2004). *Methods of Teaching ife Science*. New Delhi: Discovery Publishing House. ISBN 81-7141-804-X.

Bhuvaneswar Lakshmi, G. and K. Subha Rao, authors and Digumarti Bhaskara Rao, editor (2004). *Methods of Teaching Biology*. New Delhi: Discovery Publishing House. ISBN 81-7141-914-3.

Chary, K.V.N.B., author and Digumarti Bhaskara Rao, editor (2006). *Techniques of Teaching Physics*. New Delhi: Sonali Publications. ISBN 81-8411-046-4

Chowdary, S.B.J.R. and Naga Raju, author and Digumarti Bhaskara Rao, editor (2004). *Mastery of Teaching Skills*. New Delhi: Discovery Publishing House.

Dayakara Reddy, V. and Digumarti Bhaskara Rao, editor (2006). *Value-Oriented Education*. New Delhi: Discovery Publishing House.

Devraj, T.A.S., author and Digumarti Bhaskara Rao, editor (1997). *Trace Analysis of Uranium and Thorium*. New Delhi: Discovery Publishing House. ISBN 81-7141-375-7.

Durga Rani, K., author and Digumarti Bhaskara Rao, editor (2000). *Educational Aspirations and Scientific Attitudes*. New Delhi: Discovery Publishing House. ISBN 81-7141-555-5.

Dutt, B.S.V. and Digumarti Bhaskara Rao (2001). *Empowering Primary Teachers*. New Delhi: Discovery Publishing House. ISBN 81-7141-615-2.

Dutt, B.S.V., author and Digumarti Bhaskara Rao, editor (2004). *Comparative Education.* New Delhi: Discovery Publishing House. ISBN 81-7141-912-7.

Ediger, Markow and Digumarti Bhaskara Rao, editor (2004). *Science Curriculum.* New Delhi: Discovery Publishing House. ISBN 81-7141-321-8.

Ediger, Marlow and Digumarti Bhaskara Rao (2000). *Teaching Mathematics Successfully.* New Delhi: Discovery Publishing House. ISBN 81-7141-552-0.

Ediger, Marlow and Digumarti Bhaskara Rao (2001). *Teaching Science Successfully.* New Delhi: Discovery Publishing House. ISBN 81-7141-600-4.

Ediger, Marlow and Digumarti Bhaskara Rao (2001). *Teaching Social Studies Successfully.* New Delhi: Discovery Publishing House. ISBN 81-7141-596-2.

Ediger, Marlow and Digumarti Bhaskara Rao (2002). *Philosophy and Curriculum.* New Delhi: Discovery Publishing House. ISBN 81-7141-631-4.

Ediger, Marlow and Digumarti Bhaskara Rao (2002). Improving School Administration. New Delhi: Discovery Publishing House. ISBN 81-7141-658-6.

Ediger, Marlow and Digumarti Bhaskara Rao (2003). *Language Arts Curriculum.* New Delhi: Discovery Publishing House. ISBN 81-7141-657-8.

Ediger, Marlow and Digumarti Bhaskara Rao (2003). *Psychology and Curriculum.* New Delhi: Discovery Publishing House. ISBN 81-7141-691-8.

Ediger, Marlow and Digumarti Bhaskara Rao (2003). *Teaching Language Arts Successfully.* New Delhi: Discovery Publishing House.

Ediger, Marlow and Digumarti Bhaskara Rao (2003). *School Curriculum and Administration.* New Delhi: Discovery Publishing House. ISBN 81-7141-709-4.

Ediger, Marlow and Digumarti Bhaskara Rao (2003). *Teaching Mathematics in Elementary Schools*. New Delhi: Discovery Publishing House. ISBN 81-7141-687-X.

Ediger, Marlow and Digumarti Bhaskara Rao (2003). *Teaching Science in Elementary Schools*. New Delhi: Discovery Publishing House. ISBN 81-7141-698-5.

Ediger, Marlow and Digumarti Bhaskara Rao (2003). *School Curriculum and Administration*. New Delhi: Discovery Publishing House. ISBN 81-7141-709-4.

Ediger, Marlow and Digumarti Bhaskara Rao (2003). *Elementary Curriculum Improvement*. New Delhi: Discovery Publishing House. ISBN 81-7141-740-X.

Ediger, Marlow and Digumarti Bhaskara Rao (2004). *Modern Elementary School*. New Delhi: Discovery Publishing House.

Ediger, Marlow and Digumarti Bhaskara Rao (2004). *School Organisation*. New Delhi: Discovery Publishing House. ISBN 81-7141-843-0.

Ediger, Marlow and Digumarti Bhaskara Rao (2004). *Relevancy in Elementary Curriculum*. New Delhi: Discovery Publishing House. ISBN 81-7141-845-9.

Ediger, Marlow and Digumarti Bhaskara Rao (2005). *Quality School Education*. New Delhi: Discovery Publishing House. ISBN 81-8356-022-9.

Ediger, Marlow and Digumarti Bhaskara Rao (2006). *Successful School Education*. New Delhi: Discovery Publishing House. ISBN 81-8356-054-7.

Ediger, Marlow and Digumarti Bhaskara Rao (2006). *Successful School Administration*. New Delhi: Discovery Publishing House. ISBN 81-8356-046-6.

Ediger, Marlow and Digumarti Bhaskara Rao (20056). *Issues in School Curruculum*. New Delhi: Discovery Publishing House. ISBN 81-8356-052-0.

Ediger, Marlow and Digumarti Bhaskara Rao (2006). *Community College-Curriculum and Teaching*. New Delhi: Discovery Publishing House. ISBN 81-8356-053-9.

Ediger, Marlow and Digumarti Bhaskara Rao (2006). *Administration of Schools.* New Delhi: Discovery Publishing House.

Ediger, Marlow and Digumarti Bhaskara Rao (2006). *Reading Curriculum and Instruction.* New Delhi: Discovery Publishing House.

Ediger, Marlow and Digumarti Bhaskara Rao (2006). *Curriculum Organisation.* New Delhi: Discovery Publishing House.

Ediger, Marlow and Digumarti Bhaskara Rao (2006). *Curriculum of School Subjects.* New Delhi: Discovery Publishing House.

Ediger, Marlow, B.S.V. Dutt and Digumarti Bhaskara Rao (2003). *Teaching English Successfully.* New Delhi: Discovery Publishing House. ISBN 81-7141-707-8.

Elizabeth, M.B.S., author and Digumarti Bhaskara Rao, editor (2004). *Methods of Teaching English.* New Delhi: Discovery Publishing House. ISBN 81-7141-809-0.

Elizabeth, M.B.S., author and Digumarti Bhaskara Rao, editor (2004). *Acquisition of English Vocabulary.* New Delhi: Discovery Publishing House.

Fatima. Sk. author and Digumarti Bhaskara Rao, editor (2007). *Reasoning Ability of School Students.* New Delhi: Discovery Publishing House.

Gopala Krishna M., author and Digumarti Bhaskara Rao, editor (2007). *Teachniques of Teaching Physical Education.* New Delhi: Discovery Publishing House. ISBN 81-8411-044-8.

Gopala Krishna M., author and Digumarti Bhaskara Rao, editor (2007). *Teachniques of Teaching Education.* New Delhi: Discovery Publishing House. ISBN 81-8411-062-6.

Harshitha, Digumarti author and Digumarti Bhaskara Rao, editor (2004). *Methods of Teaching Information Technology.* New Delhi: Discovery Publishing House. ISBN 81-7141-805-8.

Harshitha, Digumarti author and Digumarti Bhaskara Rao, editor (2007). *Techniques of Teaching Computer Science.* New Delhi: Sonali Publications. ISBN 81-8411-036-7.

Harshitha, Digumarti and Digumarti Bhaskara Rao, editor (2004). *Educational Innovations.* New Delhi: Discovery Publishing House.

Indira Devi, author and J. Prasanth Kumara and Digumarti Bhaskara Rao, editor (2004). *Values in Language Text Books.* New Delhi: APH Publishing Corporation.

Jalaja Kumari, G., author and Digumarti Bhaskara Rao, editor (2004). *Methods of Teaching Technology.* New Delhi: Discovery Publishing House. ISBN 81-7141-810-4.

Jalaja Kumari, G., author and Digumarti Bhaskara Rao, editor (2007). *Job Satisfaction of Teachers.* New Delhi: Discovery Publishing House.

Janardhan Reddy, B., author and Digumarti Bhaskara Rao, editor (2006). *Techniques of Teaching Sociology.* New Delhi: Sonali Publications. ISBN 81-8411-042-1.

Jayasree,R., author and Digumarti Bhaskara Rao, editor (1999). *Methods Correlatse of Socialisation.* New Delhi: Discovery Publishing House. ISBN 81-7141-517-2.

Jayasree,R., author and Digumarti Bhaskara Rao, editor (2004). *Methods of Teaching Science.* New Delhi: Discovery Publishing House. ISBN 81-7141-801-5.

John Babu G., author and T.J.R. Prasad, G.M. Madhukar and Digumarti Bhaskara Rao, editors (1996). *Problem Solving in Mathematics.* New Delhi: APH Publishing Corporation. ISBN 81-7648-273-0.

Joseph Raju, B., and G.A. Anitha, author and Digumarti Bhaskara Rao, editor (2004). *Population Education.* New Delhi: Discovery Publishing House. ISBN 81-8883-632-3.

Lalitha, T., author and R.S. Prabhakaram, D.S.N. Sastry and Digumarti Bhaskara Rao, editor (2004). *Educational*

Philosophic Beliefs. New Delhi: Discovery Publishing House. ISBN 81-7141-765-5.

Krishna G., author and Digumarti Bhaskara Rao, editor (2006). *Techniques of Teaching Physical Education*. New Delhi: Discovery Publishing House. ISBN 81-8411-044-8.

Kumar Raju G., author and Digumarti Bhaskara Rao, editor (2007). *Principles of Primary School*. New Delhi: Sonali Publications. ISBN 81-8411-054-5.

Lakshmi Kumari, V., author and Digumarti Bhaskara Rao, editor (2006). *Techniques of Teaching Home Science*. New Delhi: Discovery Publishing House. ISBN 81-8411-048-0.

Madhu Babu Jampla, author and Digumarti Bhaskara Rao, editor (2004). *Adjustment Problems of Hearing Impaired*. New Delhi: Discovery Publishing House. ISBN 81-7141-831-7.

Madhu Babu Jampla, author and Digumarti Bhaskara Rao, editor (2004). *Methods of Teaching Exceptional Children*. New Delhi: Discovery Publishing House. ISBN 81-7141-802-3.

Madhu Babu Jampla, author and Digumarti Bhaskara Rao, editor (2007). *Adjustment, Achievement Motivation and Academic Achievement of Hearing Impaired Students*. New Delhi: Discovery Publishing House.

Majra, Tabi and Digumarti Bhaskara Rao, editors (1996). *Educational Leadership and Social Changes*. New Delhi: Discovery Publishing House. ISBN 81-7141-320-X.

Nageswara Rao, P. and M. Srihari, author and Digumarti Bhaskara Rao, editor (2004). *Guidance and Counselling*. New Delhi: Discovery Publishing House. ISBN 81-7141-840-6.

Nageswara Rao, P., author and Digumarti Bhaskara Rao, editor (2006). *Teachniques of Teaching Phychology*. New Delhi: Discovery Publishing House. ISBN 81-8411-040-5.

Nageswara Rao, P. and P. Sridhari, author and Digumarti Bhaskara Rao, editor (2004). *Methods and Techniques of Teaching*. New Delhi: Sonali Publications. ISBN 81-8883-633-8.

Nirmala Jyothi, M., author and Digumarti Bhaskara Rao, editor (2003). *Non-detention System in School Education.* New Delhi: Discovery Publishing House. ISBN 81-7141-654-3.

Padma Tulasi, G., author and Digumarti Bhaskara Rao, editor (2004). *Methods of Teaching Elementary Science.* New Delhi: Discovery Publishing House. ISBN 81-7141-871-6.

Pitchi Reddy, M., author and Digumarti Bhaskara Rao, editor (2007). *Techniques of Teaching Social Science.* New Delhi: Sonali Publications. ISBN 81-7141-066-X.

Prasad Babu, B., author and P. Madhu and Digumarti Bhaskara Rao, editors (2006). *Psychological Adjustment and Wed-being of Tuberculosis Patients.* New Delhi: Discovery Publishing House.

Prasad Babu, B., author and M.V.R. Raju and Digumarti Bhaskara Rao, editors (2006). *Behavioural Problem of School Children.* New Delhi: Discovery Publishing House.

Prasad Babu, B., author and K.N. Rani and Digumarti Bhaskara Rao, editors (2004). *India Pakistan: Partition Perspectives in Indo-English Novels.* New Delhi: Discovery Publishing House. ISBN 81-7141-871-6.

Prabhakaran, K.S., author and Digumarti Bhaskara Rao, editors (1998). *Concept Attainment Model in Mathematics Teaching.* New Delhi: Discovery Publishing House. ISBN 81-7141-424-9.

Prasanth Kumar, J., author and Digumarti Bhaskara Rao, editor (1998). *Effectiveness of Distance Education System.* New Delhi: Discovery Publishing House. ISBN 81-7141-437-0.

Prasanth Kumar, J., author and Digumarti Bhaskara Rao, editor (2004). *Methdos of Teaching Civics.* New Delhi: Discovery Publishing House. ISBN 81-7141-806-6.

Prasanth Kumar, J., author and G. Sundara Rao and Digumarti Bhaskara Rao, editors (2000). *Open University Student Support Services.* New Delhi: Discovery Publishing House. ISBN 81-7141-550-4.

Raja Kumar, M.A. and D.R.S. Sundari, author and Digumarti Bhaskara Rao, editor (2004). *Special Education.* New Delhi: Discovery Publishing House. ISBN 81-7141-846-5.

Raja Kumar, M.A. and D.R.S. Sundari, author and Digumarti Bhaskara Rao, editor (2004). *Methods of Teaching Educational Psychology.* New Delhi: Discovery Publishing House.

Ramatulasamma K., author and Digumarti Bhaskara Rao, editor (2002). *Job Satisfaction of Teacher Educators.* New Delhi: Discovery Publishing House. ISBN 81-7141-655-1.

Rama Krishnaiah, D., author and Digumarti Bhaskara Rao, editor (1998). *Job Satisfaction of College Teachers.* New Delhi: Discovery Publishing House. ISBN 81-7141-438-9.

Rama Kumar Ranam M.V., author and Digumarti Bhaskara Rao, editor (1998). *Dukkha: Suffering in Early Buddhism.* New Delhi: Discovery Publishing House. ISBN 81-7141-653-5.

Rama Krishna Prasad and P. Vide Sagar, author and Digumarti Bhaskara Rao, editor (2004). *Methods of Teaching Physical Education.* New Delhi: Discovery Publishing House.

Rama Seshaiah, M., author and Digumarti Bhaskara Rao, editor (2004). *Methods of Teaching Home Science.* New Delhi: Discovery Publishing House. ISBN 81-7141-916-X.

Rama Swamy, K., author and Digumarti Bhaskara Rao, editor (2007). *Techniques of Teaching Environmental Science.* New Delhi: Sonali Publications. ISBN 81-8411-035-9.

Ramesh, A.R., author and Digumarti Bhaskara Rao, editor (2006). *Techniques of Teaching Commerce.* New Delhi: Sonali Publications. ISBN 81-8411-043-X.

Ramesh, Ghama and Digumarti Bhaskara Rao, editors (1998). *Environmental Education: Problems and Prospect.* New Delhi: Discovery Publishing House. ISBN 81-7141-423-0.

Ranga Rao, B., author and Digumarti Bhaskara Rao, editor (2007). *Techniques of Teaching Economics.* New Delhi: Sonali Publications. ISBN 81-8411-056-1.

Ranga Rao, R., author and Digumarti Bhaskara Rao, editor (2004). *Methods of Teacher Teaching.* New Delhi: Discovery Publishing House. ISBN 81-7141-812-0.

Rani, S.S., author and Digumarti Bhaskara Rao, editor (2006). *Techniques of Teaching Botany.* New Delhi: Discovery Publishing House. ISBN 81-8411-037-5.

Rathaiah, Lavu and Digumarti Bhaskara Rao, editors (1996). *International Innovations in Education.* New Delhi: Discovery Publishing House. ISBN 81-7141-359-5.

Rathaiah, Lavu and Digumarti Bhaskara Rao (1997). *Achievement Correlates.* New Delhi: Discovery Publishing House. ISBN 81-7141-385-4.

Ravi Krishna, M., author and Digumarti Bhaskara Rao, editors (2004). *Examination System.* New Delhi: Discovery Publishing House. ISBN 81-7141-824-4.

Ravi Krishna, M., author and Digumarti Bhaskara Rao, editors (2004). *Methods of Teaching Computer Science.* New Delhi: Discovery Publishing House. ISBN 81-7141-823-6.

Rudramamba, B., author and Digumarti Bhaskara Rao, editor (2003). *Problems of Teaching.* New Delhi: Discovery Publishing Corporation. ISBN 81-7648-462-8.

Rudramamba, B. and V. Lakshmi Kumari, author and Digumarti Bhaskara Rao, editors (2004). *Methods of Teaching Economics.* New Delhi: Discovery Publishing House. ISBN 81-7141-900-3.

Sambasiva Rao, B., author and Digumarti Bhaskara Rao, editor (2007). *Techniques of Teaching Psychology.* New Delhi: Sonali Publications. ISBN 81-8411-040-5.

Sanjeeva Rao, P.C., author and Digumarti Bhaskara Rao, editor (1996). *A Text Book of Geology.* New Delhi: Discovery Publishing House. ISBN 81-7141-313-7.

Santhanam. T., B. Prasad Babu and S. Sugandhi, author and Digumarti Bhaskara Rao, editor (2007). *Children with Learning Disabilities.* New Delhi: Discovery Publishing House.

Sarala M.M.O., author and Digumarti Bhaskara Rao, editor (2006). *Techniques of Teaching English.* New Delhi: Sonali Publications. ISBN 81-8411-047-2.

Satya Narayana, V., author and Digumarti Bhaskara Rao, editor (2001). *Physical Education, Social Attitudes and Leadership Qualities.* New Delhi: Discovery Publishing House. ISBN 81-7141-593-8.

Satya Narayana, B.V.V. and G. Krishna, author and Digumarti Bhaskara Rao, editor (2004). *Curriculum Development and Management.* New Delhi: Discovery Publishing House. ISBN 81-7141-813-9.

Shamsuddhin, Sk. and V. Dayakara Reddy, author and Digumarti Bhaskara Rao, editor (2007). *Academic Achievement and Values.* New Delhi: Discovery Publishing House.

Singh Y.C., author and Digumarti Bhaskara Rao, editor (2006). *Techniques of Teaching Science.* New Delhi: Sonali Publications. ISBN 81-8411-041-3.

Sirisha Rani, S., author and Digumarti Bhaskara Rao, editor (2007). *Techniques of Teaching Botany.* New Delhi: Sonali Publications. ISBN 81-8411-037-5.

Sivaratnam Reddy, M., author and Digumarti Bhaskara Rao, editor (2004). *Creativity in College Students.* New Delhi: Discovery Publishing House. ISBN 81-7141-697-7.

Siva Lakshmi, G.V. and G.L. Subbaiah, author and Digumarti Bhaskara Rao, editor (2004). *Methods of Teaching Environmental Science.* New Delhi: Discovery Publishing House. ISBN 81-7141-839-2.

Srinivas, G., author and Digumarti Bhaskara Rao, editor (2007). *Anxiety of Prospective Teachers.* New Delhi: Discovery Publishing House.

Srinivas, M. and L. Prasada Rao, author and Digumarti Bhaskara Rao, editor (2004). *Methods of Teaching History.* New Delhi: Discovery Publishing House.

Srinivas Rao, P., author and Digumarti Bhaskara Rao, editor (2007). *Principles of Secondary School.* New Delhi: Discovery Publishing House. ISBN 81-8411-058-8.

Srinivasulu Reddy, L., and K.R.S. Sambasiva Rao, author and Digumarti Bhaskara Rao, editor (1999). *A Text Book of Aquaculture.* New Delhi: Discovery Publishing House. ISBN 81-7141-482-6.

Srinivasa Rao, Landababu, author and Digumarti Bhaskara Rao, editor (2003). *Achievement Motivation and Achievement in Mathematics.* New Delhi: Discovery Publishing House. ISBN 81-7141-674-8.

Srihari, M., author and Digumarti Bhaskara Rao, editor (2003). *Values of Propspective Teachers.* New Delhi: Discovery Publishing House.

Subba Rao, K., author and Digumarti Bhaskara Rao, editor (2007). *School Education Policy.* New Delhi: Discovery Publishing House.

Subba Rao, K., author and Digumarti Bhaskara Rao, editor (2007). *Education Planning.* New Delhi: Sonali Publication. ISBN 81-8411-053-7.

Sudhakar Reddy, M., author and Digumarti Bhaskara Rao, editor (2003). *Creativity in Adolescents.* New Delhi: Discovery Publishing House. ISBN 81-7141-659-4.

Sunil Kumar, K. and K. Rana Krishana, author and Digumarti Bhaskara Rao, editor (2004). *Methods of Teaching Chemistry.* New Delhi: Discovery Publishing House. ISBN 81-7141-913-5.

Sunita, B. and B. Samadeva Rao, author and Digumarti Bhaskara Rao, editor (2004). *Methods of Teaching Mathematics.* New Delhi: Discovery Publishing House. ISBN 81-7141-915-1.

Surya Madhva, K., author and Digumarti Bhaskara Rao, editor (2006). *Techniques of Teaching Geography.* New Delhi: Discovery Publishing House. ISBN 81-8411-034-0.

Surya Madhava, K., author and Digumarti Bhaskara Rao, editor (2007). *Techniques of Teaching Political Science.* New Delhi: Discovery Publishing House. ISBN 81-8411-061-8.

Swamy, K.R., author and Digumarti Bhaskara Rao, editor (2006). *Techniques of Teaching Environmental Science.* New Delhi: Discovery Publishing House. ISBN 81-8411-035-9.

Swarna Jyoti, R., author and Digumarti Bhaskara Rao, editor (2007). *Educational Research.* New Delhi: Discovery Publishing House. ISBN 81-8411-063-4.

Swarna Latha, K., author and Digumarti Bhaskara Rao, editors (2006). *Encyclopedia of Biotechnology,* 5 volume. New Delhi: Discovery Publishing House. ISBN 81-8356-168-3. (set).

Swarup, Rani, K., author and Digumarti Bhaskara Rao, editor (2004). *Educational Measurement and Evaluation.* New Delhi: Discovery Publishing House. ISBN 81-7141-859-7.

Vanaja, M., author and Digumarti Bhaskara Rao, editor (1999). *Inquiry Training Model.* New Delhi: Discovery Publishing House. ISBN 81-7141-515-6.

Vanaja, M., author and Digumarti Bhaskara Rao, editor (2004). *Methods of Teaching Physics.* New Delhi: Discovery Publishing House. ISBN 81-7141-867-8.

Vanaja, M. and K. Sneha Latha, author and Digumarti Bhaskara Rao, editor (2004). *Student Shyness.* New Delhi: APH Publishing House.

Valeri V. Koushouk, author and Digumarti Bhaskara Rao, editor (2002). *A Text Book of Cryogenics.* New Delhi: Discovery Publishing House. ISBN 81-7141-642-X.

Vamsi Krishna, K., author and Digumarti Bhaskara Rao, editor (2004). *School Psychology.* New Delhi: Discovery Publishing House. ISBN 81-7141-880-5.

Veena Kumar, author and Digumarti Bhaskara Rao, editor (1996). *Operation Black Board.* New Delhi: APH Publishing House. ISBN 81-7024-711-X.

Veena Kumar, Balusu, author and Digumarti Bhaskara Rao, editor (2004). *Methods of Teaching Social Studies.* New Delhi: Discovery Publishing House. ISBN 81-7141-899-9.

Veena Kumar, Balusu, author and Digumarti Bhaskara Rao, editor (2000). *Psycho-Social Correlates of Achievement.* New Delhi: Discovery Publishing House. ISBN 81-7141-547-4.

Venkat Rao, B., author and Digumarti Bhaskara Rao, editor (2007). *Techniques of Teaching Chemistry.* New Delhi: Sonali Publications. ISBN 81-8411-057-X.

Venkat, Rao, B., author and Digumarti Bhaskara Rao (1989). *A Text Book of Zoology—Junior Intermediate.* New Delhi: Vignan Publishers.

Venkat, Rao, B., author and Digumarti Bhaskara Rao (1989). *A Text Book of Zoology—Senior Intermediate.* New Delhi: Vignan Publishers.

Venkatshvara Rao, V., author and Digumarti Bhaskara Rao, editor (2004). *Problems of Education.* New Delhi: Discovery Publishing House. ISBN 81-7141-841-4.

Venkatshvara Rao, V., V. Vijaya Lakshmi and V. Vamsi Krishna, author and Digumarti Bhaskara Rao, editor (2004). *Education for All.* New Delhi: Sonali Publications. ISBN 81-8883-630-3.

Venkatshvara Rao, V., V. Vijaya Lakshmi and V. Vamsi Krishna, author and Digumarti Bhaskara Rao, editor (2004). *Education in India.* New Delhi: Sonali Publications. ISBN 81-8883-858-9.

Venkatshvara Reddy, V. and Narayana, M.L., author and Digumarti Bhaskara Rao, editor (2004). *Eduation for Deths.* New Delhi: Discovery Publishing House. ISBN 81-7141-872-4.

Venkatshvara Reddy, L. and Narayana, M.L., author and Digumarti Bhaskara Rao, editor (2004). *Method of Teaching Rural Sociology.* New Delhi: Discovery Publishing House. ISBN 81-7141-811-2.

Venkashvaralu, K. and S.J. Basha, author and Digumarti Bhaskara Rao, editor (2004). *Methods of Teaching*

Commerce. New Delhi: Discovery Publishing House. ISBN 81-7141-808-2.

Venugapala Rao, K., author and Digumarti Bhaskara Rao, editor (2000). *Teacher Morale in Secondary School.* New Delhi: Discovery Publishing House. ISBN 81-7141-551-2.

Venugapala Rao, K., author and Digumarti Bhaskara Rao, editor (2007). *Techniques of Teaching History.* New Delhi: Sonali Publications. ISBN 81-8411-059-6.

Vidya, C., author and Digumarti Bhaskara Rao, editor (1996). *A Text Book of Nutrtion.* New Delhi: Discovery Publishing House. ISBN 81-7141-309-9.

Vimala, K.D., author and Digumarti Bhaskara Rao, editors (2007). *Stree, Coping and Management.* New Delhi: Discovery Publishing House.

Vijaya Bharathi, K., author and Digumarti Bhaskara Rao, editor (2000). *Educational Philosophies of Swami Vivekananda and John Dewey.* New Delhi: APH Publishing House. ISBN 81-7648-309-9.

Vijaya Bharathi, K., author and Digumarti Bhaskara Rao, editor (2005). *Educational Philosophy of John Dewey.* New Delhi: Discovery Publishing House. ISBN 81-8356-024-5.

Vijaya Bharathi, K., author and Digumarti Bhaskara Rao, editor (2005). *Educational Philosophy of Swami Vivekananda.* New Delhi: Discovery Publishing House. ISBN 81-8356-023-7.

Vijaya Lakshmi, K., author and Digumarti Bhaskara Rao, editor (2004). *Basic Education.* New Delhi: Discovery Publishing House. ISBN 81-7141-881-3.

Vijaya Lakshmi, K., author and Digumarti Bhaskara Rao, editor (2006). *Techniques of Teaching Music.* New Delhi: Discovery Publishing House. ISBN 81-8411-038-3.

Vijaya Kumar, S.J., author and Digumarti Bhaskara Rao, editor (2006). *Techniques of Teaching Mathematics.* New Delhi: Sonali Publications. ISBN 81-8411-039-1.

Visalaka, K., author and Digumarti Bhaskara Rao, editor (2006). *Techniques of Teaching Biology*. New Delhi: Sonali Publications. ISBN 81-8411-045-6.

Visalaka, K., author and Digumarti Bhaskara Rao, editor (2007). *Techniques of Teaching Zoology*. New Delhi: Sonali Publications. ISBN 81-8411-055-3.

Telugu Language

Bhaskara Rao, Digumarti (1986). *Dhrushya Sravana Bodhanapakaranalu* (Audio Visual Teaching Aids). Guntur: Nagarjuna Publishers.

Bhaskara Rao, Digumarti (1993). *Jeevasashtra Bodhana* (Teaching of Biology). Guntur: Nagarjuna Publishers.

Bhaskara Rao, Digumarti (1997). *Vignanasasthra Bodhana* (Teaching of Science). Guntur: Nagarjuna Publishers.

Bhaskara Rao, Digumarti (1997). *Vidya Manovignana Sastram* (Educational Psychology). Guntur: Creative Press.

Bhaskara Rao, Digumarti (1998). *DSC Study Material*. Guntur: Nagarjuna Publishers.

Bhaskara Rao, Digumarti (1998). *Upadhyayudu Vidya* (Teacher and Education). Guntur: Nagarjuna Publishers.

Bhaskara Rao, Digumarti (1998). *Vidya Drukpadalu* (Perspectives of Education). Guntur: Nagarjuna Publishers.

Bhaskara Rao, Digumarti (1999). *EdCET Teaching Aptitude*. Guntur: Nagarjuna Publishers.

Bhaskara Rao, Digumarti (2001). *Bhoutika Sastra Bodhana Padhatulu* (Methods of Teaching Physical Science). Guntur: Sri Nagarjuna Publishers.

Bhaskara Rao, Digumarti (2001). *Jeeva Sastra Bodhana Padhatulu* (Methods of Teaching Biology). Guntur: Sri Nagarjuna Publishers.

Bhaskara Rao, Digumarti (2001). *Vidya Manovignana Sastram* (Educational Psychology). Guntur: Sri Nagarjuna Publishers.

Bhaskara Rao, Digumarti (2003). *Patasala Yajamanyam / Paripalana* (School Management and Administration). Guntur: Sri Nagarjuna Publishers.

Gopala Krishna, G., A. Rama Krishna, K. Subba Rao and Bhaskara Rao, Digumarti (2004). *Jeevasashtra Bodhana Padhatulu* (Methods of Teaching of Biological Science). Guntur: Sri Nagarjuna Publishers.

Krishna Murthy, V., K.S. Sudheer Reddy and Bhaskara Rao, Digumarti (2004). *Vidya Manovignana Sastra Adharalu* (Foundations of Educational Psychology). Guntur: Sri Nagarjuna Publishers.

Lalini, V., V. Dayakara Reddy, M. Srihari and Bhaskara Rao, Digumarti (2004). *Vidya Adharalu* (Foundations of Education). Guntur: Sri Nagarjuna Publishers.

Subba Rao, K.P., P. Ayodhya and Bhaskara Rao, Digumarti (2004). *Patasala Yajamanyam—Vidhya Vyavasthalu* (School Management and Systems of Education). Guntur: Sri Nagarjuna Publishers.

Sudhakar, V., B. Ravindra Babu, D.S. Kumar and Bhaskara Rao, Digumarti (2004). *Vidya Sanketika Sastram—Computer Vidhya* (Educational Technology and Computer Education). Guntur: Sri Nagarjuna Publishers.

Index

P

Q

R

❑❑❑